FAMILIES COPING WITH SCHIZOPHRENIA

A Practitioner's Guide
to Family Groups

Jacqueline M. Atkinson

and

Denise A. Coia

University of Glasgow, UK

JOHN WILEY & SONS

Chichester · New York · Brisbane · Toronto · Singapore

Other Wiley Editorial Offices

John Wiley & Sons, Inc., 605 Third Avenue,
New York, NY 10158-0012, USA

Jacaranda Wiley Ltd, 33 Park Road, Milton,
Queensland 4064, Australia

John Wiley & Sons (Canada) Ltd, 22 Worcester Road,
Rexdale, Ontario M9W 1L1, Canada

John Wiley & Sons (SEA) Pte Ltd, 37 Jalan Pemimpin #05-04,
Block B, Union Industrial Building, Singapore 2057

Library of Congress Cataloging-in-Publication Data

Atkinson, Jacqueline M.
    Families coping with schizophrenia : a practitioner's guide to
family groups / Jacqueline M. Atkinson and Denise A. Coia.
            p. cm.
    Includes bibliographical references and index.
    ISBN 0-471-94181-6
    1. Schizophrenics—Family relationships. 2. Schizophrenics—Home
care—Study and teaching. 3. Family services. 4. Group counseling.
5.Schizophrenics—Services for. I. Coia, Denise A. II. Title.
RC514.A838 1995   94–33593
616.89′82—dc20   CIP

British Library Cataloguing in Publication Data

A catalogue record for this book is available from the British Library

ISBN 0-471-94181-6

Typeset in 11/13pt Palatino by Production Technology Department
John Wiley & Sons Ltd
Printed and bound in Great Britain by Bookcraft (Bath) Ltd

CONTENTS

Preface vii

Acknowledgements ix

 1 The relationship between schizophrenia and the family 1

 2 The response of the family to schizophrenia 23

 3 The family in therapy 45

 4 Education for relatives 69

 5 The family as carer 91

 6 Self-help groups for relatives 114

 7 Education groups 138

 8 Organising relatives' groups 157

 9 Training staff 179

10 The ethics, values and politics of caring 203

References 222

Appendix 1. Notes for relatives 245

Appendix 2. Notes for Group Leaders—Running Groups . . . 269

Index 281

PREFACE

For at least the last 50 years there has been considerable interest in the relationship between the development and course of schizophrenia and the family. Fashions in theories change, from a dynamic causal role to a family systems maintenance one, but the family is always there, sometimes only as a hazy background relationship, sometimes centre-stage. Even the current popularity of theories of schizophrenia as an organic brain disease involve the family through the medium of genet-ics. For anyone who is planning to work with people with schizophre-nia, to try to avoid the family (where it exists) is to make a nonsense of treatment plans. As the concept of community care becomes reality, the family is increasingly seen as the focus of management and care. Families are frequently the primary carers for their ill relative, and as such their role in the future of the person with schizophrenia cannot be ignored.

All too often families are left alone to care as best they can. Although there is a considerable body of research work on interactions between family and the course of schizophrenia, this is often ignored in the development of services. The philosophical, economic and political mood which has encouraged the development of community care in the West has frequently come to mean little more than care by the family. A historical perspective shows that for much of the past the ill were kept with their family, but Mrs. Rochester, locked away in the attic, is not a model of community care for our time.

If people with schizophrenia are to do more than merely survive in the community then not only do they need adequate services and resources appropriate to their varying needs, but so too do their relatives, not least in their role as informal carers. We have barely begun to explore the resources needed by families, let alone the way they can be incorporated into planning and service provision.

In this book we examine one service for relatives, education groups, which might be seen as the basis from which other more elaborate or specialised services could grow. To do this we examine first the research on the relationship between the family and schizophrenia and the family therapies which have grown from this. From there we look at the support which is currently available to families, including that from the voluntary organisations and self-help groups.

All this forms the background to the development of education groups for relatives. We draw on our own research and experience and that of others to provide a comprehensive guide to setting up relatives' education groups, whether as a catchment-wide service within the NHS, as one-off, local groups provided by a variety of agencies or as a service sold to other agencies in the new Trust hospitals or within the North American context. As well as detailing the practical problems and issues, we also look at the training requirements for staff who the run these groups. Last, but by no means least, we consider some of the ethical and political issues which are raised by the provision of services for, and involving, relatives.

ACKNOWLEDGEMENTS

Many people were involved with the setting up and running of the relatives group in South Glasgow to whom we owe our thanks. In particular we would like to mention Helen Anderson and Harper Gilmour for their involvement in the research, the people who ran the groups, namely Marilyn Aitken, Aileen Blower, Ian Gidley, Stephen Hodgson, Anne Joice, Paul Kerr, Robin McGillip, Catriona McGinley, May Munro, Nick Neville, John Robertson, Viv Rushworth and Trisha Taylor, and also Allan Stewart, Nursing Officer, for his enthusiasm in supporting the groups and releasing staff. We would also like to thank the various community organisations and agencies who supported the groups by making premises available. Our thanks also go to our editors at John Wiley & Sons, Michael Coombs and Wendy Hudlass, for their advice in supporting us through the writing of this book.

THE RELATIONSHIP BETWEEN SCHIZOPHRENIA AND THE FAMILY

Many illnesses are affected in a non-specific way by the family environment. Schizophrenia, however, is unusual in that relationships within the family seem specifically to influence the development and course of the illness, including relapse. What exact form this relationship takes has been a source of intense debate. The arguments have tended to fall into two schools of thought. The earlier is causal, suggesting a unidirectional linear model where families act as a 'provoking' factor to cause the illness and are thus seen as part of the problem. The later view uses a multidirectional 'vulnerability' model. This brings together various familial factors which may make the individual with a biological disposition to schizophrenia either more likely to develop the illness or more prone to relapse. This model also allows for the person with schizophrenia to affect the family's ability to care, cope and function effectively, and is thus interactionist. At this point relatives can begin to be viewed as part of the solution.

The causal model has had enormous influence over the years, and although largely discredited it is important within the historical context. For years relatives have had to live with both an 'ill' family member and also the censorial implication from professionals that they had somehow been responsible for this. Health care providers and relatives frequently found themselves in adversarial roles, to the detriment of the person with schizophrenia. The vulnerability model, because of its potential for change, is more likely to lead to a 'therapeutic partnership' between the person with schizophrenia, relatives and professionals.

In this chapter we review the historical contribution made by the early causal family theories, and describe how they set the scene for the later vulnerability and interactionist models to develop. These later models are by no means static and have themselves moved on considerably from their beginnings in the 1970s.

CAUSAL CONNECTIONS

The psychodynamic theories hypothesised that family relationships and interactions caused schizophrenia. These beliefs were based on two major assumptions.

1. Disordered communication or relationships are the *causal* factor of the illness.

2. Such difficulties are found uniquely in families with a member who has schizophrenia.

Freud, Jung and Adler all offered psychodynamic explanations of the illness relating to childhood and the impact of family and parental experiences. Sullivan (1927) was amongst the first of their followers to consider the family in therapy. In an inpatient setting, he tried to recreate the family as a way of providing patients with appropriate emotional experiences which would stand against, and correct, pathological early family interactions. Following this period some theorists investigated the quality of intrafamilial relationships in greater depth, whilst others focused more specifically on the content and quality of communications within the family.

Relationship Theories

Frieda Fromm-Reichmann (1948) is perhaps best remembered for introducing the term 'schizophrenogenic mother' to describe a mother whose relationship to her child was distant and lacking in both warmth and affection. The feelings of rejection in the child, recounted by the adult child in therapy, were believed to have hindered the development of appropriate psychological and social skills, leading to illness.

The view was popularised in the novel by Hannah Green, *I Never Promised You a Rose Garden* (1964), later made into a film of the same name (1977, New World Picture, Director Anthony Page), which is a fictionialised account of her therapy with Fromm-Reichmann.

Similarly Lidz *et al.* (1957) concluded that disturbed family functioning caused severe stress in the patient as a child and played an aetiological role in the development of schizophrenia. The disturbed relationships between the parents were described as either marital schism or marital skew. Marital schism occurs when there is emotional disharmony between the partners, who pursue their individual needs and goals at the expense of the child, often involving the child and thus dividing the child's loyalties. Marital skew occurs when one partner is excessively dominant or passive. Usually the father has yielded to a more dominant mother. Thus the father does not provide a strong masculine role model for the child.

Bowen (1960) also pursued the issue of marital disharmony in the families of adolescents with schizophrenia. The child formed an important function in the 'interdependent triad' because, although being given conflicting messages regarding their role and relationship to their parents, their presence was required to maintain the parental relationship.

Whilst marital disharmony in families has been the main focus of the psychodynamic theories, a slightly different approach was taken by Alanen and Kinnuman (1975), who addressed the marital relationship between a person with schizophrenia and their spouse. They identified three types of relationship which they considered unsatisfactory.

Type I. The person with schizophrenia is passive and dependent, with the spouse being domineering.

Type II. Both partners are dependent on each other in an infantile way and so are unable to support each other.

Type III. The person with schizophrenia is dominant but the spouse is supportive.

Since schizophrenia developed in these patients after marriage, Alanen and Kinnuman postulate the marital dynamics may have played some role in the onset of the illness.

Communication Theories

Bateson *et al.* (1956) introduced the concept of 'the double bind'. Observing verbal and non-verbal communication in families with a member with schizophrenia, they concluded that people with schizophrenia receive conflicting messages, labelled double bind, from their relatives. These paradoxical communications throughout childhood may have led to the development of the illness. Such communications involve two incompatible messages being given. The second message is often non-verbal. (For example 'Give your mother a kiss' while non-verbally distancing self from the other person.) In time, with repeated exposure, the child loses the power to discriminate between such messages and exhibits schizophrenic behaviour. This theory has not withstood experimental testing (Hirsch and Leff 1975), and the possibility that double bind communication could arise from living with a person with schizophrenia has not been explored.

Wynne and colleagues (Wynne and Singer 1965) were another group to focus on communication problems in families, but they differed by being interested in the *form* of communication not the *content*. They observed four types of communication:

1. *Amorphous*—vague speech lacking clarity of goals.

2. *Fragmented*—a loss of flow in conversation.

3. *Mixed*—a combination of the previous two.

4. *Constricted*—where the content of the speech is understandable but aspects of reality are separated from it.

Wynne found communication disorders in both families and the person with schizophrenia, leading him to hypothesise that children growing up in such families take on the patterns of disjointed and incoherent communication. This could lead to problems with reality testing and perceptual ability which may eventually cause thought disorder and schizophrenia. Again Hirsch and Leff (1975) attempted to replicate this work, but concluded that communication disorder may be explained by the greater verbosity of the parents of people with schizophrenia.

Somewhat apart from these early theories are the writings of R.D. Laing, the only British researcher of prominence in this area, which continue to be important mainly because of the enormous influence they have had on popular, rather than academic, culture. Many artists have found his theories a useful way to counteract the inadequacy of realism when trying to convey non-rational, non-logical modes of thought and experience. This is clearly seen in the work of Doris Lessing, where the Laingian hypothesis, that so-called madness and dreams may be states of greater perception than so-called sanity, is central to three of her novels: *Briefing for a Descent into Hell* (1971), *The Summer Before Dark* (1973) and *The Memoirs of a Survivor* (1974).

Similarly, the film *Family Life* (1971, screenplay David Mercer, director Ken Loach) makes use of Laing's view that the family is a pathogenic institution and schizophrenia is a reasonable response to such pathology. In the film a 19-year-old girl is diagnosed as suffering from schizophrenia. The blame for this is put on the family, the implication being that, disapproving of her behaviour and initially viewing her as insolent, they have driven her to a 'breakdown' and she is then defined as 'ill'.

Laing's early work suggested that schizophrenia may be a natural self-protective response to a family problem (Laing 1960) and thus family therapy would be appropriate. Doubts have been expressed about the validity of the observations on which this theory was based (Hirsch and Leff 1975). Nevertheless, Laing's theories have been helpful in making us recognise that people vary in the time and conditions they need to work through their problems in a way that suits them. No doubt Laing will continue to capture public imagination and provide the basis for 'good drama'. It is a pity that some of it is at the expense of those who care most for the person with schizophrenia.

The Impact of the Causal Theories

Over the years the lack of objective experimental evidence for these psychodynamic theories has reduced their importance. Recent technological developments, leading to new biological theories of schizophrenia, have taken their place and further reduced interest, particularly in relation to their aetiological importance. One of the major problems with the psychodynamic theories stemmed from the misconception that an association implies causality. The connections or links between the family situation or relatives' behaviour may have other reasons.

Most obvious is that the family's behaviour is a response to the behaviour of the person with schizophrenia. Less obvious is that both might be linked to a third factor which contributes to both schizophrenia and family problems but there is no direct link between the two.

Although having a negative impact, by driving a rift between professionals and relatives, and creating blame and guilt, we should remember that some positive things have come from early psychodynamic work. Fromm-Reichmann, for example, was one of the first psychotherapists to demonstrate that severely mentally disturbed people might benefit from psychosocial interventions. Stress levels in families became an area of interest and research attention was focused on the family as a whole, which led to work on the family's influence on the course and prognosis of the illness, finding its greatest recognition in the form of expressed emotion. This, maybe, is their major contribution.

FAMILY AND RELAPSE—THE MAINTENANCE OF SCHIZOPHRENIA

Research into how the family affects the course of the illness has targeted two areas, expressed emotion (EE) and, to a much lesser extent, negative affective style (AS).

Expressed Emotion

Expressed emotion has caught the imagination of both clinicians and researchers, spanning the globe and spawning a variety of interventions with families. Since the late 1980s, however, a growing 'uncomfortableness' with EE has shown itself because it has not generalised into a usable service provision.

Kuipers (1992a) describes the history of EE in four stages, the initial discovery stage from 1958 to 1976, the early stage of intervention from 1977 to 1986, a negative stage around 1986–1987 and the established stage from that period on. To establish the current position of EE we have to trace its history to discover where and why it is useful and how much is applicable in routine clinical practice.

Definition of expressed emotion

Expressed emotion is defined operationally by an assessment interview. Described as negative or intrusive attitudes that relatives express about the patient, it is a measure of the 'emotional temperature' within the family (Vaughn 1989). It has three parts, critical comments (CC), hostility (H) and emotional over-involvement (EOI), from which a global EE rating is derived. The scales can, and should, be regarded as independent. Positive comments and warmth were rated in the early studies but dropped in later ones, their role being complicated by high levels of positive comments being found along with high EOI (Leff and Vaughn 1985).

Assessment of expressed emotion

Expressed emotion was first described and assessed using the Camberwell Family Interview (CFI) (Brown *et al.* 1972). An abbreviated interview was introduced by Vaughn and Leff (1976b) and is now the instrument most commonly used. It is a semi-structured interview lasting about an hour-and-a-half and is administered separately to relatives, usually following an exacerbation of symptoms in the person with schizophrenia and around the time of discharge. It is both relatively time consuming and expensive to train as a rater, and as a result of this, and the time involvement for both families and researchers, consideration has been given to the possibility of other, shorter assessments of EE. This might make assessment more accessible to others, especially clinicians wishing to assess EE in their caseload.

One scale, level of EE (LEE) (Cole and Kazarian 1988), differs significantly from others by changing the source of information from relatives to the person with schizophrenia, thus measuring 'perceived expressed emotion'. McCreadie and Robinson (1987) compared two ratings, the Patient Rejection Scale (PRS) (Kreisman *et al.* 1979) and a self-devised four-point global scale (the 'Clinician's Hunch') with the CFI. Unfortunately neither proved an adequate short cut to measuring high EE, mainly because of problems with sensitivity. The Clinician's Hunch found that clinicians had a wider concept of hostility, as they assigned many low EE relatives to a high EE category. The global scale also did not rate emotional overinvolvement. The PRS distinguished high EE and low EE categories statistically, making it useful for research purposes. It did not, however, have a clear cut-off point which would allow the clinician to identify individual relatives with high EE in a clinical setting. This problem of sensitivity to high EE has been similarly highlighted by Magãna *et al.* (1986) with their Five Minute Speech Sample (FMSS), although it has been used by some researchers (Goldstein *et al.* 1992).

Early studies measured EE when the person with schizophrenia was admitted to hospital, but later research has considered other time scales (McCreadie and Robinson 1987). This is important as it influences findings and thus the development of the concept and its predictive power and explanatory value.

If we accept the value of EE-related family groups and wish to plan for, and implement, such a clinical service in the future, there remains a need for a shorter method of assessing the families involved.

The history of expressed emotion

The 1950s saw the emergence of interest in the relationship between families and schizophrenia. In the United States this was firmly rooted in the psychodynamic tradition. At about the same time, George Brown, a sociologist in London, started his pioneering work on the role of social and situational factors within the family (Brown 1959). This work was taken up by the psychiatrist Julian Leff and clinical psychologist Christine Vaughn at the Institute of Psychiatry and led to the two, now classic, papers of 1976 (Vaughn and Leff 1976a, 1976b) which launched expressed emotion on a peculiarly receptive research community. This was a period when, despite being the heyday of social psychiatry, there was a hiatus in research on the psychosocial management of schizophrenia, in contrast to the developments in pharmacological management brought about by depot medication.

These studies showed the apparently clear relationship between expressed emotion, duration of face-to-face contact (more or less than 35 hours per week) between the relative and the person with schizophrenia, medication and relapse at nine months follow-up. Results showed a wide variation in relapse in high EE families from 15% with low contact and medication, 42% with low contact and no medication, 53% with high contact and no medication, to a staggering 92% relapse rate where there was both high contact and no medication. It was hardly surprising that EE should be greeted with optimism as a potential predictor of relapse. From there it was not far, conceptually, to question whether, *if* EE *was* a good predictor of relapse, changing EE in the family might not also change relapse rates.

From the mid-1960s to the mid-1980s there were a number of studies, predominantly British, which seemed to confirm the link between relapse rates and high EE in families (Brown *et al.* 1972; Vaughn and Leff 1976a; Leff and Vaughn 1981; Vaughn *et al.* 1984; Moline *et al.* 1985; Koenigberg and Handley 1986; Nuechterlein *et al.* 1986). Although from then on the picture became muddied, there were still studies in the late 1980s and into the 1990s supporting the connection (Tarrier *et al.* 1988a; Barrelet *et al.* 1990, Nuechterlein *et al.* 1992).

Also more recent reviews have again supported the importance of EE. Kavanagh (1992), reviewing 26 studies predicting the course of schizophrenia from EE, found that the median relapse rate over 9–12 months was 21% for low EE and 48% for high EE, thus indicating that it may be 'a phenomenon as valuable as medication'. A meta-analysis of 12 studies of the predictive value of EE (Parker and Hadzi-Pavlovic 1990) indicated that people with schizophrenia living in high EE homes were 3.7 times more likely to relapse than those in low EE homes. This trend is reducing in more recent studies, possibly due to more of these concentrating on first-episode patients in whom the predictive power of EE is less marked. One must also be aware of the publication bias of journals towards reporting positive findings.

From the mid-1980s, however, have come reviews and studies which have criticised the methodology and found results which have not supported the hypothesised association between EE and relapse (Kottgen *et al.* 1984; Hogarty *et al.* 1986; MacMillan *et al.* 1986; J. Mintz *et al.* 1987; McCreadie and Phillips 1988; Parker *et al.* 1988; Tarrier *et al.* 1989; Stirling *et al.* 1991). It is, in fact, becoming clear that good methodology is a major problem in researching EE.

Some of the methodological problems which have contributed to this confusion have been changing the cut-off point for critical comments (Moline *et al.* 1985), low pre-admission contact with families (Nuechterlein *et al.* 1986) and the patient not living with the family after discharge (Barrelet *et al.* 1990). Stirling *et al.* (1991) report re-analysing Nuechterlein *et al.*'s (1986) data using Fisher's test rather than χ^2 and finding that the results are then non-significant. McCreadie and Phillips' (1988) study is of particular interest since, as well as being a prevalence study, it measured EE at a time other than that of hospital admission for the person with schizophrenia. A 12-month follow-up reported no differences between people with schizophrenia living with high or low EE relatives or living alone. McCreadie's (1993) work also highlights the small number of families in a community sample who show high EE.

The studies of negative findings have not been without their critics either. Kottgen *et al.* (1984) have been thoroughly criticised by Vaughn (1986), while MacMillan *et al.* (1986) have been criticised on a number of occasions (Nuechterlein *et al.* 1986; Kuipers and Bebbington 1988; Stirling *et al.* 1991). What these studies have led to, however, is a concept of EE which is becoming narrower, having tighter parameters constraining it, and thus may have a useful if more limited, function.

Several studies now have identified factors which can make the predictive value of EE more powerful. Defining relapse as exacerbation of symptoms rather than admission to hospital improves predictive ability (McCreadie and Phillips 1988). Those who have a persistent high level of symptoms from the acute illness episode should be excluded (Vaughn *et al.* 1984, Vaughn 1986) since detecting a new episode or a relapse can be very difficult. Expressed emotion may have a time-limited impact, being more powerful in the first nine months after admission (Leff and Vaughn 1981, Hogarty *et al.* 1988). Tarrier *et al.*'s continuing studies found, for example, an association at nine months follow up (Tarrier *et al.* 1988a) but not when the same cohort was followed up at 24 months (Tarrier *et al.* 1989).

Expressed emotion appears to be gender-sensitive, being of better predictive value for men (Salokangas 1983; Hogarty 1985). From the early studies to the present, medication is seen to interact with EE to provide protection against the impact of EE (Vaughn and Leff 1976a; Goldstein and Kopeiken 1981). Age may be a factor as Nuechterlein *et al.* (1992) suggest that high EE may be more likely to be found in the families of patients with early onset illness. Equally these illnesses are likely to be more severe and thus more likely to lead to negative attitudes.

Lastly, there is the issue of contact with relatives, which was important in the early studies (Brown *et al.* 1972; Vaughn and Leff, 1976a; Vaughn *et al.* 1984) but has either been neglected or not been replicated since. These findings have led to the presumption, not advanced, it has to be said, by the authors of the original paper, that patients and families should spend less time together, or indeed be separated from one another. Such a suggestion has caused distress to families who already feel that EE may be used to blame them. Indeed, Leff *et al.* (1982) attempt to interpret the findings in a different light and suggest the more positive approach of advising patients and relatives to increase the time spent in independent, enjoyable activities.

The response of a person with schizophrenia to a high expressed emotion setting

For EE to have a causal connection with relapse there needs to be some mechanism or pathway which connects the two events with the most likely explanation involving stress levels and physiological arousal. This means establishing that a high EE environment causes stress or high physiological arousal in the person with schizophrenia, and then that this arousal triggers relapse. We are some way from demonstrating this.

To prove that high EE creates stress, most studies have used psychophysiological measures, notably cardiovascular activity and skin conductance (Tarrier *et al.* 1979, 1988b; Tarrier and Barrowclough 1984; Käsermann and Altorfer 1989; Tarrier 1989). The earlier studies looked at whether the pressure of a high EE relative was correlated with physiological responses, but did not relate changes in arousal to particular aspects of the interaction. Tarrier and Barrowclough (1984) showed a differential psychophysiological effect in a person living with one high EE and one low EE parent depending on which was present. However, successful change in EE after an intervention programme did not reduce arousal readings of skin conductance. Tarrier *et al.* (1988b) also could not distinguish between criticism and hostility or emotional over-involvement from the patient's psychophysiological response to the presence of a relative. It has to be said, however, that these measurements of physiological arousal are fairly crude. Nevertheless, they did allow Tarrier (1989) to put forward a more succinct definition of the purpose of EE which

> 'is not so much as a measure of family pathology or dysfunction but an operational measure of environmental stress that can be quantified in a frequently occurring environment that is the family home'.

Looking at the more particular aspects of the interaction within the family, Altorfer *et al.* (1992) examined changes in non-verbal behaviour as indicative of a stress response to high EE. Although not using a measure of EE, they attempted to show physiological changes in response to 'emotionally loaded' or 'disturbing' events and situations versus 'emotionally neutral' events and situations during conversations between parents and their children, and found that 'conversational stressors' correlated with changes in cardiovascular functioning. It should be noted that the patient group contained both people with schizophrenia and people with a bipolar manic illness. They also analysed the parents' conversation in respect of affective style (AS) and found that verbal sequences containing positive AS caused no problems for the people with schizophrenia or bipolar illness. Also, in most interactions, both parent and child referred to this statement subsequently. In contrast, where negative statements were made, more than half the children 'display evasive reactions' and, in more than half the families, the parent does not repeat this negative comment in the subsequent statement. The detail of the analysis of the non-verbal behaviour and the interaction makes for complex results, but there is some indication that it is the repetition or retention of negative AS which is important in the interactions. No doubt we will see ever more refined measures and analysis of interactions between parents and children and stress responses. This is particularly so since some researchers and clinicians are now formulating the 'problem' within families as one of stress management (Falloon *et al.* 1993) which incorporates other external stressors, such as life events, which are assumed to lead to, and operate through, a common mechanism of increased physiological arousal.

Transcultural implications

World-wide there is confirmation of a relationship between high EE and relapse rates in schizophrenia. Most Western research was based in Britain and America in the late 1980s, but since then there has been growing interest world-wide although few studies are published in English. Those that are include results from Australia (Vaughan *et al.* 1992), Brazil (Martins *et al.* 1992), Czechoslovakia (Mozny and Votypkova 1992), Germany (Buchremer *et al.* 1991), Greece (Mavreas *et al.* 1992) and French-speaking Switzerland (Barrelet *et al.* 1990). Leff *et al.* (1990) has confirmed a relationship between high EE and relapse rates in India.

There is, however, substantial evidence to indicate that the outcome for people with schizophrenia is considerably better for people in developing countries than for those in the West (Lin and Kleinmann 1988). How much of this can be attributed to EE? Expressed emotion generally appears to be higher in Western countries, and one explanation may be the greater involvement of extended families in developing countries mitigating against high EE and relapse (Wig *et al.* 1987).

A next step may be to look at minority cultural groups living in a wider society. Karno *et al.* (1987) found a relationship between high EE and relapse rates in Mexican-Americans. Birchwood *et al.* (1992b) looked at relapse/re-admission rates in a group of first-episode people with schizophrenia in England. Relapse/re-admission rates were lowest amongst the Asian population (16%) compared to the white (30%) and Afro-Caribbean (49%) populations. They did not measure EE in families, but suggest that the differential rates may result from 'rapid access to care, stable and supportive family structures, and the availability of a valued and productive social role'. The last two are the same reasons given for the differences found in India. It would be interesting to compare such levels in families living in the West with other cultural groups in the West and also with families in the different countries of origin.

Increasing interest is being shown in the theoretical concepts associated with EE (Angermeyer 1987), yet the search for the meaning of culturally defined response of family members to an ill relative has taken second place to research on the variations in EE levels in different populations.

Kuipers (1992b) reviews the European studies, including some that are unpublished or non-English, that addressed cultural variations occurring in some of the five rating scales of the CFI. Having established support for high EE predicting relapse in eight European languages, and thus transcending the language barrier, they have investigated the proportionality of two determinants, EOI and CC, in predicting relapse. Emotional over-involvement was found to be the major determinant of relapse in some cultures (Stirling *et al.* 1991, Mavreas *et al.* 1992), whilst early British studies have the proportions of CC and EOI reversed in favour of CC (Kuipers 1979). As Kuipers (1992b) pointed out, it will be important to establish whether EOI alone is predictive of outcome in particular cultures, as it suggests that an intervention geared to dealing with this aspect would be particularly necessary in such a population.

Critical comments have been examined and have proved a valuable predictive measurement across European cultures. The lack of specificity of the content of CC allows different cultures to criticise a variety of attributes in their ill relatives, and although the content of their ratings may vary it does not appear to affect the predictiveness of the measure. Whilst outcome measures have been increasingly explored through differing cultures and languages, intervention studies have tended to be limited to English-speaking countries.

Expressed emotion as an interactionist concept

Families affect patients. Patients affect families. Both contribute to high EE, but the multiplicity of contradictory research findings challenges some fundamental assumptions about EE: first, that it is a stable trait, and second, those of primacy and causality. Thus the late 1980s saw a shift in attitudes towards EE, partly to explain some of the contradictory research findings, partly because a mechanism to explain how high EE becomes translated into relapse was not forthcoming, and partly to take account of the concern that maybe EE was a response by relatives to living with someone with schizophrenia. Also there was an awareness that like other family models before it, EE could be used to blame families (Hatfield *et al.* 1987; Parker *et al.* 1988).

Research assumed that the attitudes expressed by the relative during the assessment interview were the same as, or predictive of, the long-term interactional style between the relative and the person with schizophrenia. Some studies have investigated this, although using other ratings scales such as that for AS (Miklowitz *et al.* 1983, 1989; Strachan *et al.* 1986, 1989), and have found positive connections. Other studies, however, have found that EE is not stable over time, or at least not for high-EE relatives (Dulz and Hand 1986; Tarrier *et al.* 1988a; Goldstein *et al.* 1989; Leff *et al.* 1990). That EE seems to change over time may not matter for the prediction of relapse if all studies measure it at the same point, that is, when the person with schizophrenia is experiencing an exacerbation of acute symptoms. Changes in ratings do, however, have important theoretical implications.

What do EE and changes in EE over time suggest about the relatives? Goldstein's (1987) work in the UCLA high-risk study made use of Wynne's definition of communication deviance (CD), and he suggested that high CD or high EE in a relative might be related to either onset or relapse

> 'because these measures are markers of a sub-clinical or full-blown psychopathology status in the relative. Thus, offspring of high-CD relatives may be at risk for developing schizophrenia because their parents are expressing the predisposition to the disorder through some form of sub-clinical thought disorder. In addition, CD may reflect the tendency on the relative's part to manifest overt forms of psychopathology that create stress in the intrafamilial environment and, in turn, increase the likelihood that the offspring's vulnerability to schizophrenia will ultimately be expressed'. (Goldstein et al. 1992)

They suggest that the same is true of relapse.

Although this looks suspiciously as though we are back to blaming the relative, Goldstein and his colleagues do suggest that the schizophrenia associated with high EE may be more severe, 'transmitted readily across generations' (whether by genetics or upbringing is not indicated), and have a poorer prognosis, or that 'the psychopathology associated with high EE attitudes and behaviour creates a more stressful and adversive environment'. Either of these explanations does not preclude the other. What they do not seem to be prepared to consider is that high EE may be within a 'normal' range of behaviours related to coping styles and long-term care.

McCreadie and colleagues (McCreadie 1993; McCreadie et al. 1994a) have looked at the perceived child-rearing patterns of parents, their current EE status and symptomatology in the person with schizophrenia. McCreadie et al. were interested in whether the parent's attitude to the person with schizophrenia pre-dates the illness and whether it reflects styles of parenting behaviour. They used the EMBU (Egna Minnen av Barndoms-Uppfostran), an 81-item self-report questionnaire which allows people to describe their upbringing by their parents (Perris et al. 1980; Arrindell et al. 1983). This has three scales, rejection, emotional warmth and over-protection, which make it well placed for comparison with EE. A fourth scale, favouring subject, was omitted.

Little difference was recorded between mothers and fathers, but there was a tendency for mothers to be seen as warmer and more protective. Rejection and over-protection were positively correlated, which might be thought surprising, but rejection and warmth were negatively correlated. It is suggested that rejection and over-protection represent higher orders of care. This was also found in a similar study in Germany (Arrindell *et al.* 1986). In both studies people with schizophrenia described their parents as showing less warmth than non-schizophrenic people. Parental attitudes as described by people with schizophrenia showed no significant correlations with patients' pre-morbid personality or social adjustment but did, however, show a significant correlation with current symptoms. More severe symptoms were correlated with rejection or over-protection, and less severe symptoms with warmth. This findings was particularly marked for positive symptoms of schizophrenia and general psychopathology.

Four possibilities are examined to account for this.

1. Current mental state might influence assessment of upbringing: suspicion and hostility may predispose towards recalling childhood rejection or blunt affect, and social or emotional withdrawal may lead to a perception of lack of warmth.

2. The attitude and rearing behaviour of parents may affect the severity of the illness, although this is difficult to explain in causal terms.

3. The more severely ill patients may have been 'more unusual' in childhood and, as a consequence, experienced more rejection or over-protection. This was not borne out in the measures used in this study.

4. McCreadie *et al.* (1994b) showed that not only did the people with schizophrenia have more schizoid and schizotypal traits than their siblings, but whereas siblings' social adjustment improved between childhood and adolescence, it deteriorated for people with schizophrenia. They suggest that there may be a common genetic link between rejecting and over-protective behaviours and severity of illness.

Of particular interest are the correlations with EE. There was no correlation between EE and parental rearing attitudes either on overall scores or between the subscales. When the subscale of hostility was partialed out, however, a significant correlation with EMBU rejection was found. This raises the question of whether hostility is a pre-illness trait.

McCreadie and his colleagues do draw attention to the fact that what is being reported is *perceived* parental rearing behaviour as viewed by the person with schizophrenia rather than observed behaviour, and that current symptomatology may influence this perception. It may be that more than just current symptomatology influences this. Simply receiving a diagnosis of schizophrenia might make a person reassess their past and their upbringing. This work harks back to that of Fromm-Reichmann and descriptions of the schizophrenogenic mother based on adult patient's memories.

One way forward, apart from difficult prospective studies, would be to look at the views of other siblings in high-EE homes to see if their views of parental attitudes were different from that of the person with schizophrenia. This would not necessarily answer the 'chicken-and-egg' question, but would suggest whether a general parental style was being described or a specific style dependent on the relationship between the parents and the person with schizophrenia.

Although the interest in interactive models has grown in strength since the mid-1980s (Seywert 1984; Birchwood and Smith 1987; L. Mintz *et al.* 1987), we should remember that over 20 years ago Brown *et al.* (1972) were proposing an interactive model. The response to the predictive value of EE by developing family interventions also demonstrates some allegiance to an interactive approach.

Despite this change of approach to EE it still has a negative resonance for families. As Kavanagh (1992) concludes, ' "high-EE" relatives and a "high-EE family" are correctly perceived as pejorative labels, if not for family members, at least for their coping strategies.' Even those most closely involved with EE have been aware of its potential as a 'blaming tool' and have argued against this (Vaughn, 1986, 1989; Leff and Vaughn 1987). Kavanagh goes so far as to say that we should not use it as a descriptive term of either relatives or families, but should simply speak of high-EE settings.

The future of EE

What of the future? Where will further expressed emotion research lead us? What areas remain to be explored? Expressed emotion has been used mainly as a measure of the outcome of the course of schizophrenia and a measure of the efficacy of interventions. Expressed emotion has also moved beyond the family to other groups with whom people with schizophrenia come into contact. Kavanagh (1992) found that intense supervision by staff can be likened to EOI and also carries an increased risk of relapse. For people who do not live with their family the emotional atmosphere in group homes or hostels might well be as important (L. Mintz *et al.* 1987). This should include not only staff members but also other residents. Both groups have been shown to display, at times, high levels of criticism and hostility (Higson and Kavanagh 1988).

Studies in London investigating EE levels in staff in residential and long-term day-care facilities found staff were unlikely to show emotional over-involvement, but 43% showed high EE levels to at least one patient (Moore *et al.* 1992a). This work supports the proposition that EE is not a stable trait in an individual (staff or relative) since it seems to be dependent on the attributes of the person with schizophrenia and not to staff characteristics such as stress at work, lack of job satisfaction or poor health.

The popularity of EE has also been demonstrated by researchers using it when studying a wide variety of other conditions, including depression (Hooley *et al.* 1986), bipolar disorder (Miklowitz *et al.* 1986, 1988), weight reduction (Flannigan and Wagner 1991), agoraphobia (Peter and Hand 1988) and senile dementia (Whittick 1993). This has, however, led to EE once again expanding beyond a narrow, predictive indicator of relapse. In dementia it has been used to describe a response by relatives to the process of caring, and even possibly to breakdown of care (Whittick 1993). This might well be important for the involvement of other services, but is very different from the current status of EE within schizophrenia.

Although within schizophrenia research has refined the concept of EE and recognised it as part of an interactive process in relation to relapse, as more researchers apply EE to other populations and other situations it is once again a concept running away with itself. Confusion regarding EE and its emotionally laden aura of blame may result from this. These are issues which will need to be addressed over the next few years as the usefulness of EE in other populations is explored.

Negative Affective Style

Running in parallel and based on similar premises to EE is the concept of Parental Affective Style (Doane *et al.* 1985). Affective style (AS) attempts to measure the emotional climate of the family, and Doane *et al.* (1981) showed that a measure of Family Affective Style derived from direct interaction was related to the onset of psychiatric disorder in a group of adolescents at risk of schizophrenia. The measure is derived from remarks made by the parent to their child in actual face-to-face conversations. The negative codes include criticism, guilt induction and intrusiveness. It is different from the measurement of EE in that it reflects actual *behaviour* rather than *attitudes* expressed to an interviewer in the patient's absence. Doane *et al.* (1985) found AS to be a significant predictor of relapse, and a negative AS pattern was significantly associated with decreased patient social functioning, a reduced ability of the family to absorb family intervention and a reduced capacity of the family to cope with day-to-day stressful problems. Maybe such an important intrafamilial attribute has implications for prevention of relapse and highlights a subgroup of relapse-prone people who require family-based intervention. Doane has been quick to emphasise that negative AS is not a cause of relapse, but rather that psychosocial factors may have an important contributing role in the course of the illness. Acting as a non-specific stressor, it may merely interact with other variables known to affect the clinical course of schizophrenia.

Although interesting, this is essentially the work of a small group of researchers and has not been developed by others, perhaps because of the overwhelming popularity of EE. The few studies from Goldstein, Nuechterlein and their colleagues which have employed AS as a measure have been described earlier, along with EE, because the implications for interactionist models (Goldstein *et al.* 1992) and on stress responses (Altorfer *et al.* 1992) are similar. However, they have been useful in contributing to the development of a family programme.

LIFE EVENTS

Two major forms of social environmental stress (high EE and life events) have been implicated in the course of schizophrenia. Although it is well established that high EE in families has a significant effect on relapse, studies looking at life events precipitating episodes of psychosis are more ambiguous.

An early study by Brown and Birley (1968) found an increase in the frequency of independent life events (that is, those not brought about by the person's illness) in the 3-week period before the onset or relapse of psychotic symptoms. This work has not been consistently replicated (Jacobs and Myers 1976; Al-Khani et al. 1986; Norman and Malla 1993), although the Jacobs and Myers study perhaps used an over-long (1 year) period in which to record life events. Chung et al. (1986) found a significant increase in frequency of life events for schizophreniform disorder but not for schizophrenia, and postulated that as a briefer psychosis it may be more stress-related. A recent, methodologically more stringent, study did find strong and significant relationships between antecedent life events and the onset of psychosis, but earlier: 3 months rather than 3 weeks before onset (Bebbington et al. 1993).

Are life events and high expressed emotion interrelated in respect of relapse? Do they act as separate variables or do they interact in some way to produce a cumulative effect? The only study to look at this in any detail is that of Leff and Vaughn (1980). This study simultaneously measured these two forms of environmental stress in people with schizophrenia and depression. They found people with schizophrenia living with high-EE relatives had a low rate of life events compared with those living with low-EE relatives in the 3 months preceding the onset of illness. This finding was reversed in people with depression, suggesting a different interaction between life events and high EE in the two illnesses. Leff and Vaughn hypothesised that the onset of relapse of schizophrenia appeared to be associated either with high EE or with an independent life event, whilst relapse in depression is associated with the cumulative effect of a critical relative and an independent life event. No differences were found between first and subsequent admissions.

This study had a number of methodological problems. It only looked at people who were taking drugs and living with a relative, and thus studied a selected group, unlike Brown and Birley (1968) who had a general sample of the population of people with schizophrenia. Relatives differed between the diagnostic groups, with a higher proportion of spouses, who are traditionally less involved than parents, in the depressed group. The difficulties in defining relapse in depression and inclusion of prodromal neurotic symptoms in schizophrenia relapse were also a problem.

The use of regular anti-psychotic medication further complicates the role of environmental stress in relapse. Leff *et al.* (1983) found that a significantly greater proportion of people who relapsed whilst on active neuroleptic medication had experienced an independent life event in the 5 weeks prior to relapse, in comparison with those who did not relapse but were also on active medication. This led Leff (1987) to propose that for those living in a high-EE environment but protected by medication, additional life stresses are required for relapse. That is, medication has a prophylactic effect by raising the person's threshold to relapse, a view which has also found some support from Ventura *et al.* (1992). This later study had the advantage of a prospective longitudinal design and monthly life-event assessments to limit retrospective memory bias. The results showed independent life events to be more frequent in the medication group than in those not taking medication.

THE VULNERABILITY MODEL

The picture of the interaction between environmental stress and schizophrenia is complex. Negative symptoms in schizophrenia have been viewed as a strategy for avoiding stress (Wing and Brown 1970). As such, they should reduce the rate of events in psychosis, but Schwartz and Myers (1977) found that people with schizophrenia experience events more frequently. The studies discussed in this section rate only independent events. These events show a tendency to increase as the time of onset of illness is approached, which supports the hypothesis that life events are exerting an aetiological effect on relapse.

Leff and Vaughn's (1980) study indicated that two environmental stressors, independent life events and high expressed emotion, are not cumulative but act as independent variables, exerting separate aetiological effects on relapse. Both variables do share the property of having their effects on relapse modified by medication.

These findings provide some support for a vulnerability stress model of schizophrenia, as proposed by Zubin and Spring (1977) and Nuechterlein and Dawson (1984). An interactive model of the course of schizophrenia (Kavanagh 1992) builds on these earlier models and incorporates a biological vulnerability, with social and life events having an impact on the individual's social perceptions, emotional reactions, coping skills and self-efficacy. These, in turn, affect symptoms and problem behaviour which further affect vulnerability. The behaviour of the person with schizophrenia, including symptoms, has an effect on other people in terms of how they cope and respond to it. Sometimes coping will be less than optimal, and critical, hostile or over-involved responses will result. As we have already discussed, these responses can exacerbate symptoms and induce relapse.

Much of the interest in EE and relapse stems from the belief that changing EE levels will reduce relapse. We should remember, however, that EE is only one of a number of factors which contribute to an individual's vulnerability to relapse. Indeed, one recent review on vulnerability to relapse does not mention EE specifically at all (Zubin *et al.* 1992). Others describe EE as one indicator for possible early intervention.

We have discussed life events and EE specifically in relation to the course of schizophrenia. Surprisingly little work has been done looking at specific forms of stress in relation to 'family coping', particularly in relation to life events. If families become stressed and are not coping, this may not necessarily be a response to the illness but perhaps to other life events. Equally the role of dependent, or illness-related, life events has not been explored in relation to family. There are clearly many avenues in this field worth further investigation.

BIOLOGY, FAMILY AND SCHIZOPHRENIA

There is an increasing body of evidence to suggest that schizophrenia (or at least some forms of it) is a biological condition. Research has included as causes, genetics, neuropathology, neurochemistry, neurophysiology, obstetric complications and virology. To discuss these is outside the scope of this book, although the impact of this work on vulnerability models, the family, and for education programmes is clear. Blame may be seen to have moved from upbringing and family relationships to inheritance, but the psychological consequences of 'guilt' still remain.

2

THE RESPONSE OF THE FAMILY TO SCHIZOPHRENIA

The way a family reacts to a member developing schizophrenia must, in part, depend on the way they perceive mental illness and the practical impact of the illness on themselves.

ATTITUDES TO MENTAL ILLNESS

Attitudes reflect an underlying philosophy or system of beliefs which partly derives from popular culture, possibly modified by experience. Thus the family's attitude to schizophrenia must be seen in the wider context of society's attitude.

Society's Attitudes to Mental Illness

Prevalent in Western societies is the social interpretation of the nature of mental illness. Based on social causal theories, this has led to a greater emphasis on personal responsibility, autonomy and the belief that much severe mental disorder can be prevented through education focusing on achieving positive mental health and a society more tolerant of nonconformity.

Wing (1978) has written

'The persistence of unitary concepts of "mental illness" is a grave handicap to the demythologising and demystification of psychiatry. "Schizophrenia" is not synonymous with "madness".'

Unfortunately, most of the studies looking at community attitudes focus on 'the mentally ill' rather than a specific diagnosis, and it is not always clear whether the public is *un*informed or *mis*informed about mental illness.

Negative attitudes by society to mental illness can be re-interpreted as stigmatisation. Its original meaning of external distinguishing markings as a visible sign of disgrace, later also applied to disease, is perhaps best seen in the drug side effects of facial rigidity, stiffness and odd gait that mark out the patient on long-term intramuscular medication. Stigma is currently more popularly used to indicate a degree of social distance that pushes those 'stigmatised' to the fringes of society, in some cases disqualifying them from full rights as a citizen. Most recently we can look to the defeat of the Civil Rights (Disabled Persons) Bill in the British House of Commons, and compare this with the acclaimed Americans with Disabilities Act in the United States, passed by George Bush in 1990.

From the 1950s to the 1970s there seems to be broad agreement about how the general community views people with mental illness. The methods of investigation have followed two main paths: either asking respondents how far they agree, or not, with a range of statements, or describing short case histories and asking questions about those.

Using the first method, studies conclude that stigma exists (e.g. Nunnally 1961; Maclean 1969). 'There is a strong "negative halo" associated with the mentally ill; they are considered all things "bad" ' (Nunnally 1961). Dangerousness and unpredictability are commonly held to be the cornerstones of the public's attitude, but this is not the whole picture (Maclean 1969). Nunnally suggests that the unpredictability felt by the public may have as much to do with people with mental illness behaving in an embarrassing way as with them behaving dangerously.

The use of case studies to examine the public's recognition of symptoms began with a national survey in the United States by Star in 1950 (described by Cumming and Cumming 1957). The vignettes which she developed have since been used by a number of other researchers. The vignettes used were paranoid schizophrenia, simple schizophrenia, chronic anxiety neurotic, compulsive phobic, alcoholic and a 12-year-old with a behaviour disorder. In Star's study only the person with paranoid schizophrenia was recognised as mentally ill, this being upheld by Cumming and Cumming (1957). Since then, most other studies have found both types of schizophrenia and alcoholics being described as mentally ill. One survey, however (D'Arcy and Brockman 1976), gave different results. These researchers went back to the Saskatchewan town (pseudonym Blackfoot) where the Cummingses had carried out their survey and found little change in public recognition of psychiatric symptoms since the study 20 years earlier. They suggest that changes in methodology, including the way questions are asked, may have contributed more to the changes in findings than a real change in the public's attitudes.

It is very difficult to judge with any degree of accuracy whether the public's view has changed or not. Where it is thought to have 'improved' the conclusion is still expressed with caution. Gurin *et al.* (1960) suggested that although knowledge had improved, attitudes and emotional response had not caught up with this knowledge. Using Nunnally's scale (with some misgivings) over 20 years later, Ahmed and Vishwanathan (1984) still found the public largely uneducated about mental illness, with only slight shifts in attitude.

The changes in services for people with mental health problems and the move to community care over the last decade may have had an impact on the public's view of mental illness and we need to look at a recent survey to determine this. One study in England compared two areas, one which had a 'traditional mental hospital' and one which had a 'community-based service', using statements taken from the Attitudes to Mental Illness Scale (Brockingham *et al.* 1993) and updated versions of Star's vignettes (Hall *et al.* 1993).

In analysing the responses from the statements, three factors accounted for most of the variance. The first, 'community mental health ideology' (with the theme 'fear of the mentally ill and their exclusion from residential neighbourhoods') accounted for 39% of the shared variance. With almost 85% of scores being positive, the public no longer seem to show a fear of the mentally ill. The second factor, 'authoritarianism' (identifying intolerant attitudes), accounts for 37% of the shared variance and again showed a rejection of negative attitudes, although one-third had positive scores indicating 'intolerant attitudes in a substantial minority of the community'. Statements making up the third factor (23% of the variance), broadly described as 'benevolence', were overwhelmingly accepted, with less than 2% having negative scores and 77% of respondants agreeing with the statement that 'More tax money should be spent on the care and treatment of the mentally ill'. Although being prepared to marry someone with a history of mental illness was supported by 'Only two-thirds of the interviewed population', this is still a major increase on a study by Maclean (1969) nearly 25 years earlier. She found that only 21% were prepared to admit a person with mental illness into family membership through marriage. The optimism engendered by this, however, must be tempered by the response to the vignettes, when overall only 6% would marry and 11% have a close relationship with the people described in the vignettes. As the researchers point out, responses to the statements may be biased by a 'social desirability response set'.

Demographic variables had only a small predictive power as to attitude. Of most importance is 'acquaintance with mental illness', which includes personal experience, having a relative or close friend affected or being a professional carer. Age was also important, with older people being associated with more intolerance, while young adults (25–44 years) were the most tolerant. Most worrying, however, was the finding that those below 25 years of age (including students) had the least benevolent attitudes (factor 3), which may reflect their coming to maturity during a long period of Conservative government which has consistently undermined the concept of the welfare state. Both higher occupational status and more education were associated with greater tolerance. Residence in the area with the 'traditional mental hospital' was also associated with a more tolerant attitude, 'but only slightly so'.

The response to the vignettes was less positive and does not suggest a high level of tolerance. Overall 'only 32–54% would live next door, work with, or join the same club as a person with the mental illness portrayed and only about 10% would share a house with such a person.' Knowledge of local services was low and suggested use of services and other sources of help variable.

It should be noted that there was a general low level of identification of mental illness as the 'cause' of the behaviour presented in the vignettes, with 'mental illness' mentioned by 26%, depression by 25% and schizophrenia by 3%. Identification of the cause as being mental illness was more common in women, those aged between 34 and 64 with higher social class and better education, although the effects were small. The authors suggest that 'the frequent choice of stress, insecurity, etc., may imply a relatively tolerant attitude'. Although about 75% of patients were not identified as such, it may be that not labelling people 'mentally ill' should be seen as positive and that 'more specific definition of illness creates a focus of rejection' (Turner 1986). This echoes Kirk (1974, 1975) who, studying sick role and rejection, found that 'conferring the sick role under some considerations was significantly associated with greater rejection.' Sarbin and Mancuso (1970) described the public as not ready to use the label 'mentally ill' to categorise the same behaviour that a professional would diagnose as such, which suggests that in 25 years maybe things have not changed very much.

Downey (1967) considered 'public explanations of mental illness have a cultural history and therefore may pertain to a social system which no longer exists' and offered 'a "cultural criteria" theory which assumes that once an explanation becomes *dominant* in a society it tends to persist regardless of functional consequences'. He suggests that the trend towards scientific explanation from the older folk beliefs is only partial and has to do with causes rather than symptoms. However, since moral and Freudian causes are still considered to be 'valid explanations ... it is becoming easier to be identified as mentally ill' as this seems to expand the range of behaviour so labelled.

It would be useful to know more about the impact of causal beliefs on wider attitudes. That some mental illnesses appear to run in families may be interpreted from this viewpoint as a form of familial moral degeneracy. Negative symptomatology of withdrawal, apathy and poor motivation in schizophrenia can be seen as moral choices, made voluntarily by the person, and thus as antisocial, undesirable traits, although, nevertheless, 'normal' rather than a product of the illness process.

From all of these studies we tend to be left with the overwhelming impression that the public does not much like the mentally ill, but they are becoming more careful in expressing that view and the negative characteristics they attribute to them.

Relatives' Attitudes to Schizophrenia

Relatives, not unnaturally, often share the beliefs of the general population. How, then, do they place these general attitudes in the context of a personal response to a loved one who suffers from a mental illness? Do they reject their previous opinions of mental illness, or do they develop an attitudinal dichotomy, continuing to care for their ill relative and coping with his or her behaviour in particular, whilst still incorporating general stereotyped beliefs regarding the mentally ill? Maybe they even attempt to change society's views.

It might be assumed that professionals find it much easier to accept that behaviour can be symptomatic of illness, both because the patient is not known to them outside their professional relationship and because of their specialised knowledge. They are thus in a better position to distinguish between illness and health. They see only disability, whereas parents and spouses have seen the person with schizophrenia in many roles and contexts and will always be biased and emotionally involved. This is not necessarily true, and families and staff may not be very far apart in their beliefs and behaviours.

Clausen and Yarrow (1955) noted that wives continually altered their interpretation of their husband's behaviour because of the overlap and gradual change between symptoms of mental illness and normal behaviour patterns. They also found it difficult to be viewed as the 'wife of a mental patient', which led them to experience guilt and feelings of rejection towards their spouse (Yarrow *et al.* 1955a).

Most of the work on relatives' knowledge of schizophrenia comes from the research on education and support groups for relatives. Surprisingly little work has been done on exploring the relationship between relatives' attitudes to schizophrenia and the effect of this on the general caring process. It would be reasonable to hypothesise that by not blaming the patient for his or her illness, the family would be more tolerant of the patient's problems.

The relationship between knowledge and attitudes and the impact of both on behaviour is extremely complex and at times contradictory. Freeman and Simmons (1963), for example, found that relatives who thought recovery unlikely were also more likely to blame the person with schizophrenia for their illness. Why? Does this relate to the finding that those who are nearest to the person who is ill are less likely to recognise mental illness (Sakamoto 1969) and tend to normalise the illness? That may explain one unexpected finding in an American survey which showed that 80% of relatives denied avoiding friends out of embarrassment or shame (Doll 1976). Families were, however, less sympathetic in their reactions as the severity of symptoms increased and performance deteriorated.

The concept of differential tolerance of deviance had been introduced by Freeman and Simmons (1963), who found that feelings of stigma on the part of relatives were significantly related to performance levels among males, and less strongly among females, but did not have a relationship with the person's ability to remain in the community.

Functioning may be related to family environment as much as symptoms. Freeman and Simmons (1958) found differences in male patients' post-hospital performance levels depending on the type of family with whom they lived. Patients had lower levels of performance in parental rather than marital homes. They related this to mothers interpreting symptoms/illness as equating with dependency, leading to lower expectations and an increased caring role. Patients who returned to hospital were more likely to come from marital rather than parental homes (Freeman and Simmons 1963), although the level of their functioning, or the degree of illness behaviour, was no worse.

There is a widespread assumption that stigmatisation associated with increasing isolation and alienation may lead to a poorer prognosis or outcome. Improved prognosis in developing countries is often linked to the reduced stigma there, yet the assumption that there is a causal relationship between stigma and prognosis remains unproven. Kelly (1964) found no difference between those with favourable or unfavourable attitudes on background and treatment variables considered in conjunction with outcome.

The extent to which a family feels it is stigmatised will depend on their particular community's view of mental disorder; larger, non-Western families being traditionally more tolerant (Lefley 1990). This in itself causes problems, as communities often vary considerably between principle and practice. People who have less empathy with mental illness may, in practice, not isolate the person with a mental illness. This was borne out by Doll (1976), who found that families may tolerate difficult behaviour whilst not accepting it, so that measures of rehospitalisation are low but the invisible and unmeasured toll of distress remains high.

ATTITUDES OF PEOPLE WITH SCHIZOPHRENIA TO THE FAMILY

This is an area which has been of little concern to chroniclers of family relationships, perhaps because families have been mainly of interest with regard to their role in aetiology and their effect on outcome and relapse. That the person with schizophrenia may influence both family dynamics and family health has been of secondary importance.

Scott and Montanez (1971) reported what may appear obvious, that patients living in the community appeared to view their relationship with their parents as 'tenable', whilst hospital-based patients reported their relationships to be 'untenable', seeing their parents as 'disturbed'. This group were also more likely to be admitted to hospital more quickly if a crisis developed. Although with some methodological flaws, and dealing only with parent/child relationships, this study did link the concept of patient's attitudes as a block to developing effective coping skills. Interestingly, in order for parents to be perceived as 'well' the patient had to move into the 'sick' role, with the resultant loss of autonomy. These findings propose two competing hypotheses. First, that for parents to be viewed as 'well' the child must be viewed as 'sick', and second, that adopting the sick role leads to rejection. Both hypotheses might be true, but related to different types of family interaction or views of the illness.

Furthermore, the patient's understanding and conceptualising of their illness may not coincide with that of their family. Conflicts may arise between sociological and biological viewpoints, which may lead to different degrees of perceived stigmatisation. In addition, carers understandably want to be involved in discussions over treatment and management while the patient, equally understandably, usually wants to protect privacy, confidentiality and autonomy.

THE RESPONSE TO SCHIZOPHRENIA

The illness can alter patients' and relatives' attitudes to themselves and others and challenge previous values. For a spouse or parent it may mean giving up a career for a more routine job, or leaving paid employment altogether to adopt a caring role. Plans for the future may have to be substantially reviewed. It may lead to more tolerant and sympathetic attitudes to other peoples' difficulties, or it may result in an embittered feeling of the unfairness of the situation. Conversely, it may bring understanding and a degree of satisfaction in the caring role.

It is severity and chronicity that lead relatives to experience stress in responding to, and coping with, the illness. The family's response must be addressed both as a response to the illness itself and as a response to caring. These two responses often overlap, but it is important to separate them since they cause different problems and not all family members will accept, or even need, to take on the role of care-giver, yet they may still experience difficulties (Atkinson and Coia 1989).

Despite a well-documented 30-year history of family response to schizophrenia and the difficulties of living with mental illness, and the establishment of research-based demonstration services, there has been little progress in the provision of routine catchment-wide services for relatives. This leads us to ask if there has been any real progress in changing social policy to acknowledge relatives' needs or in the provision of services to support families. We should ask whether it remains important to document how families respond to illness.

Throughout the 1960s and 1970s, research in this field was carried out in both the USA and the UK. The increasing discharge of long-term patients into the community provoked a recognition that increased 'face-to-face' contact meant greater strains on families supporting such people at home. More recently there has been a change in the way professionals view the role of the relative.

Without family involvement, statutory community services would rapidly become overloaded and unable to function. For major mental illness, 60% of first admissions now return home (MacMillan *et al.* 1986), while Creer *et al.* (1982) found that 40–50% of long-term patients are in contact with relatives. In order to maximise family functioning in this area, an increased understanding of their response to illness and their coping mechanisms as carers is needed. It must not be assumed, however, that more patients living in the community is an indication that relatives have more positive attitudes, and better adjustment, to mental illness. They may just have developed a higher threshold for tolerating symptoms. This, in turn, may result in serious emotional difficulties within the family (for example, high expressed emotion).

This raises several interesting questions. Do families wish to be viewed as carers? Is the investigation of their response to schizophrenia and how they manage it within their own family setting intrusive and a violation of their privacy? How do patients view increasing interest in their family setting? It is important to focus on the response of *all* family members to the illness, not just that of the primary carer, and to look at the effect on the more peripheral relatives such as siblings or grand-parents.

IMPACT ON THE FAMILY

How does schizophrenia in one family member affect the other members of the family? The impact depends on the resources of relatives: their physical health and age, their social assets, including their marital relationship and social network, their material assets, and their psycho-logical strengths and coping skills. It has been extensively documented that living with, and caring for, someone who is severely mentally ill can cause problems, traditionally described as 'family burden', a term that may be offensive both to people with schizophrenia and to fami-lies. The former might be unwilling to accept they are a burden, have a lack of comprehension or insight that they present a problem or, when well, be struggling to seek independence and find such a concept of dependency a retrograde step. Families may find the idea of a loved and cherished family member being burdensome extremely upsetting and the idea of considering their care stressful guilt-provoking. These issues are often neglected in the rush to describe the actuality of burden. It is also important to distinguish family hardship, a much broader concept than burden, which is specific to 'patient'-related problems. Since uniform criteria on burden have not been applied across studies, it is not possible to quantify or make absolute comparisons. Equally we have little empirical information on how burden varies with time and illness severity. We can only state with certainty that it exists and that it is a feature of the caring process in the majority of families.

Studies in the early 1960s found considerable evidence of family dis-turbance, hardship and strained social relationships (Mandelbrote and Folkard 1961; Grad and Sainsbury 1963; Wing *et al.* 1964). The concept of burden was refined into two dimensions, objective and subjective (Hoenig and Hamilton 1967). Objective burden, in terms of adverse effects on the household, is that which exists externally, can be observed by others, and includes quantifiable, measurable problems such as physical care, finance and over-crowding. Subjective burden, in contrast, is less tangible and viewed as personal, internal feelings such as guilt, shame or worry over the future, or attitudes to experiencing burden.

Interestingly, one does not automatically imply the other. Many families experiencing high levels of objective burden do not have high levels of subjective burden. Nor do they have an expectation of help, despite experiencing considerable objective burden (Hoenig and Hamilton 1967, 1969). Individuals show a great deal of variation in the relationship of objective to subjective burden (Platt 1985). Families with high levels of subjective burden tend to cope less well irrespective of their objective burden, and subjective burden also appears to be linked to high EE and thus, perhaps, to a high risk of patients' relapsing. Platt (1985) described burden somewhat differently and introduced the term 'patient relatedness burden', which implies that the burden has to arise specifically from problems of living with the patient.

Having described a structure for assessing burden, it is perhaps important to look at the information that has been amassed regarding burden. Studies on this topic are descriptive, either based on clinical observation and relatives' accounts, or on an attempt to measure the extent of burden on the family, refine the concept and identify associated factors. This has proved difficult, as many factors are not only not specific to families coping with schizophrenia, but are also cumulative rather than acting in isolation.

This traditional way of identifying burden has not led to the provision of real services for relatives, and perhaps the introduction of a good needs assessment for carers will be more effective in developing services to meet relatives' needs.

Effect on Carers of the Behaviour of a Person with Schizophrenia

There is a general consensus over the behavioural problems which cause most distress in relatives (Mills 1962; Grad and Sainsbury 1963; Hoenig and Hamilton 1967; Creer and Wing 1974; Lefley 1987). These fall into two categories: acute, socially disturbing or embarrassing behaviour, and social withdrawal. Whereas disruptive behaviour precipitated by positive symptoms of delusions and hallucinations may cause acute apprehension and stress in relatives, it is the negative symptoms resulting in social withdrawal, apathy and self-neglect that cause more long-term conflict and disruption. This occurs for a number of reasons.

1. Families feel that they have lost the mutual relationship between themselves and the person with schizophrenia (Birchwood and Smith 1987).

2. Families may also be more likely to attribute negative symptoms personally to the individual, rather than to the illness, viewing such symptoms as a lack of control or a personality deficit.

Long term support and respite care (MacCarthy *et al.* 1989a) have been identified as the most appropriate strategies for coping with negative symptomatology. Planned respite interrupts the complex cycle of relapse and re-admission to extend the stable period by reducing relatives' subjective stress (Geiser *et al.* 1988). Current community services within Britain focusing on more acute provision (for example, 24-hour crisis intervention) do not appear adequate to meet this need.

Relatives' Own Mental Health

Few studies have examined in any detail, or assessed adequately, mental health problems occurring in relatives as a result of their caring role. Yet with increasing numbers of relatives replacing statutory services as providers of care, now would seem to be the time to document more fully this aspect of burden. In depressive disorder there is a direct association between the severity of a person's depression and mental health problems in their spouse, as measured on the GHQ (General Health Questionnaire). Whilst we are aware that relatives of people with schizophrenia experience considerable levels of stress, the extent of this and in whom it translates into measurable psychiatric disorder is unclear.

Studies on general populations of carers that have been carried out using instruments such as the GHQ and the PSE (Present State

Examination) find at least one-third of relatives have incurred major psychiatric symptomatology, in particular anxiety and depression, related to their caring role (Wing *et al.* 1974, 1981; Goldberg and Hillier 1979; Creer *et al.* 1982; Fadden *et al.* 1987a, b; Oldridge and Hughes 1992). Subjective emotional distress appears to be highest amongst new carers, perhaps because having just taken up their caring role they are more involved and less resigned (Gibbons *et al.* 1984). Such emotional disturbance was found to be greater in families whose relative was community- rather than hospital-based (Grad and Sainsbury 1963). This led MacCarthy (1988) to point out that when calculating the cost of maintaining long-term patients in the community, the cost of psychiatric provision to one-third of their carers should be added.

Relatives' Social Functioning

Families of people with schizophrenia experience increasing social isolation, which usually means limitation of the families' social and leisure activities. Yarrow *et al.* (1955a) noted a policy of 'aggressive concealment' in one-third of patients' wives, who made drastic changes to their lives or moved house in order to avoid friends. Also, only one-third told family or close friends of their husband's illness. He related this to fears of being 'stigmatised' or socially discriminated against. Similar findings of diminished social activity and a reduction in relatives' natural social networks were found by other studies (Mandelbrote and Folkard 1961; Beels 1975).

Social isolation is rated more burdensome than financial and employment difficulties. MacCarthy (1988) suggests that it may be more destructive of the relationship between the carer and the person with schizophrenia and reduce coping resources. Two caveats have to be added.

1. The difference between objective social isolation and the subjective perception of one's social situation has to be made.

2. There is an implied assumption that social support via a social network is beneficial in reducing stress.

Paradoxically, the relatives' illness-related network may expand with time during the course of the illness as they continue to seek outside help in their role as care-giver. This network may also help reduce social isolation. Groups of other family care-givers, such as the

National Schizophrenia Fellowship in Britain and the National Alliance for the Mentally Ill in the USA, fulfil such a role for many people as well as helping to improve self-confidence.

Financial and Employment Problems

Relatives report practical, objective problems related to loss of employment and financial hardship. These problems appear to be worse when the carer is a spouse, has a partner who was formerly earning, and who had good pre-morbid functioning (Yarrow et al. 1955a; Fadden et al. 1987b). The reason that spouses may find material hardship more difficult to bear is that they have experienced a relationship that is reciprocal and have built up commitments and plans for the future. They may not have expected, or be able, to take over the role of primary earner, and come to resent this. The situation is different for parents when the person with schizophrenia may never have achieved financial independence. Thus a more gradual adaptation to financial hardship may occur, even though the person with schizophrenia who has early onset illness experiences a longer period of loss of earning.

Unemployment may also extend to carers who have to give up work or limit opportunities at work, to look after their relatives, and this again increases the vicious circle of social isolation and lack of time away from their ill relative. For those initially unemployed this may prove a less stressful exercise (Gilleard 1984).

Relationship Problems Within the Family

Two related problems, the loss of reciprocity and increasing reliance on relatives, leads carers to seek outside help with caring (Kuipers et al. 1992). This loss of mutuality and failure to meet the shared obligations normally present in healthy relationships can vary in importance depending on the relationship, spouse, parent or sibling, but has been likened to a 'living bereavement'.

Spouses

Spouses, with their higher expectations than parents, may find the increasing 'emotional deadness' (Hatfield 1990) in their marriage a particular problem. Inequality within the relationship may lead them to think about divorce, even if they do not act upon it. The divorce rate for women with mental illness had been found to be three times the national average, and that for men four times (Brown and Rutter 1966). There is contradictory evidence on the impact on the family depending on the gender of the person with schizophrenia. Wives with schizophrenia tend to disrupt the family life more than husbands and are coped with less well at home (Rodger and Hollingshead 1965). Thus the threshold for hospitalisation may be lower for women, although this may also be due to less stigmatisation. Niskanen and Pihkanen (1972), however, found that families exercised a more tolerant attitude towards a mentally ill female relative than towards a male relative.

Parents

Parents, like spouses, tend to be the main or primary carers with considerable burden placed upon them. They may, in fact, cope better with the loss of reciprocity within the relationship than spouses, since a relationship with a child is historically unequal. Parents' worries may centre more around guilt, feelings they have caused or contributed to the illness and fears for the future. Neither the health nor the social services have been prepared to take up this last issue since emphasis is still placed on people coming out of hospital who have no family involved with them. Less is offered to those living in the community with relatives.

Primary care-givers tend to be female and tend all too readily to take on the emotional attachments of the role—guilt, self-blame, fear and frustration. Life outside this role becomes increasingly narrow. Where parents view the illness differently, this can further increase marital disharmony.

Siblings

Hatfield (1990) describes three tiers of care-giving, parent or spouse being in the first tier and siblings in the second tier, as they are part of the immediate family household but not directly responsible for the ill member, and are able to remove themselves regularly from the situation. The needs of this group are often neglected by professionals as they are seen as less important to the care-giving process. Nevertheless, they face considerable problems including guilt, fear, shame and anger (Dearth et al. 1986). 'Perceived burden' may be the greater due to the intermittent nature of 'actual burden', as they are freer to come and go within the household. Family relationships become altered. Parents coping with a mentally ill child may pay less attention to other children and expect more of them at an earlier age. This can lead to resentment, which may be directed towards the illness itself, leaving them ambivalent about mental illness and sometimes misunderstanding the problems. Such attitudes may persist into adulthood and colour their attitudes towards their ill sibling. They may leave home early to avoid either sharing or taking on the burden of caring. Sadly, this may reduce their involvement with the primary care-giver, thus increasing the isolation (Meissner 1970; Hoover and Franz 1972). In addition, constant contact with their ill sibling may also engender fears that they may be 'like them'—'will I develop the illness?'—leading to feelings of self-doubt and altered self-perceptions. Guilt may occur over their inability to improve the situation and their own success (often not properly acknowledged within the family), whilst their sibling continues to make little progress (Fadden *et al.* 1987a).

Little is known of siblings needs and desire for information. Landeen *et al.* (1992) found that the majority wanted information. Information about heredity risks was wanted by three-quarters of siblings, and aetiology and prognosis were other popular requests. Most reported that although they had communication difficulties at times with the person with schizophrenia their ill sibling did not disrupt their lives on a day-to-day basis, nor were they particularly interested in meeting siblings of other schizophrenia sufferers. As might be expected, great concern was expressed by all siblings about the future, and whether the person with schizophrenia would remain independent, i.e. independent of current service provision.

On a more optimistic note, siblings may ultimately prove effective care-givers, often being slightly detached and less likely to become over-involved. Some verbatim accounts of siblings responses are given in Dearth *et al.* (1986).

Other relatives

The third tier of care-giving describes 'peripheral relatives', grandparents, cousins and others, who may be concerned but who live outside the immediate household. They often try to support the primary carer and, because the burden is intermittent, may prove a useful support and resource from time to time. Problems may arise because of their reduced contact with the person with schizophrenia, which leads them to misunderstand the illness and offer inappropriate advice. Equally this partial involvement may make them feel helpless and frustrated, and result in conflict with the immediate family over how they manage the person with schizophrenia.

Children

Surprisingly little is written about the responses of a child to living with one or two ill parents or even an older sibling. This is despite a body of research into the influences on family development and child-rearing which stresses that one capable parent is necessary for effective parenting. As might be expected, there is more research on mothers than on fathers with mental illness, although this is only partly to do with post-partum mental illness. Illness in a parent may reflect on the child directly through marital problems or repeated hospitalisation (Rutter and Quinton 1984). Both positive and negative symptoms of schizophrenia can cause problems in mothering behaviour; acute episodes can lead to distraction and neglect, and if there are any delusions or hallucinations concerning a baby or child then close supervision is indicated. Pre-morbid social adjustment obviously plays a part, but the lack of warmth, and rigid or anxious styles of mothering which can occur during an acute episode, may take anything up to a year to be replaced with more appropriate styles (Rodnick and Goldstein 1974). The flattened or incongruous affect, apathy, disturbed behaviour and lack of responsiveness to the child's cues which are part of the chronic condition may all lead to problems in mother–child bonding, with the worrying consequences of impaired social functioning and problem solving (Pastor 1981; Egeland and Stroufe 1981).

These studies are concerned primarily with the post-partum period and early childhood. They are complicated by there being little agreement on how best to assess maternal competency, and by most assessments being carried out in mother and baby units. Despite this, psychiatrists are likely to be asked to assess a woman's mothering skills, often in response to a request from social workers who are acting under ever-growing public pressure to protect children, and who have the responsibility to do so in law (Appleby and Dickens 1993).

Older children may become concerned that they may have caused or contributed to the illness, yet still feel anger and resentment at not being given appropriate care. Puberty and adolescence, in itself a difficult period of change and adjustment, may be made more so by the continued health problems of a parent or the breakdown of an older sibling.

Personality may seem an obvious factor in both coping and effective care-giving but, as described in later chapters, it is usually of less importance than the characteristics of the illness and specific caring tasks. The quality of the relationship before the illness would also seem relevant, but is little researched. Relatives in difficult relationships prior to the illness tend to be more critical (Leff and Vaughn 1985). Why many relatives find unsuspected strengths when faced with the burden of caring is unknown. Gillis and Keer (1965) describe families who continue to care as 'somewhat odd' due to their own needs, personalities and expectations being subjugated over a period of chronic adjustment to accommodate the ill family member.

FAMILIES' ADJUSTMENT TO THE ILLNESS

For the family the strange behaviour of the person with schizophrenia is a 'new experience' which has to be understood and responded to. The emotional impact of this behaviour continues to be underestimated. For each family the totality of the impact will be different, but there are some common pathways.

The way families respond to the illness varies in time, although there is little empirical research of this longitudinal adjustment process (Kreisman and Joy 1974). Families usually start with ignorance of the illness, and strange behaviour is not recognised as illness but seen as an extension of normal personality or denied as presenting a problem (Jackson et al. 1990). Some relatives ask patients to 'own' their behaviour, seeing them as difficult or lazy. Such relatives often have high EE ratings (Leff and Vaughn 1985). Eventually the behaviour reaches a threshold where the family can no longer cope. Family anxiety and fear increases markedly and they will seek help, which may in turn antagonise the person seen as having the problem. The difficult phase of first contact with professionals begins.

This contact should initiate and establish a therapeutic and supportive partnership between the person with schizophrenia, the professionals and the relatives. Unfortunately it all too often goes wrong. The person who is thought to have the problem may reject help, not believing themselves ill, and if the course of the illness fluctuates relatives will be both confused and increasingly anxious. Usually by this time there is an acute incident that transforms the ill person into 'official patient' status, with all the implications such diagnostic and social labelling involves. The family begins to realise that this disorder will not just go away. Understandably they search for a cause of the problem either internally, through familial interaction, attaching blame and guilt to various members, or externally, for biological explanations. Conflict can occur when different family members favour different approaches. Such a search may have different outcomes. Those who favour a biological approach (except birth injury) tend to attach less guilt or blame to themselves or their ill relative. However, in their search for effective treatment they are more liable to 'therapeutic despair' at the lack of major progress in scientific research into aetiology or therapeutics. Family members who favour an internal approach via family dynamics may become destructive to one another in their attempt to change the behaviour they perceive as damaging, but are less likely to feel resignation or despair.

Living with the established illness brings the realisation that things will never be as before, and that there has to be an adjustment to the actual level of functioning of the person with schizophrenia. There is sadness and mourning (bereavement) for the loss of the person they knew before the illness (Fadden *et al.* 1987a), anger and resent-ment at having their own lives altered or curtailed (Creer and Wing 1974), shame and stigma leading to narrowing social contacts, and poor understanding from those outside the immediate circle. Both over-protection and resignation can lead to continuing reduction in the patient's social functioning and networks, and increases the downward spiral.

Responses probably vary with the phases of the illness. During the acute phase relatives tend to be sympathetic, supportive and make considerable effort to hold things together, but the chronic phase of the illness can present more difficult problems. The person who withdraws may make relatives feel devalued and less respected, particularly if their opinions regarding treatment and management of the illness are ignored. Fortunately, however, relatives often become increasingly tolerant of episodes of treatment rejection. This episodic pattern makes stable coping mechanisms difficult to cultivate and is extremely distressing for relatives (Hatfield 1978).

Finally, some attempt is made to pick up the pieces. Continuous care at home makes this cumulatively difficult, whilst the intermittent absence of the person with schizophrenia makes it easier to restrict the effect of the ill member on family life. Such absence may only be provided in future by respite care, which is likely to become ever more important as we move into new service delivery (Geiser *et al.* 1988) through the implementation of community care.

RELATIONSHIP OF PROFESSIONALS AND RELATIVES IN THE CARING PROCESS

If we accept that it is appropriate and beneficial for increasing numbers of patients to live in the community, it becomes essential that the partnership between professionals and relatives is strengthened to provide maximum care with minimum stress. In the past this relationship has often been uneasy, and we need to break down the boundaries that both professionals and relatives erect around themselves and re-examine how each may best help the other.

Services in Britain are patient-orientated and confidentiality is only one of the reasons put forward for not involving relatives (Atkinson and Coia 1989). Families may often view service interventions as inappropriate to their clinical needs. Relatives' attitudes are often set by their first experience of services. First contact with professionals may mean relatives are ignored, despite their knowledge and lifetime involvement with the patient. Yet, despite not being consulted, they are expected to care for the patient once the acute episode of the illness has passed. When they are not given their place, their involvement acknowledged, their expectations, fears and anxieties discussed, and information exchanged, they may develop negative attitudes towards professionals that colour future interactions with services and are less than helpful to patient management.

In addition, professionals tend to forget that families often deal with multiple agencies, medical, social and legal, all of whom have different views on, and attitudes to, mental illness. From these multiple contacts they have to distil information, take what is helpful in managing their particular problems, and reject what is not. In addition, whilst continuously responding to the information demands of these professionals, they are often fearful of criticising any service provision in case it is withdrawn. No matter how poor the service, families rarely complain (Hoenig and Hamilton 1966, 1969). Concerns have been raised (Brown and Rutter 1966) that this lack of complaint may presume too much of families in the drive to community care.

On the other hand, some families may never be satisfied by the services provided, no matter how excellent. Their demands may be beyond any service provision, addressed to the wrong service, or not be in the patient's best interests. They may continue to search endlessly, with false expectations, for 'cures'. Such behaviour is understandable given the distressing nature of schizophrenia, and may be a form of self-protection for families unable to cope with someone who may not get much better. Such distress has to be dealt with patiently, and families helped and empowered to feel they have some control and contribution to make in aiding the person with schizophrenia to maximise their functioning, no matter how limited. Families ask for information, but what relatives want to know and what professionals think they should know can be very different. What value is information to families? It is assumed that it allows them to feel involved, not shut out by professionals, and that it influences behaviour and coping skills. This is not necessarily the case, and will be discussed in detail in Chapters 3 and 4.

Another frustration for families occurs with the lack of continuity of the staff involved. Frequent staff changes require patients and relatives continually to repeat their case histories, give up trusting relationships and start again with another person. Repeated requests that statutory services should place a higher priority on maintaining staff continuity for patients with chronic illnesses, and offer a more personalised service, have so far been ignored despite the growing prominence of the consumer movement.

In addition, professionals tend to place less emphasis on, and are less interested in, the more chronic aspects of schizophrenia. Relatives report that they often feel more able to seek and obtain help during acute relapse, yet are most in need of support during more chronic phases of the illness. Creer and Wing (1974) found that families obtained little support from their GP or social worker at this time. In contrast, during the acute episode doctors tended to take over responsibility for patient care and management completely. Such unequal, unbalanced relationships at different times in the course of the illness have led to a wariness and reluctance on the part of relatives to interact with staff. This reluctance, in turn, results in staff becoming negative towards them (Birley and Hudson 1983).

Families need constant support throughout the illness and become rightly wary of short-term, intensive interactions that leave them feeling let down when they end. Little is known about their specific long-term requirements (Atkinson 1986), but providing long-term, low-key support may prove an important first step. Chapter 3 looks at how families have been involved in therapy, and Chapter 5 reviews the role of relative as carer.

3

THE FAMILY IN THERAPY

Families can be ignored in therapy for two reasons. If it is believed they play no part in either the development or course of the illness, relatives may be useful to describe symptoms and individual and family history, but beyond that have little to contribute apart from (possibly) ensuring that the patient takes medication. Relatives are thus benignly ignored. If, however, schizophrenia is caused by psychological factors in the family's functioning, then to remove the 'patient' from the noxious family environment for individual therapy might make (at least super-ficial) sense. Where patients want continued relationships with their family or have nowhere else to live, they are returned to the environ-ment which initially caused the problem. Although it could be assumed that therapy will help the person cope better, it would seem to put undue strain on someone who has already shown themself to be vulnerable. This individual-therapy approach may lead to relatives being actively shunned rather than ignored.

A newer approach includes the family in the treatment process with a view to changing their interaction with the patient and thus reducing relapse or improving the patient's functioning. This approach can be one that is positive and supportive of both patient and relatives, or can still lead to relatives' feeling responsible and being blamed. The ap-proaches described here span dynamic, behavioural, educational indi-vidual and group approaches.

FAMILY AND CHANGE

The aim of therapy is to bring about change. We need to consider who or what changes, and what outcome is taken as indicative of change.

In family therapy the family is taken as a unit and is the target of change. Commonly, however, outcome is measured by the impact on one person—the designated patient. If the family as a 'system' is being 'treated', then should not the 'system' be the focus of measures of outcome? Expressed emotion might be measured in the family but the primary outcome is always patient relapse, however imperfectly defined.

The family being 'in therapy' for their sake rather than the patient's is rarely discussed in these approaches. Families may well become involved with the intention of 'helping the patient' without necessarily understanding the implications for change for themselves. This is not to suggest that therapists are acting unethically, that procedures are not explained to clients, or that if they did explain families would not take part. Rather it is to try to highlight the differences between therapy, support and education.

Skynner (1989) describes family therapy as essentially a paradigm shift. He uses an analogy from astronomy:

> 'it is more akin to the change from the geocentric to the heliocentric view of the solar system at the time of Galileo, which changed our whole concept of the universe, than to the mere discovery of a new planet.'

He describes it as a

> 'remarkable meeting ground permitting fruitful cross-fertilization between disciplines . . . including psychiatry, psychoanalysis, sociology and social work, anthropology, communication theory, mathematics, systems theory'.

Family-orientated treatment programmes, however, are best seen as those that involve the family in the treatment process, but not in ways which could be defined as therapy. Individual therapy for the patient may include the family to deal with specific behaviour.

Family support, in contrast, may be seen as enabling the family to deal with unusual and difficult conditions. It includes counselling, advice regarding management of the patient's behaviour, alternative choices of intervention, and problem-solving skills. Although it may encompass advice which alters behaviour or attitudes, it does not occur within a therapeutic framework.

Education can be part of wider support or can stand alone. Education about the illness, its causes, symptoms, treatment, prognosis and rehabilitation, may be given to alleviate anxiety, give people a basis from which to make informed decisions, or with the hope that it might influence behaviour. Or it may be given as part of a philosophy which promotes the individual's (here the patient and/or the relative) right to know as much about the condition they are being treated for as possible (Atkinson 1989; Atkinson and Coia 1989). Health education and promotion seek to alter the lifestyles of individuals with the clear aim of altering health outcomes, but there is no suggestion that this is therapy. Years of research in social psychology demonstrate that changing attitudes and changing behaviour are two different things, and that giving people information does not necessarily affect behaviour.

Family-orientated treatment programmes and family support, like family therapy, draw on a number of disciplines. It is to be hoped that they can also resist a move towards polarisation but retain a broadly collective approach characterised by the positive involvement of families.

PSYCHODYNAMIC PSYCHOTHERAPY AND THE FAMILY

Two different beliefs influenced the early family therapies of the 1960s and 1970s. The first suggested that if schizophrenia was the result of conflicts within the family, then exposing those conflicts would mean that the person identified as having schizophrenia would no longer need to 'act crazy'. This end point could then justify any techniques, 'no matter how confrontational or manipulative' to bring conflict out into the open. The second approach, which saw pathological family communication as the underlying cause of schizophrenia, meant that therapists 'were understandably intent on aggressively altering these aberrant behaviours'. Personal confidentiality was abolished. Not everyone who viewed these sessions saw them positively. Although some people saw a 'wonderful new therapeutic tool for assisting patient and family', to others the sessions were more disturbing and they 'felt troubled by what they saw as abuse rather than assistance of families' (Steinglass 1987).

Laing's view of schizophrenia as a potentially self-healing process led to the development of a form of existential family therapy (Esterson *et al.* 1965). A pioneering project in London extended the concept of a therapeutic community. A crisis unit provided support for patients and families during acute episodes. Existential therapists attempted to understand delusions and hallucinations within the family context, which often led to the scapegoating of family members. Later treatment programmes, in both Britain and the United States, saw the psychotic episode as a valid and valued experience from which new insights could be gained. Staff, who were often young and untrained mental health workers, lived with the people with schizophrenia. They worked with them through the psychological disturbance, being tolerant of inappropriate behaviour. It was seen as important that time was given to develop the suppressed and more imaginative parts of the person with schizophrenia rather than further suppressing them with drugs. How difficult this could be has been described by a young psychiatrist (Barnes and Berke 1971).

Reflecting on seminars with Laing, Esterson and Cooper in the early 1960s, Scott (1991) recalls,

> 'These sessions were very charismatic. They led to an in-depth understanding of the patient and the role of the family in his illness. Later I came to realise a limitation involved. It concerns the idealisation of the patient who was basically seen as an innocent victim of his parents and of society. This diminished his genuine agency—his status as a human being. The status of the parents was also diminished—they caused schizophrenia. They were seen as being schizophrenogenic.'

There is little evidence to suggest that psychodynamic psychotherapy adds anything very much to conventional treatment with psychotropic drugs (Kottgen *et al.* 1984; Dulz and Hand 1986; McFarlane 1990). One explanation is that an insight-orientated approach is usually believed to be too stimulating or stressful for psychotic patients as it can exacerbate delusional thinking and contribute to psychotic regression (Strachan 1986; Vaughn 1986). Neither do these studies stand up to methodological scrutiny, because either they do not employ good design, being case studies or having small numbers, they lack objective outcome measures or they have no follow up.

Working with the families of people with schizophrenia is not always easy. The difficulty, if not impossibility, of involving families as 'allies' in psychodynamic psychotherapy is described by Kanter and Lin (1980). Keith and Whitaker (1980) suggest that if, as sometimes happens,

> 'the treatment demand comes from the family, it is usually to protect their *status quo* in hope of improved adaptation. When the demand stays at this level, it is unlikely that psychological growth or family creativity will advance. In order to bring the family alive the therapists need first to confront the family's chaos.'

FAMILY INTERVENTION PROGRAMMES

Many of the early family intervention programmes also did not employ good experimental designs, notably non-randomised assignment to therapeutic situations, variable attrition rates, poor outcome assessment, and a design which made it impossible to determine the independent effect of each component. Nevertheless, they do show some interesting results which are worth considering since they have informed later, better designed, studies. They share an orientation which is behavioural, educational and skills-focused rather than analytical and interpretive, and forms part of a continuing care package. Families are treated with respect and helped to develop strategies for coping. A biosocial approach is taken, putting schizophrenia within a vulnerability–stress–coping–competence model. Within the intervention programmes, however, a number of distinct strands can be described.

The first of the random assignment family intervention programmes was that of Goldstein *et al.* (1978). The family involvement was through short-term, crisis-intervention family therapy while the patient was on either a low or medium dosage of long acting phenothiazines. The patients were predominantly young and 69% were first admissions. The family sessions, which involved a co-therapist and the patient, were weekly for six weeks, and held in the out-patient clinic following discharge. They were based on family crisis intervention therapy designed to enable the family to understand the events around the crisis, and thus to improve future coping. This involved identifying the stressful events preceding breakdown, making links between them, moving on to identifying two or three situations currently stressful to the patient, and developing strategies for coping with, or avoiding, these events. Homework during the week included putting these plans into action and reporting back. Lastly, plans were made to anticipate future crises and to develop coping strategies in advance of such crises. The most important topic was the emergence of psychiatric symptoms, but others included making friends, resuming employment and planning future living arrangements.

There were interactions between drug dosage and family therapy, with the greatest effects showing at the extremes. Short-term changes were not maintained at six months, with the only significant change being in withdrawal, and this was found only in the group with the higher drug dosage. Long-term follow up of three years plus showed no differences.

Glick *et al.* (1985) and Haas *et al.* (1988) ran a programme while the patient was still in hospital. The sessions, of one hour, had an educational, supportive and forward-planning focus. Although overall there were significantly lower levels of psychiatric symptomatology at discharge for those in the family psycho-education programme, the effects were much smaller for people with schizophrenia than for those with a major affective disorder, and those with poor pre-morbid functioning showed no benefit. Thus, overall, only about one-third of those with a diagnosis of schizophrenia showed a benefit. Although relatives rated themselves as having benefited, there was an interesting relationship between sex of patient, pre-morbid functioning and response. Families of both males and females with good pre-morbid functioning and females with poor pre-morbid functioning reported improvements with the family psycho-education groups. The families of poor pre-morbid functioning males showed more improvement with the standard in-patient care.

A three-phase approach is described by Reiss (1988) involving in Phase I an attempt to connect with patient and family to lay 'the foundation for the entire process of treatment'. This took place as early as possible, with four aims:

'(1) to develop a working alliance among the clinician, the patient and the family; (2) to maximise and emphasise family strengths and resources rather than focus on weakness and deficits; (3) to gain an understanding of any problems that might contribute to the stress levels of the patient or other family members; (4) to establish the rules and expectations of treatment through the creation of a contract with mutual, specific and attainable goals.'

Phase II was a one-day, multi-family 'survival skills' workshop, and Phase III was individual sessions with the family.

REDUCING EXPRESSED EMOTION

One of the important differences between families was that high-EE relatives believed the person could, if they so wished, control their behaviour. This was associated with believing that the 'illness' was not really an illness, and that the behaviour of the person with schizophrenia was somehow deliberate or malicious. By contrast, the low-EE relatives accepted the problem as a legitimate illness and thus that bizarre or difficult behaviour was outside the person's control. With this information, it is not surprising that there should be a move to change these beliefs and lower expressed emotion in high EE families with the aim of reducing relapse.

Leff and colleagues developed an intervention to this end, involving three parts: education, a relatives' group and family therapy (Berkowitz *et al.* 1981; Leff *et al.* 1982). Education (Berkowitz *et al.* 1984) was presented to relatives at home and is described later. The groups were held fortnightly, were led by two professionals and included both low- and high-EE relatives. The hope was that the more effective coping mechanisms modelled by the low-EE relatives would be demonstrated to the high-EE relatives and be adopted by them. In the event the low-EE relatives tended to drop out of the groups. Consequently the group leaders had to take a more active role in helping relatives develop coping strategies. The family therapy aspect included the patient, was conducted in the family home, and was intended to deal with family dynamics using a pragmatic, flexible approach. The number of these sessions varied; every family had at least one session, with an average of five.

The design of the study means that the impact of each therapeutic element cannot be assessed separately, but taken as a whole the relapse rate of people with schizophrenia living in high-EE homes was reduced to 8%, the same as for those in low-EE homes. Those patients in the control group, and high-EE families, had a relapse rate which remained at 50%. The expression of EE decreased from high to low in 6 out of 12 families. At two years follow-up (Leff *et al.* 1985), 33% of the treatment group compared to 75% of the comparison group had relapsed.

Some patients stopped taking medication during this period and the data analysed without these patients showed results which were even more significant, with only 20% of the family intervention group compared with 78% of the standard out-patient treatment group relapsing. Differential attrition rates over time, between conditions and for a variety of resources do, however, make comparison difficult, as follow-up can look like poorly matched sample groups.

The next stage was to try to establish which part of the package was most responsible for success, particularly in respect of professional resources (Leff et al. 1989). Family therapy at home was compared to a relatives' group with both receiving education at the outset. Both groups and family therapy were held fortnightly, although the overall number of sessions held/attended varied between families. The investigators found it harder to recruit families to the groups than to therapy (6 out of 11 versus 11 out of 12), although in some cases this was not necessarily because of lack of interest. Relatives had work commitments and one was agoraphobic. The small number in the education group makes extrapolation from the data difficult.

Decrease in relapse rates and critical comments was comparable for both groups. The increased professional resources required for family therapy together with results from earlier studies lead the authors to conclude that 'relatives' groups be set up in conjunction with one or more initial family therapy sessions in the home.' They suggest that the problem of families who are reluctant to attend groups or interact with professionals might be overcome by 'organising regular family sessions in the home'.

Other people have also been developing interventions to reduce expressed emotion. Liberman et al. (1984) used a brief behavioural family intervention in a multi-family setting together with social skills training in 14 patients from high-EE families. Compared with a no-treatment group, relapse rates were 21% and 56%. Expressed emotion in the families was also shown to drop.

Hogarty et al. (1986) and Reiss (1988) used a similar intervention with a larger number of patients. Their study compared four treatment conditions: medication alone; medication and family treatment; medication and social skills treatment; and medication, family treatment and social skills training. All the patients lived with high-EE relatives and 23% were first admissions. Withdrawal from the programme was comparatively low. The explicit aim was to reduce the emotional atmosphere within the home and maintain reasonable expectations of the patients' functioning (Anderson *et al.* 1986).

The family treatment had four phases. The first, while the patient was acutely ill and briefly hospitalised, involved two sessions per week with the relatives. It was aimed at developing a relationship with the relatives and also at reducing anxiety, guilt and frustration. The family therapist also fulfilled the role as mediator between the hospital, the treatment system and family. Education (phase two) for the family was provided in a one-day 'survival skills' workshop. Meeting at the hospital, four or five families learnt about the illness, received concrete management suggestions, and were encouraged to maintain or develop lives of their own. The multi-family aspect was seen as very important, the informal interaction with other families supporting a sense of togetherness and, possibly, the beginnings of a support network. Phase three, the family therapy stage, involved fortnightly meetings for a minimum of six months, with both relatives and the patient. Strategies from the survival skills workshop were encouraged, including reinforcing the boundaries between the patient and relatives, developing friendships and community connections, and encouraging patient responsibility, together with developing more realistic family expectations. The last stage depended on both the family and their response to treatment. They could either continue family therapy dealing with further problems, or they could begin disengagement. The team, however, remained available, either for maintenance sessions or for crisis management.

The other aspect of the treatment programme for the patients was social skills training following previously established interventions (Wallace *et al.* 1980; Liberman *et al.* 1985) of instruction, modelling, role play, feedback and homework. In this case particular emphasis was placed on improving skills in interacting with other family members.

At one year follow-up, patients who had only received medication had a relapse rate of 41% compared with no relapses in those who received medication, family intervention and social skills training. Family treatment and social skills alone had relapse rates of 19% and 20%, respectively. Expressed emotion was measured at follow-up and it is noteworthy that in families which decreased from high to low EE there were no relapses. In the families where EE remained high it was only where there was both family intervention and social skills training that relapse was prevented. Not surprisingly, decrease in EE was shown most in the families which had been involved in family therapy.

Tarrier *et al.* (1988a, 1989) compared two types of behavioural interventions with education only or with routine treatment controls for families with at least one high-EE member, while families with low EE ratings were only allocated to the latter two conditions. The two behavioural interventions (symbolic and enactive) significantly reduced the relapse rates of patients in high-EE families, whereas education alone had no effect. Although significant decreases in criticism and emotional over-involvement were found in the high-EE families, these were greatest in the families involved with the behavioural interventions. However, a significant decrease in hostility was only found in the families in the behavioural programmes.

BEHAVIOURAL PROGRAMMES

The late 1960s and early 1970s saw behavioural techniques used with people with schizophrenia for the management of symptoms and behavioural problems. Relatives were sometimes included, acting as the 'therapeutic agent', having been taught basic behavioural principles and then expected to apply them (Cheek *et al.* 1971). O'Brien and Azrin (1973) used response priming and reinforcer sampling to reinstate patient–family relationships with three hospitalised patients who had lost virtually all contact with their family. Hudson (1975) and Atkinson (1982, 1986) used a variety of behavioural techniques in a home-based programme comparing one which involved a relative with one which did not. Although both groups improved, the behaviours involved were different.

The person who did most to promote family behavioural programmes was Liberman and his colleagues (e.g. Liberman *et al.* 1973), most notably Falloon (e.g. Falloon and Liberman 1983). The programme became very skills-based, focusing on changing the inappropriate communication of feelings (Falloon *et al.* 1981) and including social skills training for the patient.

The programme developed by Falloon had, like others, several parts. The main focus was behavioural family management with the whole family to develop family problem-solving and communication skills using structured problem-solving tasks with the aim of enabling the family to shield the patient from stress, and is now defined very much as cognitive and behavioural strategies for stress management (Falloon *et al.* 1993). The first two sessions, which included the patient, were educational, giving information about schizophrenia and a rationale for the programme. The patient remained on oral medication given flexibly and at the lowest dose possible, as this would promote a better response to psychological intervention, and because of an earlier finding that depot drugs may impair social functioning more than oral medication (Falloon *et al.* 1978). The sessions were held at the family home and were weekly for the first three months, fortnightly for the next three months, and thereafter monthly for three months. At the end of this intervention period families were invited to attend multi-family groups held on a monthly basis.

Families were explicitly taught problem-solving skills; identify a problem, generate solutions, evaluate potential consequences, agree on a best solution/strategy, implement the solution and finally review outcome. The family was expected to work on problems between meetings. Communication training was aimed at changing the way emotion was expressed and encouraged active listening, making specific requests, and expressing both positive and negative feelings clearly. An important part of Falloon's programme is the availability of a 24-hour on-call service for crisis management.

The comparison treatment, carried out by the same therapists, was individual case management consisting of education and supportive therapy with an emphasis on everyday problems. All the patients were living in families with attitudes similar to high EE or high family tension, and one-third were first admissions.

At the nine-month follow-up, 6% of the family management group had relapsed compared with 44% in the individual treatment group, and at two years 17% of the family management group had relapsed compared with 83% of the individual group, both differences being highly significant. At both follow-ups patients in family management had fewer hospitalisations, less behavioural disturbance, better reported family relations and more friends. The number of critical or intrusive remarks made by the family decreased, and was associated with increases in problem-solving statements (Doane *et al.* 1985).

The family can be used in behavioural programmes with patients as an indirect method of communication when direct confrontation with the patient over his or her perceptions is not possible or contra-indicated. Jenner (1991) describes several instances of making use of relatives in this way during crisis intervention with hallucinating patients.

Miller (1989) describes a 'group sociotherapy model' which is begun as early as possible and includes, as well as medication, education about schizophrenia and relatives' responsibilities for both relatives and people with schizophrenia, social skills training, training in coping skills, health and nutrition, effective living and community resources.

METHODOLOGICAL PROBLEMS AND THE DEVELOPMENT OF CLINICAL SERVICES

What is it about these studies which still urges caution? The research from all the various family intervention studies (including education, covered in the next chapter) has a number of issues in common when translating them into clinical services.

Sample Population

Many studies have strict criteria for both patients and relatives before they are invited to take part in programmes. This includes current florid symptoms or hospital admission (Glick et al. 1985; Goldstein and Strachan 1986; Hogarty et al. 1986), and living with a high-EE relative (Falloon et al. 1982, 1985; Leff et al. 1982, 1985, 1989; Kottgen et al. 1984; Hogarty et al. 1988). While this makes for 'good' research, in that tighter parameters give clearer results, it can handicap the development of clinical services. Expressed emotion is a difficult and time-consuming measure to use in a clinical setting, and poses several questions.

1. How easy is it to provide a service only for these families?

2. Is it only high-EE relatives who complain of neglect by professionals?

3. If not, do other relatives also warrant consideration and services?

4. If so, what?

The neglect of low-EE relatives means we have little understanding of their impact on people with schizophrenia. Their interaction style may not contribute to exacerbation of acute symptoms or rehospitalisation, but maybe it maintains negative symptoms or poor social functioning.

From a design point of view many of the early studies did not employ random assignment to conditions (e.g. Weakland *et al.* 1974; Palazzoli *et al.* 1978), and it is disappointing from a research perspective, although perfectly understandable from a service delivery one, that this is still happening (Birchwood *et al.* 1992b).

Loss to Follow-up and Drop-out Rates

Drop-out rates and length of interventions varies considerably. Even where samples have been well matched across conditions, in some studies there is a substantial loss of relatives/patients, which complicates analysis of results by being variable across interventions. Thus what may have been matched groups at outset is not by the time of follow-up (Hogarty *et al.* 1986; Leff *et al.* 1989). Many studies report difficulty in both engaging relatives and keeping them in interventions. This may be exacerbated by, for example, low-EE relatives seeing the intervention as inappropriate (Berkowitz *et al.* 1984).

Outcome Measures

On the whole, standard clinical measures are used to assess symptoms, burden and social functioning. Individual research groups have developed assessments to measure knowledge about schizophrenia (Berkowitz *et al.* 1984; Barrowclough *et al.* 1987). Ideally raters should be independent and blind to the patient's/relative's involvement in clinical programmes. Few studies manage this (Falloon 1985; Wallace and Liberman 1985). Even when this is attempted, it is difficult to maintain. Relapse is usually assessed by the clinician involved in management, and is, in some cases, made retrospectively. The time scale used for follow-up varies enormously, ranging from the immediate, post-intervention assessment to two years. Long-term follow-up is complicated by the other components which have been part of the whole package. Outcome for the person with schizophrenia is usually confined to 'relapse', variously measured as exacerbation of acute symptoms or admission to hospital. Admission to hospital does not usually distinguish between symptom exacerbation or breakdown in care by the relatives. This might be relevant in relation to the nature of EE and its interactive role in both contributing to relapse and being a response by carers.

One area of neglect is the social functioning of the person with schizophrenia, which might be affected by changes in the negative behaviour and attitudes of family members even more than by the symptoms. Studies involving social skills training have, not unexpectedly, measured this (Falloon 1985; Wallace and Liberman 1985; Hogarty *et al.* 1991), but others are now beginning to consider it (Barrowclough and Tarrier 1990). For both people with schizophrenia and relatives quality of life may be independent of acute episodes, and more attention should be paid to this.

Likewise it is surprising how little outcome for relatives has been measured, given the focus in the interventions on carer involvement. In part this was because earlier studies assumed that lack of knowledge was the underlying factor influencing behaviour such as high EE, and so this was all that was assessed (McGill et al. 1983; Berkowitz et al. 1984; Barrowclough et al. 1987). Although some studies have reported reduction in burden, the changes were not always maintained or measured at follow-up (Abramowitz and Coursey 1989; Cozolino et al. 1988). Falloon reports decreases in family burden across a number of studies at both 9 and 24 months follow-up (Falloon et al. 1985) and improved social functioning on the part of relatives. None of these studies has paid attention to the process of change in families in relation to specific aspects of interventions.

Intervention Strategies and Procedures

None of the studies use exactly the same design, interventions or education. Comparison is thus difficult, but broad generalisations are possible. Furthermore, the strategies involved tend not to have been given in any detail. This is changing, with research groups producing books which detail their programmes (Hatfield 1990; Barrowclough and Tarrier 1992; Kuipers *et al.* 1992; Falloon *et al.* 1993) and distributing copies of their education programmes (Smith and Birchwood 1985). Both replication of studies and the development of a clinical service is thus difficult, especially when not all components can be included. The 24-hour crisis intervention offered by Falloon's group, for example, must have a greater impact on how families see the illness and services than occasional crisis-team involvement.

Drug compliance might be important, but in most studies patients receive depot medication and compliance does not seem to be an issue (Leff *et al.* 1985; Hogarty *et al.* 1988). Tarrier *et al.* (1988a) ruled out improved drug compliance as being responsible for their outcomes.

Content and intensity of programmes to individual families will inevitably vary, and for some participants there will be partial withdrawal. The person with schizophrenia may stay on medication, for example, while the family drops out of the programme, or vice versa. How are the results of partial interventions to be analysed? When looking at outcome data, questions are raised as to who is included in follow-up. Outcome from all people assigned to each intervention should be included, so that drop-out from programmes can be assessed for its relevance to service delivery along with possible implications for clinical outcomes. More analysis of subgroups of relatives and people with schizophrenia would be welcome.

The question of control groups must also be raised. Very often the family intervention programmes are simply compared to 'standard treatment'. While this might give acceptable comparisons for that clinical setting, standard treatment varies between centres and between clinicians within centres. Whether standard treatment can be seen as optimal management is debatable.

Training

Although a number of studies report that training was available for staff, this is rarely evaluated. Little is known about the skills of those involved in delivering the interventions beyond their being members of highly motivated, highly skilled, well-respected research teams. Training packages have been developed, the most established being that of Falloon, but others include that of Tarrier and Barrowclough and that of the MRC Social and Community Psychiatry Unit developed by Leff. What we await now is evidence from 'average' staff in 'average' clinical settings to support the current findings.

Non-specific Treatment Factors

As well as the specific strategies and interventions in therapy, there are many non-specific factors which influence treatment and outcome. The old adage that a new treatment should be used 'while it still works' sums up the dilemma many find in introducing a new intervention which shows early promise. Most studies have not controlled for time spent with the therapist. Many studies report the discipline of therapists, but other therapist factors are not taken into account. Falloon (1985) uses the same therapists to provide interventions for both the new, specific family interventions and for the control group. In all research groups, contact between members of the therapeutic team as part of the research study may have led to better liaison and prompter response to potential problems, and thus reduced the possibility of major problems or even relapse. These non-specific factors maybe require a little more consideration.

THE TREATMENT PACKAGE

The specific components of the treatment packages range from education to problem solving, from social skills to reducing expressed emotion, and in multi- or single-family settings, with or without the patient. There are some commonalities: a positive approach to relatives and a genuine desire to form a working relationship with them, a programme which aims for structure and stability, a focus on the 'here and now', the use of family concepts as a starting point, cognitive restructuring, a behavioural approach, and improving communication within the family. Lam (1991) suggests that two psychological theories could inform psychosocial family treatment in schizophrenia, these being the general theory of coping, as described by Lazarus and Folkman (1984), and Folkman (1984), and attribution theory (Weiner 1986).

Medication and Drug Compliance

Family treatment is not seen as an alternative to drug therapy but as an adjunct, since between 30% and 40% of people with schizophrenia still relapse while on medication (Johnson 1976). Where compliance is low it has been suggested that family involvement may increase compliance and that this will, in turn, reduce relapse. Patients in the programmes of both Leff and Goldstein were compliant and yet family treatment still decreased relapse, as it did for Hogarty's patients regardless of whether they were compliant or not. The amount of drugs used decreased in the Falloon studies, while compliance improved.

Some studies have looked specifically at medication and early intervention. Carpenter and Heinrichs (1983) had patients medication-free until prodromal signs of relapse occurred. Medication was then restarted and then stopped again when the patient had become stabilised. Since this required those close to the patient to respond promptly to prodromal signs, this regime was coupled with a psycho-educational programme for relatives. Results suggested that there could be a significant reduction in medication without increased relapse, but that the cooperation of the families was essential.

Two studies have also looked at withdrawing maintenance therapy and providing brief pharmacotherapy when prodromal signs occurred (Carpenter et al. 1990; Jolley et al. 1990). Patients were educated in signs of relapse and the effect of early medication, since recognition of their own prodromes was very much their (and their family's) responsibility. In both studies intermittent medication was less effective. In the Jolley study, relapse was rated as more severe and the number of relapses preceded by identified prodromes decreased over time. They suggested that maybe a 'single teaching session at the start of the study does not provide patients and families with an adequate grasp of the intermittent paradigm' and that psycho-education needs to be on-going.

Carpenter et al. (1990) also found that intermittent medication was less popular, with 50% refusing to continue with the regime against 20% who were maintained on continuous medication. This is especially interesting since it goes against the 'received wisdom' that people with schizophrenia generally do not like staying on medication. The reasons given for this were not only the more obvious ones of higher rates of prodromal symptoms and hospitalisations, but also that the responsibility on the person with schizophrenia to recognise their prodromal symptoms was something they found stressful, and even excessive.

Marder et al. (1987) considered whether a targeted regime at prodromal signs combined with low dose maintenance medication would compensate for the risks inherent in medication reduction. They found that those taking the lower doses had fewer side effects but were slightly more likely to relapse. This was eliminated if the medication dose was doubled at the onset of prodromal signs. Reviewing the literature, Birchwood (1992) suggested that although these strategies 'have yet to be properly tested', the results 'do give cause for optimism'. One important question is the amount and type of education needed by the person with schizophrenia and their relatives to enable them to recognise prodromes, and how the responsibility for this recognition can best be shared between the person with schizophrenia, relatives and professionals.

Family–Therapist Relationship

For some relatives this was their first opportunity to enter into a real dialogue with a professional. Relatives are asked to describe *their* experience of both the patient's behaviour and its impact on them, allowing relatives openly to acknowledge that such problems exist, as well as having them legitimised by the programme. Being in an environment which expects relatives to ask questions, receive answers and discuss implications will be novel, and is probably liberating. Carer groups have long described themselves as 'the experts', and for the first time relatives may feel they are being taken seriously by staff. Where relatives believe that they have been blamed or rejected in the past, family support or education may be experienced as being more positive than 'family therapy', which implies that there is something wrong with family members. Strachan *et al.* (1986) suggests using the term 'family meetings'.

We think that everyone working within the broad area of family psycho-education would support the need to engage with relatives and understand their situation, although this may vary. Steinglass (1987) sees a difference in the attitude of Anderson and her colleagues

> 'from the more purely behaviourally oriented treatment approaches of Falloon and Robert Liberman . . . Succinctly put, the attitude is one of *empathy* for the extraordinary stresses and disappointments experienced by families with schizophrenic members, complemented by a genuine respect for the efforts family members have put forth in trying to deal with an intractable and at times overwhelming situation.'

The therapist–relative relationship will be affected by the role assigned to the relative: carer or simply kin, co-worker or client. Although in psychosocial family interventions families are no longer implicated in aetiology and their major role of caring is acknowledged, this does not mean that a discussion of EE will not be experienced as blame by relatives and treating them as 'clients' may contribute to them experiencing themselves as part of the problem. Developing a good working relationship with relatives can only be achieved by respecting them and the contribution they make.

Defining the Problem

Involving the family means that problems can be examined from different perspectives and the family's search after meaning can be redefined as a biosocial illness. We have already noted that relatives may hold views which will not be altered by education, especially regarding aetiology. Although for some it may not be possible to help them reframe the problems, or even give up patently false beliefs, for others the freedom of discussion coupled with information will be a release from an unhelpful framework of beliefs.

Knowledge more commonly leads to relief than to worry, and is frequently better than the worst imaginings. Uncertainty and lack of control are underlying contributors to stress, and increased information can reduce both of these. It is easier for the relative to have more realistic expectations, including their own ability to influence the situation, when they have an informed framework in which to speculate. Worries about the patient becoming 'addicted' to their medication, for example, are better dealt with when schizophrenia is understood as an illness managed by medication than by simple reassurance.

Different perspectives mean that high EE can be examined from the relatives' viewpoint while placing it in the context of its consequences. 'Emotional over-involvement' is thus seen as 'concern' or even 'protectiveness' and part of the relatives' effort to care or 'be helpful', but which, in these circumstances, has adverse consequences. Redefining issues means that a problem is no longer seen as belonging to either the patient or the relative, but rather to them both and their way of relating.

Present Versus Past

The family programmes focus on what is going on in the family at the moment rather than on establishing what went on in the past. This reinforces the problems as one of interaction. Analysis of problems and exploration of coping or alternative strategies is then the natural focus.

Family Communication

Programmes to reduce expressed emotion focus on communication. Even where there is no direct intervention on expressed emotion, family programmes show a reduction in tension or criticism and a change in interaction patterns (Doane *et al.* 1985; Goldstein and Strachan 1986). Improved communication may change the family environment in terms of both over- and under-stimulation as a greater understanding of the other's *experience and perception* of events is improved. Problem-solving is a specific technique taught in some programmes which will also influence communication.

INVOLVING AND MAINTAINING FAMILIES IN INTERVENTION PROGRAMMES

Almost all researchers comment that engaging relatives in family programmes and maintaining this involvement is difficult. Why should this be so? The voluntary organisations tell us that families complain of being ignored, something backed up by most people's clinical experience. So why are families not flocking to intervention or education programmes? Smith and Birchwood (1990) report that the refusal rate for families is 7–21%, the range for withdrawal from programmes is 7–14% and total non-compliance is 8–35%. MacCarthy *et al.* (1989b) reported a 31% (4 out of 13) non-engagement rate for a counselling and support group for relatives. Studies which make a distinction show that eliminating 'partial takers' improves relapse rates (Hogarty *et al.* 1986; Tarrier *et al.* 1988a). This should increase our concern about understanding why some families seem not to want to engage in family interventions since people with schizophrenia in these families appear to be at increased risk of relapse. The difference found by Leff *et al.* (1989) between education and relatives' groups compared to education and family therapy are worth noting. Can the difference be attributed to family therapy being seen as more relevant or, as is usually suggested, family therapy taking place in the family's home compared to the family having to travel to a relatives' group?

Tarrier (1991) reviews families' adherence to intervention programmes using Meichenbaum and Turk's (1987) five general categories:

- Characteristics of the client,

- Characteristics of the treatment regime,

- Characteristics of the disease,

- The relationship between the health care provider and the client,

- The clinical setting,

We follow the same framework.

Client Characteristics

Here the client is the carer. Many are elderly parents who feel that involvement is not possible because of their own infirmities or even general lack of energy. Some relatives are house-bound and the person with schizophrenia may act as a carer to them. In saying that services have come 'too late', some relatives may be expressing the belief that 'you can't teach an old dog new tricks' as much as anything else. There is no data from the research on whether older relatives change more or less than younger ones.

For younger relatives there are other compelling demands on their time, particularly employment or child-care. Evening groups are welcomed by some people but are by no means the answer for all. Providing transport may improve attendance for some, but not all, relatives. Tarrier (1991) notes that lack of a stable residence for either the person with schizophrenia or the family may contribute to non-engagement. All this may interact with apathy, pessimism, absence of support and high levels of burden to make programmes seem less than attractive. Unwillingness to leave the person with schizophrenia alone in the house may be a realistic assessment of the situation, over-protectiveness brought about by past 'bad experiences', or a rationalisation for not wanting to attend groups. Relatives' idiosyncratic beliefs about schizophrenia may mean that the intervention offered is seen as irrelevant. Or it may simply be that after years of negative experiences and nothing much changing, the relative has learnt resignation and a (realistic?) pessimism and is reluctant to give up this hard-won emotional stability. Or the programme may be seen as one more burden or responsibility. Given the history many relatives have of interaction with services, it is not surprising that many of them are wary and slow to engage in new projects. They have been ignored and let down too often in the past.

Almost nothing is known about cultural influences. Although Falloon does include Afro-Caribbean Americans in his programmes in the United States, and Tunnell reports on a predominantly black population, minority and ethnic groups are largely ignored. Pakenham and Dadds (1987) restricted their education groups to those who 'spoke English at home'.

Characteristics of the Treatment

There is little data on this. Despite relatives who stayed in programmes rating them positively, this does not mean that those who dropped out viewed them negatively. Personal beliefs of relatives or different views to those put forward in the interventions may play a part, but this is not clear. Relatives may find it difficult to adapt to the new behaviours and give up out of a sense of failure or hopelessness. Without prolonged support it is unlikely that many of the new behaviours would be maintained. Where interventions did continue, positive outcomes were maintained.

The information on low-stress environments and high-EE behaviour may still be experienced as 'blaming' by some relatives despite precautions by staff. Over-protective relatives, in particular, may find it very threatening to be expected to 'let go'. If there have been very disruptive episodes in the past, especially with major financial consequences or injury to people, a reluctance to allow any change which would risk this again may be present. Or the relative may be so locked into a life which revolves around the person with schizophrenia that not only can they see no other lifestyle, they want no other. To alter the *status quo* not only takes away their role, it also takes away everything which fills their time. Such relatives may require an intervention which enables them to rebuild an independent life as much as the person with schizophrenia.

Characteristics of the Disease

Most studies have recruited families at times of acute exacerbation of symptoms and/or hospital admission, and this seems the most appropriate time to engage relatives. Both Hudson (1975) and McCreadie *et al.* (1991) reported problems in engaging families from a fairly stable community population. Where people with schizophrenia show predominantly negative behaviours, relatives may believe that neither the programme nor their actions will affect this (Fadden *et al.* 1987a).

Although many of the programmes explicitly deal with aggression and violence, these behaviours may prevent relatives' involvement either through fear or through being unwilling to upset a currently stable situation. If the person with schizophrenia is negative about the programme or their relatives' involvement, families may be reluctant to go against their wishes and risk what may be a fragile relationship. Gaskill and Cooney (1992) report that of 26 spouses of people with schizophrenia offered an education group, nine refused to be interviewed. 'The major reason . . . appeared to be their partner's symptoms of paranoia'.

The Relationship Between the Service and the Client

Despite trying to promote a 'therapeutic alliance', families who saw the intervention as 'too little, too late' may see such an approach as patronising, especially where they now view themselves as experts in the management of their ill relative. Families who have experienced blame, hostility or even just neglect in the past may be slow to give their trust, and time, to what they may (rightly) see as 'the latest fad'.

The Clinical Setting

The clinical setting of services may also be relevant. It is commonly assumed that relatives feel stigmatised by attending psychiatric facilities, and other health settings may be more appropriate. Clearly time of sessions, travel and general 'ambience' will influence some relatives, but this may have more impact on those who already have low interest than on others.

IMPROVING RELATIVES' ENGAGEMENT WITH INTERVENTIONS

The foregoing indicates some of the many difficulties experienced in engaging relatives in family intervention programmes. However, it is not altogether clear what would definitely increase take-up and decrease drop-out. Generally, making the service accessible and 'user friendly' must be positive, but probably only affects a small number. Visiting relatives at home for an initial interview seems important in aiding take-up, as does holding sessions in the family's home. However, this is time-consuming for staff and the potential benefits of a number of relatives/families coming together are lost. Contacting relatives at times of acute disturbance looks as though it is more fruitful than at other times. Falloon's (1992) work on prodromal signs and very early interventions also bears further scrutiny.

We need to know more about the impact of the different aspects of the various packages and how some of these, particularly education, might be delivered. Educational aspects will be discussed in the next chapter. An individualised, flexible intervention which responds to relatives' needs and priorities and is within all appropriate cultural frameworks seems important. Above all, these interventions need to be seen as part of a wider hierarchy of services which can be tapped into more easily and more quickly to meet individual needs.

Lastly, however, we have to question the underlying emphasis of such packages. To improve patient well-being is unquestioned, but improving the role of relatives as informal carers is more open to debate. Simply providing education and a few skills to relatives is not a substitute for other community services. It is not necessarily the only service relatives require; neither does it ask them if they want to be 'better carers', or even carers at all. To look at service provision is outside the scope of this book, but Chapter 5 looks in more detail at support for relatives and their role as carers.

4

EDUCATION FOR RELATIVES

Psycho-education appears to be ubiquitous while at the same time having no formal definition. Anderson *et al.* (1986) made the following attempt:

'care that provides attention to the family system without sacrificing the potential contributions of biological, psychological and vocational systems'

and which will

'aim to develop a good therapeutic alliance which will sustain patients in the community, and minimalize relapse *without* undue stress on family members themselves'.

All well and good, but this does not explain how psycho-education differs from 'family counselling', 'family therapy' or 'family consultation' (Hatfield 1988).

The effects of education about schizophrenia on families are usually embedded in the wider treatment packages. Few have studied education alone. The major aims of an education programme are as follows:

1. The passing on of information with the goals of giving a rationale for treatment, including medication.

2. Reducing relatives' guilt and/or blame, particularly about aetiology.

3. Encouraging realistic expectations regarding prognosis.

4. Giving practical advice about management including ways of reducing expressed emotion.

Before we look at the impact of education we should consider the content and style of the programmes.

CONTENT OF EDUCATION PROGRAMMES

Despite minor variations, educational packages have more similarities than differences. The common themes are:

1. The nature of schizophrenia, including diagnosis, symptoms, aetiology and course of illness;

2. Treatment, including medication and family management;

3. The interaction between the family and schizophrenia;

4. Available services.

Information about Schizophrenia

Berkowitz et al. (1984) describe the 'Education Programme' in the Leff studies as consisting of 'the Knowledge Interview and the education itself'. The Knowledge Interview consists of 21 open-ended questions. The four short talks which make up the education package are delivered in two sessions and cover:

- Diagnosis;

- Symptomatology;

- Aetiology and course of illness;

- Treatment.

They describe the illness from both a standard, medical approach and also from the perspective of the person with schizophrenia and the relatives. The relatives' influence on the course of the illness is outlined in the third session. In their discussion, however, Berkowitz et al. report that

> 'We became aware at the end of the programme of our caution in telling relatives about EE in an open way.'

Since knowledge of high EE is associated with change, they suggest that

> 'relatives value and can use tips about how to deal with the patient; thus, education should perhaps be more explicit in this particular area.'

Falloon (1985) has the patient present during the two education sessions, and runs them in the family's home. Each session lasts for 2–3 hours and occurs as soon as the person is discharged from hospital. The first session is on the nature of schizophrenia and the second on issues related to medication. They summarise the first session, 'What is schizophrenia?' as follows.

'1. Schizophrenia is a major mental illness that affects one in 100 people.

2. The symptoms include delusions—false beliefs, hallucinations—false perceptions, usually voices, difficulties in thinking, feeling and behaviour.

3. The exact cause is not known, but appears to produce an imbalance of the brain chemistry.

4. Stress and tension make the symptoms worse and possibly trigger exacerbations of the illness.

5. People who develop schizophrenia possibly have a weakness which may run in families, that increases their risk of getting schizophrenia.

6. Some people recover from schizophrenia completely, but most have some difficulties and may suffer relapses.

7. Although there are no complete cures available relapses can be prevented and life difficulties overcome.

8. Family and friends can be most helpful by encouraging the person suffering from this illness to gradually regain former skills and to cope with them more effectively.'

The second session they summarise as medication management:

'1. *Regular* tablet taking is the mainstay of the treatment of schizophrenia.

2. Major tranquilizers are very effective medicine for the treatment of schizophrenia.

3. In low doses, they also protect a person from relapse or symptoms.

4. Side effects are usually mild and can be coped with.

5. Street drugs make schizophrenia worse.'

A newer programme by Falloon (1992) is aimed at early intervention for people experiencing a first episode of schizophrenia. General practitioners were trained to recognise eight prodromal features of schizophrenia:

- Marked peculiar behaviour;

- Inappropriate or loss of affect;

- Vague, rambling speech;

- Marked poverty of speech and thought;

- Preoccupation with odd ideas;

- Ideas of reference;

- Depersonalisation or derealisation;

- Perceptual disturbances.

A 24-hour assessment team was available which 'ensured that assessment could be made within an hour of referral, usually within a few minutes of the request'.

For people who were thought to be in the early stages of an acute episode the intervention programmes included education, comprehensive stress management and neuroleptic medication. Education was immediate, in fact

> 'Within 24 hours of detection the patient and his or her key caregivers were provided with an educational seminar that provided a rationale for the early intervention program.'

During this they were told that the patient was showing behaviours which

> *'were possible early signs of an impending florid episode of schizophrenia'*

and certain treatment strategies

> 'might ameliorate the current condition'.

Furthermore,

> 'Although it was emphasised that the person's current features might be found in a range of disorders, including benign stress responses, the characteristic symptoms of schizophrenia, theories of etiology, prognosis, and effective integrated drug and psychosocial treatment methods were outlined in an informal discussion in the home'.

Positive aspects were emphasised including the 'high rates of remission and recovery from long-term application of effective treatment methods', and the benefits of 'continued support from family/friends' together with back-up from a 24-hour 'well-trained, committed domiciliary mental health service'. One of the aims of this education session was 'to foster an optimal therapeutic alliance and minimise fears about schizophrenia'. At the end of the session what was now 'informed consent' was sought from both patient and 'key caregivers' to proceed with the intervention programme. Falloon reports that 'In every case this was granted with alacrity.'

Although Falloon is positive about the impact of this intervention preventing first episodes, he recommends that 'extreme caution should be applied to its interpretation' because of major methodological problems. What is of particular interest to us here is the speed with which relatives were told that their child might have schizophrenia and the amount of information given. In view of the common complaints by relatives that they are not told a diagnosis early enough, we could assume that this would be greeted positively. In this paper we are not given any information regarding how relatives, or patients, viewed the unusual amount of information being given so quickly.

The education package put together by Anderson and colleagues is possibly the most comprehensive (Anderson *et al.* 1986), using, as it does, a historical context in which to set the information and show that, over time, there is both an arbitrariness and limitations to the understanding of schizophrenia. The day-long session is divided into the following subsections.

1. Schizophrenia: What is it? Information on the history and epidemiology, personal experiences, public experiences and psychobiology.

2. Treatment of schizophrenia, including the use of antipsychotic medication, psychosocial treatments, effects on the course of the illness, other treatments and management.

3. The family and schizophrenia, covering the needs of both patient and family, common problems that face patients and families, and what families can do to help (revise expectations, create barriers to over-stimulation, set limits, selectively ignore certain behaviours, keep communication simple, support medication regime, normalise family routine, recognise signals for help and use professionals).

An eight-week workshop held by Zelitch (1980) consisted of one-and-a-half-hour weekly sessions covering the following points.

- Services available, including crisis intervention.
- Definitions of psychosis, neurosis, depression, hallucinations and delusions. A discussion of aetiology. Descriptions of mental health personnel. The different types of therapy, including psychoanalysis, behaviour modification, supportive therapy and medication.
- Behaviour management and family expectations.
- Discussion of personal management problems.
- Guilt and stigma and community supports.
- Particular problems raised by relatives (two sessions).
- Review and discussion.

The package put together by Abramowitz and Coursey (1989) covered the usual aspects of understanding the illness, medication, developing appropriate expectations, management, community resources including advocacy groups, and developing family networks and supports, but also included a specific session on problem-solving skills and cognitive therapy.

The NYU/Bellevue Family Psychoeducation Project (Tunnell *et al.* 1988) involved a series of ten, 90-minute lectures, these being:

1. An overview of schizophrenia (including diagnosis and cause).
2. The course of schizophrenia.
3. Medications: their purposes and their side effects.
4. Coping with specific symptoms and troublesome behaviours.
5. Developing general coping skills.
6. Improving communication.
7. Problem solving.
8. Becoming an advocate for the mentally ill (guest presentation by representatives from Friends and Advocates of the Mentally Ill).
9. Community resources (presented by a guest social worker).
10. Review and evaluation.

The Brentwood Family Treatment Programme (West *et al.* 1985) took 2 hours to present an education package in four parts, each taken by a different team member.

1. Introduction to family education (chief psychiatrist).

2. Diagnosis and symptoms (clinical psychologist).

3. Biology, neurophysiology and pharmacology (psychiatry resident).

4. Family and social factors (head nurse and/or social worker).

Handouts were used, including information about community resources and family support groups (transcripts are given in their paper).

A 'survival skills' workshop is described by Reiss (1988) as being presented from 'the internal perspective of patients' as well as the 'outward manifestations' of schizophrenia. In an all-day, multi-family session, the usual types of 'phenomenology, onset, course, treatment, and outcome of the illness' are described. 'Data that suggest a cognitive and perceptual impairment and a hypersensitivity to stimulation are emphasised' as background information to management techniques, including reducing 'family members' tendencies to react emotionally to each change in the patient's behaviour, and begin to refocus some of their energies on their lives apart from the patient.' Although it is emphasised to families that they do not *cause* schizophrenia 'it is stressed that there is evidence that families have the power to influence the course of the illness'. This is followed by individual family sessions, including homework.

Birchwood and Smith went further than most in producing back-up material for their education programme, and producing a series of pamphlets with the local health authority (Smith and Birchwood 1985). These cover four main questions.

1. What is schizophrenia?

2. What are the symptoms of schizophrenia?

3. What treatments are there for schizophrenia?

4. What can help?

This package was later modified (Sidley *et al.* 1991) to take account of the fact that some relatives retain their own versions of aetiology even after an education programme. The modified education package was aimed at relatives of people with long-term schizophrenia, and included greater emphasis on negative symptoms and how these affect behaviour.

> 'The main aim was to relate common behaviours of the patient (for example, staying in bed for long periods) to genuine symptoms of schizophrenia.'

The second change was the introduction of 'quality of life' issues, suggesting that

> 'the family plays the most crucial role with regards to improving quality of life through their endeavours to encourage worthwhile activities, independent living and social mixing'.

A third modification was to give more detail about myths, stereotypes and misconceptions, and finally a section was included on the management of hallucinations and delusions.

Barrowclough and Tarrier (1992) report a 'more collaborative approach' than any of the other investigators. They suggest that

> 'an understanding of the relatives' beliefs and attitudes about the illness in general and the symptoms of the patient in particular is a necessary precondition to establishing an interactive mode of information presentation rather than delivering a lecture about schizophrenia'.

Information is collected and assessed from an initial interview using the Knowledge About Schizophrenia Interview (KASI) which covers six areas:

- Diagnosis;
- Symptomatology;
- Aetiology;
- Medication;
- Prognosis;
- Management.

Information is structured around relatives' knowledge, beliefs and misconceptions. Attention is paid to the relatives assimilating the knowledge, particularly where previously held beliefs are contradicted by new information. They point out that after the interview a test of knowledge is helpful in assessing 'where further attitude or belief change will be important, since it is unlikely that relatives, particularly those where patients have a long history of illness, will change all their views after a brief education component'.

As well as describing what schizophrenia is, most programmes also detail what it is not, exploding myths of violence and, particularly, split personality. As well as giving information, the programmes aim to make relatives feel less isolated, not only by actively meeting other relatives but also by giving incidence and prevalence rates, supporting the view that schizophrenia is 'a common illness'. Medication, its effectiveness and side effects, is an important component of the programmes, although the amount of information on the aetiology, particularly the psychobiology of schizophrenia, varies. Most programmes place strong emphasis on the fact that relatives do not cause schizophrenia. All the programmes take a fairly mainstream, medical orientation. Before we discuss the implications of this, however, it is worth briefly looking at some other information given by some programmes.

Information about Services

Not all programmes focus on information about schizophrenia. 'Family Night' (Stern and Agacinski 1986) focused on an overview of the day hospital programme, a discussion of the daily schedule and an explanation of occupational and recreational therapy, as well as family responses to mental illness and psychiatric treatment.

Scharfstein and Libbey (1982) describe a 'multiple family orientation group' held for relatives shortly after admission. Early information was given about the psychiatric unit, which included 'roles of the staff members and how they could be contacted, procedures for obtaining passes, visiting rules, the ward schedule, and the unit's rules and regulations . . . Sources for legal, medical, social service, and financial or insurance information . . . average length of stay, discharge, and follow-up procedures'. The 'treatment philosophy' was explained, 'distilled into three major areas . . . Verbalization of problems . . . Assumptions of responsibility . . . Involvement of the patient's family'.

A meeting is held once or twice a year for relatives of people with chronic mental illness at the Maudsley Hospital in London (Mullen *et al.* 1992). It has two broad aims: to break down any isolation by getting relatives 'to know each other and to share their concerns about their role in caring for the patient', and also to 'bring members of the team face-to-face with relatives in a pleasant, sociable and nonthreatening setting and allow them to receive suggestions from relatives about offering a better service'. The numbers are very small, but nevertheless improvements in understanding the service, their relative's problems and their role in the care of their relative are reported by relatives. Two people, however, thought their understanding of their relative's problems had worsened, and two that their understanding of their own role had worsened. Despite this, all reported themselves to be interested in further meetings. Such meetings are two-way communications and an issue of which the staff were not previously aware was raised, namely the lack of access to recreational facilities for relatives. Relatives felt that this 'would make a visit more like a *normal* social occasion and ease the progress of what are sometimes awkward meetings'.

STYLE OF PROGRAMMES

Information is generally presented in a way which makes it credible, relevant and useful, relating it to the family situation, the families becoming 'collaborators' in 'management'. Despite similarity of content, the way in which it is delivered has been wide-ranging, including: individual family sessions (with patient present) (McGill *et al.* 1983; Falloon 1985), individual education for relatives (with patient absent) (Leff *et al.* 1982), separate and then joint sessions (Barrowclough *et al.* 1987), family workshops (Zelitch 1980; Anderson *et al.* 1986), relatives' groups (Smith and Birchwood 1987; Abramowitz and Coursey 1989; Cazzullo *et al.* 1989; Coia and Atkinson 1989) and multi-family groups with patients (Cole and Jacobs 1988). The style of the presentations includes 'lectures' (Leff *et al.* 1982), oral presentation and written handouts (McGill *et al.* 1983), 'lectures', discussion and course manual (Coia and Atkinson 1989), handouts alone (Smith and Birchwood 1987), and video (Birchwood *et al.* 1992b), and many have included homework (Zelitch 1980; Birchwood *et al.* 1992b; Falloon *et al.* 1993). The information has been given over varying amounts of time and number of sessions, ranging from two (Leff *et al.* 1982; McGill *et al.* 1983; Falloon 1985) to ten (Tunnell *et al.* 1988; Coia and Atkinson 1989), and from the brief (West *et al.* 1985; Cozolino *et al.* 1988) to all day (Anderson *et al.* 1986; Reiss 1988). Where patients are included, they are encouraged to talk about their experiences and psychotic symptoms to aid relatives' understanding, particularly regarding lack of control (Cole and Jacobs 1988). Relatives have been targetted at different times: during hospital-isation of the patient (Berkowitz *et al.* 1984), as a part of aftercare when the patient has been stabilised on medication (McGill *et al.* 1983) or simply as a new service open to all (Coia and Atkinson 1989). The latter part of this book describes our intervention in more detail.

Few studies have attempted to partial out aspects of psychoeducation groups. One study in the United States (Reilly *et al.* 1988) looked at the impact of the patient being in the group or not, and compared the workshop programme with a relatives' tour of the hospital and no involvement of relatives at all. The education workshop lasted two hours, focused on 'the symptoms, treatment and probable aetiology of major mental illness in a stress–diathesis framework', and was pre-sented while the patient was still in hospital. Despite receiving high satisfaction scores from participants there were no differences between the psycho-education and control groups, nor between patient present and patient absent groups, on outcome measures of future patient relapse and rehospitalisation, or on relatives' commitment to out-pa-tient therapy after discharge. Relatives in the education groups did not show any change on questionnaire measures of illness attribution, or criticism or rejection of the patient pre- and post-workshops. How much change can realistically be expected, or measured, from such brief interventions is debatable. There were differences in the group process with patients present or absent. In the patient-absent groups relatives made more personal and topic-relevant comments. Patient contributions are recorded as being 'often disruptive'. The relatives in the patient-present groups rate the professionals as significantly more helpful than those in the patient-absent group. Overall acceptance to attend the group was low, but was lower in the patient-present condi-tion (25%) than in the patient-absent condition (33%).

The most comprehensive study of the impact of the way in which information is presented is that of Birchwood *et al.* (1992b) in Birming-ham, England. They compared written material alone, written materi-als and video, and written material and group discussions. In each condition half the families were given homework to complete. The information was presented over four sessions with four booklets. The complex design of the study was spoilt by non-random assignment to conditions, the group condition being filled first. Amongst other problems, this led to uneven numbers across conditions. As with previous studies, relatives gained information, had reduced anxiety and increased optimism about their role in maintaining the well-being of the person with schizophrenia, and had improvements in various types of social functioning and independence, all of which were maintained at six months follow-up. There were short-term improvements in reducing the stress and fear of the patient. The non-specific effects were correlated with a gain in knowledge, which Birchwood *et al.* suggest

> 'clearly points to information "content" as the important medium of change, suggesting that these non-specific changes were in fact specific and direct effects of having more accurate knowledge.'

In the short term, relatives in the groups showed greatest improvements in their knowledge, although there were no other significant differences and at six months follow-up this difference had disappeared.

The 8% of relatives who dropped out of the programme were significantly more knowledgeable at the outset than those who stayed in the programme, despite the most knowledgeable 25% being excluded from the programme in the first place. It would be useful to know more about these apparently knowledgeable relatives, including where such knowledge came from, and whether they might not have been interested in a more 'advanced' course, or even been actively involved in educating others. One-third of relatives did not return follow-up data, and these tended to be those who were most stressed and more likely to believe that the illness is within the patient's control. The additional stress of assessment coupled with a medical model of the illness which accords poorly with their beliefs would seem to be important factors for relatives' drop-out.

THE IMPACT OF EDUCATION ON RELATIVES

The studies which have looked solely at education packages indicate some useful, if limited, results, for example those of Birchwood *et al.* reported in the previous section. Similar findings were reported by Pakenham and Dadds (1987), with increased understanding and short-term reduction of family burden, distress and isolation. Reduction of anxiety and distress was also reported by Abramowitz and Coursey (1989), together with improvements in coping through the use of community resources and more effective management of home life. Set against these is the study by Cozolino *et al.* (1988), who found no increase in knowledge after two months. Nevertheless, relatives did report an increased sense of support and decreased feelings of personal responsibility and guilt in respect of family and aetiology. Where education is a component of a more intensive family intervention programme, findings are similar—that there is limited acquisition of information. Both Berkowitz *et al.* (1984) and Barrowclough *et al.* (1987) report that relatives have a tendency to retain their own individual, not to say 'idiosyncratic', beliefs, especially about aetiology. Berkowitz *et al.* suggest that this may be because aetiology 'is an area which is so well defended that education makes little impression.' Although we know that anxiety does interfere with learning, since the studies report a lowering of guilt feelings, we must assume that a complex relationship exists between education which both increases and decreases anxiety, its retention as information, and the effects of the information (retained or not).

Tarrier and Barrowclough (1986) found that the greatest impact of education is on the relatives of people with a shorter, rather than a longer, period of illness. This is probably not surprising if it means that relatives have had less time to be exposed to a variety of information from other sources, and less time rehearsing alternative explanations.

The *functional* value of information was stressed by Barrowclough *et al.* (1987) for aspects such as the perceptions and attitudes of relatives and their reported behaviour. A related paper (Tarrier *et al.* 1988a) reported that education alone did not influence relapse rates. Reilly *et al.* (1988) also found no change, and concluded that it remains to be demonstrated that 'psycho-*education per se* is an active ingredient' in the change involved in psycho-education programmes.

Although these studies can be taken as a negative finding for education, it is maybe of more importance to ask why education of relatives *should* have an impact on patients' relapse rate. To do so, the chain of events demands some very strong associations and effects:

- education must affect relatives' behaviour;

- this, in turn, must affect some aspect of the person with schizophrenia;

- this effect must be directly or indirectly linked to relapse.

Since health-promotion programmes testify to the low-level impact of giving information on, for example, the effects of smoking *on the person who smokes*, let alone others, it seems to be asking a lot of education about schizophrenia, *alone*, to affect relapse.

Reilly *et al.* (1988) suggest that being generic—'major mental illness'—rather than specific may have had an effect, and that the project was in a State mental hospital where patients tend to be poor and chronic, and relations between the hospital and local mental health centres are sometimes 'strained'. A frequently reiterated theme of family intervention and psycho-education is that of developing new, more cooperative relationships between hospital staff and relatives, and that this is one of the non-specific factors of the intervention package. There is nothing in this package that clearly suggested how this was done, especially in the light of the previously 'strained' relationships. To expect a two-hour presentation to affect future patient relapse, or even relatives' commitment to out-patient therapy, is maybe naive. Education alone should be aimed at more limited outcomes, and because it does not have an impact on major outcomes does not mean that it does not contribute in valuable ways to the overall programme or have other benefits.

Overall, the message from these studies is that involving the relative in programmes is 'a good thing' and something which should happen, if not routinely, then frequently. Is the picture quite this rosy, or is it coloured by a view of relatives, either as contributing to relapse or as carers, which demands that they be incorporated into the clinical situation? The role of relatives will be taken up in a later chapter. For the moment we will concentrate on the benefits of, and the limitations in, the programmes just described. The methodological criticisms of the studies have been covered in the previous chapter.

Reviewing six studies, Lam (1991) concludes that, although describing

'labour-intensive packages . . . the beneficial effect of preventing relapse in the first 9 months has been established repeatedly. Even allowing for the intense efforts by the therapeutic teams, the interventions were cost-effective compared to hospital in-patient treatment.'

Fewer hospital admissions can also be seen as having beneficial effects for patients, their lives being less disrupted and less stigmatised.

In a review of ten controlled studies published since 1980 which 'meet minimal standards of research design, with follow-up for at least 1 year', Falloon and Brooker (1992) conclude that

'the early optimism for psychosocial intervention strategies should be tempered by recognition of the limitations of methodology of most studies, and awareness of the need for longer term interventions to establish whether enduring clinical remission and social recovery can be achieved.'

This is despite combining the results of nine studies which show that of patients having florid episodes within one year, 50% were receiving drugs plus support or education, and 30% were receiving drugs plus carer-based stress management. Falloon and Brooker suggest that this is a 'highly conservative estimate of benefits' having 'equated attrition with all indices of unsuccessful outcome'. Eight of the studies with a two-year follow-up have combined results which show that 64% of patients receiving drugs and support or education had an acute episode. This may suggest that exacerbations of the illness are inevitable, and that psychosocial intervention merely delays them, in the same way that medication delays them. However, since relapse can bring with it additional problems, delaying an acute episode must be seen as positive and worthwhile. Whether an intervention which continues at the same level of intensity for a longer period of time would have any further benefits is unclear.

MODELS OF INFORMATION

As previously noted, the educational content presented to families is a fairly standard, medically orientated approach to schizophrenia, which is not surprising since the programmes were designed and run mainly by psychiatrists and clinical psychologists. This approach is also taken by the self-help groups and voluntary organisations. It has been argued that it is inevitable that relatives will be drawn to biological interpretations of schizophrenia, since this removes them from any blame. We are not suggesting that this is not the right approach to take, but it does raise a number of issues both in relation to relatives as carers and to the way in which such information is processed and used by both relatives and patients. Lam (1991) made the distinction between 'gain in knowledge' and 'change in belief system', and suggests that while a general gain in knowledge is reported, there is little evidence to suggest that education alone had much impact on the relatives' belief system.

Although giving relatives information about schizophrenia and advice on management can be seen as sensible, practical, appropriate and even necessary, it can also be seen as firmly casting relatives in the role of co-worker. This may be appropriate, it may even be necessary, but it nevertheless represents a subtle shift in the balance between 'relative as carer' and 'relative as relative'. The person with schizophrenia is, after all, first and foremost a member of the family. Some might suggest that there is a very fine line between living with a relative who has a severe mental illness, and caring for a relative and becoming a quasi-professional. In some instances, particularly regarding autonomy and responsibility, this line may be more visible to the person with schizophrenia than to the relative.

The reasons *why* information is given may also influence *how* it is given, although many of the assumptions here are, at the very least, unspoken. Tarrier and Barrowclough (1986) suggest that there are two models which can be applied to the practical reasons for giving information, namely a simple deficit model and a more complex interaction model. They state that the

> 'basic premise of the simple deficit model is that lack of information plays a causative role in producing behaviour detrimental to health; providing relevant information, and so eliminating the deficit would also eliminate (at least partially) the undesirable behaviour and consequent health risk'.

This model can best be applied to the concept of high EE, and is made explicit in Berkowitz *et al.* (1984). Bizarre and difficult behaviour is rated by high-EE relatives as being, if not overtly deliberate, at least controllable (Vaughn and Leff 1981). Falloon and colleagues (McGill *et al.* 1983) also hypothesise that better knowledge means better care. It can also be assumed to reduce stress in carers. Reiss (1988) explicitly described the aims of a family education workshop as being 'designed to decrease the family's anxiety, sense of helplessness, and feelings of stigma or isolation.' The justification for believing that this might happen is given as: 'Knowledge can, in itself, be a stress-reducer by allowing the person to develop a sense of cognitive mastery'.

The interaction model proposed by Tarrier and Barrowclough is based on the difference between 'disease' as an external, objective entity, and 'illness' as the internal, subjective, personal perception of the person with the disease. Thus, information coming from a professional will be rooted in a disease model, but will be received by both patients and relatives within a subjective illness framework. Lay models of illness are particularly likely to be powerful in relation to mental illness, as symptoms are shown through changes in behaviour rather than physical pathology.

Clearly these two models suggest that information should be presented differently, but they also have implications for the aims of information-giving as a service, as well as the way in which such a service is received. We know that relatives frequently retain their original, 'idiosyncratic' information. Since there is little difference between high- and low-EE relatives in their amount of knowledge (Berkowitz *et al.* 1984), the deficit model would not seem to apply. Tarrier and Barrow-clough conclude that the interaction model is the most appropriate to adopt, and that information should be tailored to meet individual family needs rather than presenting general information on psychopathology. They also suggest that this means that such information-giving should be evaluated more widely than simple gain of information, including 'feelings about the provision of information', changes in behaviour as a result of information gain, patient variables including relapse and hospital admission, and changes in interactions within the family.

EDUCATION AND PSYCHO-EDUCATION

If we are to consider the differential impact of an education package which presents general information and one which makes use of more personalised information, we need to relate these to concepts of education and psycho-education, and ask whether this is the only difference between the two.

Most of us understand a model of education based on the acquisition of knowledge, with the added hope that such acquisition is long-term, that it will assist the person who has learnt it in both present and future problem solving, or simply that it will add to their understanding and appreciation of the world. Taking an educational model to illness is in stark contrast to a purely medical model, if we take the latter to mean that problems/illness are best helped/treated by external experts. As health-care budgets run out of control in the West, we are having to learn that the medical model is not the answer to all our problems, that help cannot be provided for everyone who needs or wants it, and that many problems (or even illnesses) do not have a real resolution, let alone a cure. It means moving away from the purely pathological to include questions of social, personal and moral values. Over recent years our explanations regarding the cause of schizophrenia have moved from a consideration of these areas to one that is more concerned with inherent pathology. This does not mean, however, that medical management of this pathology is the only intervention necessary. If education groups are to move away from the medical model, what new conditions, restrictions or demands does this pose? An educational model may make it easier for both sides (educator and recipient) to see the culture-bound value judgments which are made, and which are prone to being lost in the medical model. Indeed, it could be argued that implicit in an educational model is the need to make value judgments explicit.

The spiralling costs of health care also mean that in the future greater interest will undoubtedly be shown in interventions aimed at groups rather than individuals, and by low-cost staff. It is almost certain that this shift in emphasis will go too far, and warning notes have already been sounded. Hogarty (1993) suggested that recent developments in community care in the United States were *ad hoc* interventions with untrained staff providing neither good nor cost-effective care. The development of services depending on short-term funding and relying on largely untrained sessional workers has also occurred in Britain, with current funding policy making this practically the only way to develop new community-based services.

Within this reassessment of health care, the case can now be made for an educational model with educational interventions. Can we make any distinctions between an educational approach and psycho-educa-tion? Snyder (1984) has attempted this, pointing out that education models have their roots in health education, take place in classes or workshops and use strategies such as didactic teaching, assigned reading and general problem-solving. Hatfield (1990) adds to this the long-term retention of information, and generalisation to everyday situations. The language of involvement is different, with members being called 'leader' or 'instructor' and 'participant' or 'adult learner'.

Hatfield argues that psycho-education, in contrast, retains a model of deficit, most notably around high EE. Since there is a diagnosis involved, it would seem to be rooted in the medical model and words such as 'treatment' and 'therapy' abound. People with schizophrenia are still, by and large, patients. She believes that educational approaches are more likely to take the needs of the family as the starting point, and that the aim of the education is to maximise the family situation for all members. In contrast, psycho-education puts the 'patient' at the core, the benefit of the programme is overwhelmingly for the patient, measured in clinical outcome, and relatives are recruited as co-workers. She sums this up as meaning that 'the burden of keeping the patient from relapsing is placed upon the shoulders of the family'. This is a very individual view of psycho-education. Barker (1984), for example, described it much more simply as

> 'the use of educational techniques, methods and approaches to aid in the recovery from the disabling effects of mental illness or as an adjunct to the treatment of the mentally ill, usually within the framework of another ongoing approach'.

Pointing out the confusion currently within psycho-education, Hatfield asks, 'Is it an educational model or a medical one? Perhaps it is neither and needs to create the concepts and language that will define it as a totally new approach.' Berheim and Lehman (1985) had already warned that 'caution must be exercised to avoid dressing up old, negative attitudes in new terms'. When we look at current, mainline views on schizophrenia, with the emphasis on organic pathology within a stress–diathesis model, maybe the question we should be asking is whether it is possible to present an essentially medical model of schizophrenia within an educational framework.

THE FUTURE OF EDUCATION FOR RELATIVES

Reviewing the literature on education (or psycho-education, whichever term you prefer) for relatives of people with schizophrenia, it is easy to be left with contradictory thoughts and feelings. Yes, it probably does contribute to relatives' knowledge, but maybe does not affect some of the more 'idiosyncratic' core beliefs. Yes, relatives are likely to report benefits in terms of reduced anxiety and personal distress, and increased support, but such outcomes are unlikely to be maintained over long periods. Yes, relatives tend to like the groups. No, education does not, in and of itself, lead to a reduction in relapse rates. Clearly, whatever else the education does, it only forms part of a package of services which should be available to relatives.

Why, then, is there still a sense that education for relatives is 'a good thing'? Maybe part of the reason lies in the fact that there is a sense in which current outcome measures are not necessarily the right ones. Can we realistically expect brief education to profoundly affect relatives' behaviour when nothing else in their environment is changing, and attitudes and behaviour are undoubtedly being rewarded and maintained in the way they were previously? Probably not. So if education is not going to affect relatives' attitudes and behaviour, and thus not change relapse rates in the designated patient (and primary recipient/concern of the health service), why is there still such interest in education? Is it nothing more than some atavistic attachment to the view that 'education' or 'knowledge' is, in itself, 'a good thing'? Is this a reflection of a group of professional people who have spent a varying, but considerable, number of years in higher and further education justifying education for its own sake?

Within science there is a jostling for position between theoretical and applied aspects. Is the need to demonstrate the applied relevance of education for relatives in such far-reaching practical outcomes a reflection of the need to justify our acceptance of 'education'? Is it a wholly pragmatic position that is acknowledging that purchasers are not going to buy a service which cannot show a clear cost-effective benefit? If so, it is going to be difficult to justify education on these grounds alone, although there is some evidence that education packages may help to engage relatives in other family interventions.

The position for education becomes stronger if we take a different perspective and argue for education not only on the grounds that it might improve both relatives' and patients' 'quality of life', but also on ethical grounds: people have a right to know as much about their illness, or the illness of the person they care for, as possible, or as much as they wish. Another, related, answer may be to take education out of the hands of the health service and clinicians and to give the responsibility for informing both relatives and patients about their illness to other groups.

DELIVERY OF GROUPS

Health promotion may have a role in the future, although to date it has been reluctant to get involved in this kind of work, preferring what is seen as mental health promotion to mental illness prevention. Groups for relatives could, of course, be marketed as health promotion strategies (and thus tap a different source of funding) if they were shown to reduce the negative impact of caring on the carers' health. Community mental health centres would be another potential site, although currently they spend little time on health promotion. The changes and expansion of the General Practitioner service may also be an appropriate setting for education and carer groups.

It is worth considering, however, that these groups need not be exclusively within the health service. Social work is one obvious alternative. In Chapter 6, we describe how the self-help movement has spread, developing relatives' support groups. Educational interventions could be organised in conjunction with voluntary groups, or they could be run in the same way as other adult education courses, through community education, university extra-mural classes or other educational groups. One of us (JMA) ran a ten week evening class through a university adult education programme and tapped a group of relatives who had not been engaged in either hospital programmes or the self-help movement. Another possibility might be that large companies who have a health promotion policy and who already run groups (for example in stress management) could run groups for carers. The combination of an ageing population, care in the community, and a higher proportion of women working means that ever larger numbers of people will be trying to combine work and carer roles. Eventually employers may have to confront possibilities such as more flexible hours for carers, or even 'carer leave' in the same way that there is maternity (and paternity) leave. In the face of this, supportive educational groups may seem like a cheap option.

Education groups, whether within a health-care setting or outside it, may prove to be more acceptable to a wide range of potential recipients (whether relatives or erstwhile patients) if the service is seen as less stigmatising. If, however, the relative or patient is committed to a medical model an educational approach may be less attractive and may even be viewed as inappropriate. Thus the presentation and delivery of the groups may be just as important as their content.

5

THE FAMILY AS CARER

COMMUNITY CARE AS CARE BY THE FAMILY

Families have always cared for their ill, elderly and disabled members, if only because there was no other choice. The rise of asylums was a reflection of a custom which pushed people with problems out of society, caring for them under a policy of segregation. This book is not the place to chart the rise of, or the influences on, community care, but it does have a central role in the approach to families. Despite many assertions to the contrary, the development of generic community care has been largely cost-driven (Parker 1990) as the ability and willingness of the state to meet the growing burden of expensive institutional care has declined.

There is a fairly fundamental lack of information on basic care-giving, despite the work on burden reported in Chapter 2, whether it is carer characteristics, the tasks performed, or the costs and benefits, to both the family and the national purse, of their role. More information is available on carers of elderly people than other groups, presumably because of their greater numbers. In this chapter we want to concentrate first on the wider issues of caring and coping.

INFORMAL CARERS

Towards the end of the 1980s it became increasingly common to hear relatives referred to as 'informal carers', and it is their role as such that underpins recent policy. This term is not universally accepted; the Carers National Association campaign against it as making the caring task sound unskilled or unstructured. It was Sir Roy Griffiths (1988) who fully legitimised them in this role in his report *Community Care:*

Agenda for Action: ' . . . building first on the available contribution of informal carers and neighbourhood support'.

If relatives are to be viewed as a legitimate source of care, what role do they take in care? This is often difficult to ascertain, and global statistics on carers give a picture more readily applied to the elderly population than to those with schizophrenia (Green 1988). Although a generic approach is common, focusing on the undifferentiated nature of care-giving, it is difficult to sustain. Carers of mentally and physically disabled children are excluded because responsibility for a child is very different from that for another adult. Carers of mentally ill people are also excluded because the type of care is different, focusing around responsibility for the person, rather than direct care tasks (Twigg *et al.* 1990). There are thus major difficulties in extrapolating from such findings to carers of people with schizophrenia.

There is no widely accepted definition of informal care and no satisfactory term for relatives caring for dependants, reflecting not only a certain ambivalence in public policy towards relatives as carers, but also in carers themselves, as described in statements such as 'I'm his wife, not a carer.'

> 'Care' can be seen as 'an expression of concern, an attempt to manipulate, a laudable sacrifice on the part of the giver, an indication of the friendship between the two participants, the recipient's due, or a reflection of the receiver's dependence and incompetence.' (Thompson and Pitts 1992)

One person in a family is usually singled out as the carer, and this person carries the bulk of the responsibility for care. When care is shared, or help given, it is most likely given by another member of the household (Green 1988). There is very little evidence to support the notion of a caring community, and this suggests that community care is, in reality, care by the family, usually by women (Walker 1982; Finch 1984; Ungerson 1987; Parker 1990). Demographic changes such as the declining birth rate, and changes in the role of women and family structure, mean that there are fewer adults in the family to care. The traditional family carer, the unmarried daughter, is a declining species.

Before we can look at the support which is given to relatives in their informal carer role, we need briefly to consider models of care-giving.

Models of Care

If policy views relatives as carers, then a model for this role is necessary to assess what services might be necessary and how they might be delivered. Twigg and Atkin (1991) suggest four different models of carers: as resources, as co-workers, as co-clients and as superceded carers.

The first model is reflected in the Griffiths' Report and the White Paper, *Caring for People*, when they refer to care by relatives as the natural order of things. Relatives are taken for granted, a background of care against which other services, voluntary or statutory, are provided. The aim is to maintain or marginally increase the level of informal care. Services are centred on the dependant, with little thought being given to the needs or well-being of the carer. The second model is essentially instrumental: agencies aim to maintain and improve informal care by recognising some of the needs of the carer, particularly regarding morale, assuming that good morale increases the likelihood that care will continue. Education for relatives of people with schizophrenia may fall into this category when it aims to make care more 'appropriate'. This has consequences for the type of service provided. Relatives have been used to monitor the signs which predict relapse (Birchwood *et al.* 1989), since this requires close knowledge of the patient. The burden of responsibility on the family and patient to recognise and diagnose the early relapse process has been noted. MacCarthy (1988) describes a convergence of views in family therapy to the situation where relatives 'are enlisted as therapeutic agents, working alongside professionals, and sharing their aims'. Although it is accepted that relatives will require services of some kind, they are seen to have made an adjustment to their role and thus not require 'continual intensive input'. This may well be true, but it begs the question of how far relatives had a choice in accepting this long-term role. MacCarthy concludes that

> 'Family work should focus on relatives' independent needs as much as on factors which facilitate the patient's adjustment if they are not to be an exploited resource in the network of community care'.

This leads us to question of whether this shades over into the third model of carers as co-clients.

In the third model carers become 'indirect clients', a legitimate focus for support and services. This can cause confusion within the health service where the status of patient is clear, in a formal sense of defining the relationship to services, staff and treatment as well as a legal relationship between doctor and patient, but it might be inappropriate to refer to carers as co-patients, that is unless a 'whole family deviance model' is being employed. Health service personnel may be unable to meet recognised needs of carers under a service aimed at treatment and rehabilitation of illness unless such services are designated preventive medicine (Atkinson and Coia 1991). The boundary between social care and health care adds to the ambiguity. In the former the behaviours, duties and responsibilities merge into those which would normally be part of family and social life. Where a mother is caring for an adult child who became ill when young and who has never established independent living, the responsibilities may not so much have been assumed, as never given up. To regard carers as co-clients in such situations may therefore be quite unreasonable, it being,

> 'on the one side, an imperialistic take-over of what are normal processes of life; and on the other, a swamping of the social care system with "ordinary misery" '. (Twigg 1989)

The fine line between the acceptable, 'normal' duty and desire of relatives to care and the burden of care which they find unacceptable will be drawn in different places by different families, and might well differ from the line drawn by service providers and governments.

In the last model, support and services are provided for the dependent person but with the aim of making him or her independent and thus not reliant on the services of a carer. This model comes into focus most frequently when the carers are parents, particularly elderly parents and the currently dependent person has to look to a future without them.

Depending on which model of care is used and how wide the net of carers is cast, people can become disenfranchised by moving from the first two wider models to the last two narrower models. Policy moves from one model to another as suits its purpose. Although the recent changes in policy and legislation have focused more attention than previously on the role of relatives as carers, relatives themselves have always been aware of the ambiguity of their position. Twenty years ago the National Schizophrenia Fellowship (1974) presented a ten point plan entitled *Social Provision for Sufferers from Chronic Schizophrenia*. The first recommendation was that 'relatives of the chronic schizophrenics living in the community who accept a caring responsibility for them are "primary care" agents and should be recognised as such in policy making and administration'.

PROVIDING SERVICES FOR RELATIVES

The Griffiths' Report (1988) and the White Paper, *Care in the Community* (Secretaries of State for Health, Social Security, Wales and Scotland 1989) merely reflected a wider perspective of Government views put forward from the early 1980s, including the 1984 initiative *Helping the Community to Care* and the Social Work Services Group (1984) publication *Supporting the Informal Carers: Fifty Styles of Caring: models of practice for planners and practitioners.* The Disabled Persons Act 1986 required the assessment of carers' needs but was never fully implemented.

The Kings Fund produced what is essentially a guide for action with a '10-point plan' in *A New Deal for Carers* (Richardson *et al.* 1989). The following statement of need was endorsed by, among others, the National Schizophrenia Fellowship. It outlines that:

'Carers need:

1. Recognition of their contribution and of their *own* needs as individuals in their own right;

2. Services tailored to their individual circumstances, needs and views, through discussions at the time help is being planned;

3. Services which reflect an awareness of differing racial, cultural and religious backgrounds and values, equally accessible to carers of every race and ethnic origin;

4. Opportunities for a break, both for short spells (an afternoon) and for longer periods (a week or more), to relax and have time to themselves;

5. Practical help to lighten the tasks of caring, including domestic help, home adaptions, incontinence services and help with transport;

6. Someone to talk to about their own emotional needs, at the outset of caring, while they are caring and when the caring task is over;

7. Information about available benefits and services as well as how to cope with the particular condition of the person cared for;

8. An income which covers the costs of caring and which does not preclude carers taking employment or sharing care with other people;

9. Opportunities to explore alternatives to family care both for the immediate and the long-term future;

10. Services designed through consultation with carers, at all levels of policy planning.'

We have suggested (Atkinson and Coia 1991) that carer's needs do not have to be addressed only as a subjective and objective burden, but can be viewed as problems affecting any family member who lives with someone with a severe mental illness, and those problems which are specific to the caring role. Such a divide helps to separate the roles of co-client or co-worker.

Services for carers need to exist at three levels: specific services for carers, by-products of services for the dependant, and global assumptions, rules and resource practices (Twigg and Atkin 1991). The last one encompasses all the assumptions which service providers make about carers, including their availability, duties and likely involvement. These assumptions are important because to some extent services are structured on them.

If, as it increasingly seems, the policy is to acknowledge that relatives must be included both as recipients of services and also as part of the caring team, then they must be seen as part of a management triad, along with the patient and a key staff member, which rarely happens despite the White Paper demanding that local authorities and health boards 'consult with and take account of the views of . . . users and carers'.

The fact that informal care by families exists before formal provision of care means that although there may be substitution between the two systems, preference is given to informal care, especially in social care. A residualist model is employed which responds to the deficiencies of the care network (Twigg 1989) by providing the minimum of services acceptable rather than maximising the Welfare State by taking on what is defined as the family's responsibility.

As informal carers, family, friends and neighbours are, in a very essential way, 'uncommandable' resources, in that policy cannot turn such care on and off at will. Kinship is the most common incentive for care-giving and there is little evidence that neighbours and the wider community are, or will be, prepared to fall quickly into the role of informal carer. Although pressure may come from the carer and their own sense of duty, from other relatives, or even from professional staff, there is a sense in which service providers cannot control this resource, and nor can they direct it.

When carers come to be viewed as co-workers, the inherent differences between formal and informal services are highlighted. Formal services are universalistic (at least in theory), objective and emotionally neutral, governed by rules and assessment of situations rather than by personal characteristics, and derive from formal knowledge and skill based in professional training. In contrast, informal care is individualistic, subjective, emotionally laden, often characterised by long-term reciprocity or inalienable relationships and by ascribed status judgments, and derives from a knowledge-base of daily experience which, it is assumed, is open to, and accessible by, everyone.

It is not surprising that the two systems often sit uneasily together. Again there are differences in relationships between informal carers and health and social agencies. The knowledge base in medicine and health care is probably seen as more evident. This may be important, since we frequently hear carer groups refer to families as 'the real experts'. The very real knowledge and expertise of families in day-to-day management must somehow come together with the more specialised, professional knowledge of treatment and rehabilitation. For a real working partnership to develop between professionals and families, both sides have to recognise and accept the expertise of the other and also the advantages and limitations of both the formal and informal roles.

An ethical problem arises out of seeing relatives as co-workers where the person being cared for is an adult. Relatives want information about the patient/client and, indeed, may require it if care is to be appropriate. This may be opposed by either the patient/client or the professional, or both, on grounds of confidentiality. The need to maintain or develop the autonomy of the person with schizophrenia should be central in therapeutic programmes.

Problems also arise when carers are viewed as co-clients. Providing services to 'a family' may be seen as more appropriate when the client is a child rather than an adult, although this may change as parental carers themselves grow old or infirm. In such circumstances carers may attain the status of direct co-clients rather than secondary or indirect clients. However, it is when carer and dependant are both identified as clients that the various conflicts of interest between them become most fully focused.

Twigg (1989) suggests that this produces four major areas of tension in the provision of services.

1. The tension between prevention and substitution. The desire to prevent excess stress for carers and maximise their involvement set against services forming a substitute for informal care and encouraging carers to do less. One outcome of this is that either services can be used to bolster an essentially untenable situation for carers, or services only appear at the point of breakdown of care.

2. A tension between supporting carers with the aim of continuing their ability to care, and supporting them to increase their well-being, reflecting the difference between carers as co-workers and carers as co-clients.

3. Questions concerning targeting. At its most basic, these are questions about whether services should be targeted at those with most objective burden, those with most subjective burden, or those most likely to give up caring. This is particularly important when there is not necessarily a high correlation between objective and subjective burden (Hoenig and Hamilton 1969). Studies involving the carers of elderly people suggest that the breaking point for many carers is relatively early, and that male carers withdraw care-giving at lower levels of both objective and subjective burden (Levin *et al.* 1983). 'Tolerance' of problems is also likely to be variable. Hoenig and Hamilton (1969) report that greater tolerance appears to be shown by families to people with schizophrenia than to other groups of psychiatric patients. Focusing on care-givers on the margins may well result in inequitable and discriminatory allocation of resources.

4. The problems of generalisability. Services targeted at marginal situations are not, by definition, generalisable. A family or individual threatens to withdraw care and receives services, whereas another, with equal or greater burdens, does not, and so does not receive

support. Such situations are open to manipulation by carers, introducing further inequalities as different social groups have different abilities to 'work the system'.

CARERS' VIEWS OF SERVICES

There is little research which considers the view of carers as consumers. An extremely useful, but unusual, approach is to compare the views of patient, relative and staff. Perring (1991) did this in a small survey of discharged patients who had a diagnosis of 'schizophrenia, schizoid personality disorder, or a similar term'. Assessing after-care, there were some marked differences between groups. Whereas only one-third of discharged patients reported knowing that an after-care programme even existed, all the key workers believed it provided 'at least some help' and the majority saw it as effective. Both patients and relatives criticised the lack of continuity in staffing. Of the 15 patients, only three had continuity with a key worker over a two-year period, eight reported one change, and four had multiple changes of staff. Relatives also complained that they 'did not feel involved in planning the pattern of care'. Perring reports that

> 'Some relatives believed this was a deliberate strategy to ensure that former patients felt central to the service. Even with this understanding they nevertheless felt isolated and unable to turn to a professional worker when they saw the warning signs of crisis approaching'.

It is probably not surprising that relatives saw a need for greater levels of supervision in the community than did the discharged patients, and key workers saw more need for future use of services than did the people with schizophrenia themselves.

The other area which demonstrated some major differences of opinion was income. All 15 patients were on State benefits and almost all had problems attributed to low income. However, seven said they had no problem managing their finances, although even this group were aware that 'at times of crisis their management of income went completely haywire'. Relatives, on the other hand, saw finance as more of a problem, through both 'inadequate income and inappropriate management'. It is this latter point that can cause tensions between the person with schizophrenia and their relative. Inappropriate management can simply mean making different choices, or it can describe situations which become a major financial burden for relatives. Relatives wanted to see more help and advice with budgeting. Key workers were dismissive of income as 'a salient issue'.

Families meeting services ambivalent to them can feel marginalised and blamed, although there is a wide range of opinion. There is often a mismatch between what the families want as a result of contact with professionals, and what those same professionals are prepared to offer (Hatfield *et al.* 1982). As a result, families can rate therapy as a low priority (Hatfield 1983; Spaniol *et al.* 1984). The professionals tend to concentrate on issues such as family dynamics and expressed emotion, whereas the families themselves want information and practical advice. Despite this, many families still look for more contact with professionals. Whether this is because they see no alternative to professionals, or whether they believe that more time will mean they will get the information they want, is unclear. Not all studies report high levels of dissatisfaction with the services (MacCarthy *et al.* 1989a) despite high levels of unmet need. Whether this is a cultural difference between the United States and Britain or reflects other issues is unclear.

The fourth of Twigg's models may be the most appropriate to people with chronic schizophrenia and their families. The move to deinstitutionalisation means that the demography of patients in the community is changing, with more younger, single men living in the community. A study involving members of the National Alliance for the Mentally Ill (Hatfield 1983; Williams *et al.* 1986) found that 85% of carers were parents, and that these people were in their 50s and 60s. There has been little investigation of this group, although in a review article Lefley (1987) points out

> 'three major social policy implications . . . the danger that governments will be relieved of the responsibility for care of the mentally ill; the creation of a potentially at-risk population of aging parents and other family members because of the stresses of caregiving; and the reduction of the patient's potential for optimal adaptation in the community'.

Although the research demonstrating both families' problems and the usefulness of intervention programmes has been available for some time it has had little impact on general clinical practice and has not been incorporated into routine management by psychiatric services. No doubt this is partly because the evidence so far has generally come from small, specialised research projects on highly selected families. These studies indicate the problems of getting relatives involved in groups. Spaniol *et al.* (1984) suggest a number of ways in which 'professionals can share power with families', including working as a team, pointing out family strengths, encouraging family involvement, teaching family members about mental illness and medication, knowing who provides local services, meeting with local support groups and acknowledging diverse beliefs. To integrate family interventions in order to treat families as either co-clients or co-workers requires a change in clinical practice which includes not just the delivery of services, but also changes in the use of resources, which in turn affects needs assessment, evaluation of services and staff training.

CARE OR CARING

Most of the research on care comes within a framework of service delivery, either organisational or sociological. Subjective burden may involve cognitive and emotional processes, but otherwise there is very little on the psychology of care. Why should this be? Surely the individual in the caring situation should be of prime concern? Maybe even more important is the dyad of the carer and the cared for. Since, in this context 'cared for' implies dependency, maybe we should look for another word. Unfortunately the English language, so rich in many respects, is not very helpful here.

Hall (1990) attempts a psychological analysis of caring and suggests a model of care as 'an interpersonal encounter'. The four components of this model, 'a set of beliefs or philosophies . . . a set of goals or objectives . . . a set of practices and acts . . . the emotions and feelings which accompany care', could, however, be applied as easily to an organisation providing a service as to an individual providing care. Although Hall points out that most care is provided by informal carers or 'direct-care staff who are not highly trained', and that they may have 'parental—most probably maternal—models of caring, which may emphasise passivity in the cared for and so encourage dependency', it would be quite wrong to suggest that policy makers are not also involved in the projection of their own, usually political, philosophies of care onto service delivery. In their own way, such models can be described as 'lay' as much as non-trained carers.

Maybe one of the reasons for the difficulty in defining a psychological model of care is the need to separate care and caring: care as a process/task is not the same as caring as a process/experience, or as a relationship between two people. Or maybe both 'care' and 'caring' are difficult to define without putting them first in a particular framework. So Hall says that whilst 'looking at caring relationships from a social psychological perspective' may describe 'an immediate context for the caring act', 'the act' itself is not described. This then demands that caring be 'an act' and not a relationship. Since the many guides to caring which he cites all encourage the idea that control and independence should be maintained by the cared-for, surely it is relationships which are at the heart of caring, and for formal carers as much as informal carers. The relationship, the context and the tasks performed all go to make up this thing called care, and it will always be approached best from an interdisciplinary perspective. This is not to say that there are not aspects which are predominantly psychological. Major unasked questions are:

> 'What psychological processes are involved in the vigilance, risk taking and decision making of care? Can we develop a topography of care practices which adequately describes what happens in care? What is the significance of physical touch and contact in caring? What is the subjective experience of caring over long periods, with lifetime careers in caring being a reality for some? Why do people want to care when there is no pre-existing emotional or social attachment?'

The question he asks which seems less wholly psychological is

> 'can we develop indices of care which more fully reflect more adequate philosophies of care?'

Furthermore, we need to consider whether a model of care which is appropriate for a formal carer will be suitable for an informal carer.

The 'significance of physical touch and contact', for example, may be different for a trained professional, an untrained formal worker and a relative, and be experienced differently by the person being touched. Or it may not. Or it may depend on the context of the touching. Is physical restraint easier? Harder? For a relative at home or for a nurse on a ward? When the person is a danger to themselves or to others? Should we describe caring as a series of dimensions within which carers and/or caring relationships fall? To describe care thus would produce a profile on a number of variables rather than seeing it as a unidimensional activity.

If we try to apply this to people with schizophrenia and their relatives, we quickly realise how limited is our information and how blinkered our outlook. We know little about the relationship between people with schizophrenia and their families apart from that presented within a medical, problem-orientated framework. Expressed emotion tells us something, but is limited. We have not asked the person with schizophrenia how they experience this, apart from assuming that it is probably stressful and measuring physiological change (Tarrier 1989). Where is the descriptive or analytical research which explores why a (for example) mother and son stay together in what to outsiders is a mutually dependent and mutually destructive relationship? There are first-person accounts from people with schizophrenia about their illness, their treatment by professionals and by 'the system'. Families appear, relationships are discussed, but the 'care' aspects tend to receive little attention. The user movement emphasises independence and control of the treatment/care process without necessary recourse to relatives. All this has an impact on care, just as much as the tasks performed. Only two aspects of the caring relationship have been considered in some detail, burden and dependency.

Burden

The responsibility of the family to care is often referred to, in the research literature and elsewhere, as 'burden', as described in Chapter 2. Platt (1985) describes four dimensions of burden: objective burden, present regardless of cause or present only if attributable to the patient, and subjective burden, arising directly out of the patient's behaviour or arising as a consequence of (elevated) objective burden. He also describes eleven areas of burden, ten being the effect on aspects of family life (work/employment, social life/leisure, physical health, emotional/mental health, finances/income, family routine, family/household interaction, schooling/education, children, and interaction with others outside the family/household). The eleventh area is the patient's behaviour itself perceived as burden. Lastly, he describes five groups of people to whom the burden relates, namely, the informant, specific others in the household, the informant's household as a totality, specific people outside the household, and non-specific others outside the household including the community.

Despite such 'academic' definitions, 'burden' is not a neutral word and may be seen as carrying negative overtones, particularly so by the people with schizophrenia themselves, who resent being described as a 'burden'. This view rarely reaches print, but is vocalised at conferences. If people with schizophrenia are not involved in developing their aftercare, or there is no alternative to living with family, then 'burden' may be seen as doubly harsh as they have no choice either.

The situation might be eased if a clear separation is made between the person and the impact of their behaviour or illness. It must be possible to admit to the sometimes overwhelming pressures which accompany the caring role without negatively labeling the individual. This may relate to how the behaviour itself is viewed. We expect adults to know what they are doing, to understand its impact on others, and thus to exercise some control. As we saw earlier, where families believe that the person with schizophrenia *has* control over their actions they are more likely to hold negative views towards them, as expressed in high EE.

Unlike some agencies, relatives who are carers do not have an option of withdrawing care, or passing the responsibility on to a more 'high dependency' agency if the burden becomes more than they can carry. This means that both the duty to care, and the strain this puts on carers, should be the focus of service providers.

The use of 'burden' to describe the impact of caring is not only emotionally negative, but serves to limit the role of carer. A more neutral term might be 'support', as proposed by Creer *et al.* (1982), which may include the more positive side of caring. Elsewhere the term 'impact' has been used (Perring *et al.* 1990). Although some relatives speak of burden, many do not; how do they conceptualise their caring role? How is 'burden' viewed by the 'dependant'?

Dependency

As elsewhere, most investigation has focused on carers of the elderly. Although many people with schizophrenia are unable to live fully independent lives, this does not necessarily cast them in the role of dependant. The need to maintain the adult role and also the accumulating evidence that dependency contributes to 'depression-proneness' (Birtchnell 1988) confirm our interest in dependency.

Confusion over the role of carer adds to the confusion on dependency. If relatives are co-clients where does dependency fit? When the relative is a resource, or a co-worker, or when the definition of carer becomes being responsible for tasks or for the person, then dependency is an inevitable factor. Perring *et al.* (1990) describe three categories of caring tasks: practical tasks, coping with difficult behaviour and new responsibilities. These echo Creer *et al.*'s (1982) consideration of what relatives do in terms of the practical tasks which people normally do for themselves, behaviour which needs supervision, and whether the person can be left alone. Overall the caring role was described as that of assuming responsibility for their 'dependant' rather than being involved in practical tasks. However, this dependency does vary with the course of the illness. Carers take on new tasks and responsibilities in respect of their relative, resulting in changes in their relationship. Either or both sides might resent the shift in responsibility and thus in the dynamics of power in the relationship.

An issue rarely addressed is how far dependency might be encouraged, consciously or unconsciously, by a carer. Over-involvement, as described in high EE, may be seen as an allied concept, but it does not address the need some carers might have to maintain dependency. Nor does it consider how dependency might be the preferred option (by carer or dependant) rather than the risk-taking involved in becoming or maintaining independence. Carers who are socially isolated, who live alone with the dependant, may be as locked into their role as the patient is to the illness, and may not be able to tolerate the separation implied in giving up the role.

Although there are legal safeguards to protect patients' rights, these tend to apply at the extremes of behaviour. Few guardianship orders are granted, for example, in comparison with the number of day-to-day responsibilities taken by carers and the restraints put on the cared for. The variable nature of schizophrenia not only makes decision making in these areas more difficult than for more static conditions, but makes the necessity to debate them even more vital.

CARING AND COPING

An interest in the caring process inevitably means a concomitant interest in the coping process, and a framework to understand this for carers of people with schizophrenia involves EE, the coping ability of relatives, levels of burden, the spectre of relapse and even the decision to relinquish care. This, in turn, raises the question of how we define coping. The Oxford English Dictionary describes coping as dealing effectively with a person or a task, or successfully managing a situation or a problem. Folkman and Lazarus (1980) are more specific, describing coping as the cognitive and behavioural efforts made to master, tolerate or reduce external and internal demands and the conflicts between them. Both definitions indicate a positive outcome. In chronic illness we must ask, outcome for whom? A positive outcome for the carer may not always mean the best outcome for the cared for and *vice versa*.

The first step is to consider whether coping is a state or a trait. Since traits are normally defined as constant characteristics which generally indicate how someone will respond under certain conditions at both a cognitive and a behavioural level, there appears little evidence to support the view of a general coping trait. Caring for someone with schizophrenia incorporates numerous sources of stress, and individuals use different coping mechanisms at different times. Thus, coping does not appear to be a process that can be measured in a static manner, but appears to be more of a 'state'. 'Coping style' is the particular response that the individual will make or the strategies they will use in their efforts to master the demands placed on them and reduce the stress engendered by those demands.

Coping Styles

One of the best known models is Folkman and Lazarus's process model of coping (1980). Coping means what an individual does in a given situation and how changes in the situation influence what the individual does. Thus the person and the environment are involved in a continuous relationship. Two forms of coping are described. Problem-focused coping aims to influence the external situation directly and alter the source of stress, while emotionfocused coping regulates or controls the internal stressful emotions, maintaining a sense of hope

and self-esteem. Both work better when used together. Coping processes are thus what the person thinks and does in a particular situation
(appraisal) and the changes in effort they make during the course of an
episode (coping). In a study of coping styles in a community sample
experiencing stressful events of daily living over one year, they identified three main types of appraisal: harm or loss (damage that had
already occurred), threat (anticipated harm or loss) and challenge
(anticipated opportunity for mastery or gain). They showed that both
problem-focused and emotion-focused coping were used in most
stressful episodes, and a considerable repertoire of coping skills was
employed. The context of the event and its perception were the main
factors affecting coping behaviour, rather than the personality of the
individual.

The effectiveness of problem-focused coping depends, however, on the
individual's ability to apply emotion-focused coping successfully. If
they cannot, then heightened emotions limit their ability to problem-
solve (Folkman 1984) and limit social support (Billings and Moos 1981).
Folkman and Lazarus (1986) showed that individuals with high numbers of depressive symptoms use more confrontational coping and
respond with anger towards others.

Pearlin and Schooler (1978) also studied a community sample and
common life stresses in four role areas: marriage partner, parent,
employee and economic manager. Coping was defined as a mediating
factor, i.e., any response to external life strains that serves to prevent,
avoid or control emotional distress. They identified three major types
of coping: responses that change the situation, responses that control
the meaning of the situation after it occurs but before stress emerges—
'cognitive neutralisation', and responses that try to control and minimise the stress as it arises rather than being overwhelmed by it. Most
individuals used a varied repertoire of coping depending on the situation and the social and psychological resources available, but cognitive neutralisation was most common.

Illfeld (1980) suggested that coping was not just a mediating factor
between life stressors and emotional distress, but that it could precede
life stressors and may thus prevent or defuse them. He identified three
coping patterns: taking direction, rationalisation and avoidance of the
stressor, and accepting the situation without attempting alteration. He
also found that individuals used a variety of responses, suggesting that

choice of coping strategy was linked to the environmental context of the events rather than the individual's personality type. Billings and Moos (1981) also emphasised the breadth of the coping repertoire, but warned against trying to identify positive or negative types of coping because of the factors that precede the stressful event in the individual's life.

Some gender differences in coping styles have been indicated. Life stress studies have shown that women use more maladaptive coping styles, particularly avoidance techniques, that often result in them experiencing more rather than less stress (Pearlin and Schooler 1978; Billings and Moos 1981). Similar maladaptive coping styles have been described amongst female carers of the dementing elderly (Gilleard 1984; Whittick 1993). Thus it seems that women tend to become involved at a higher emotional level or experience more emotional distress in stressful situations, which can be detrimental to their ability to cope in a practical way. Miller *et al.* (1985) took the gender issue further by linking women's maladaptive coping to developing health problems. They found women who responded to life stress by getting angry with themselves or with others, ruminating or using tobacco or alcohol, were more likely to become psychiatrically ill within the year. This did not depend on the level of stress and could occur even when stress was minimal.

This work may have important implications in caring for someone with schizophrenia where patient behaviour and its context is of more importance than relatives' personality in influencing coping styles. Several studies have found problem-focused coping and positive reappraisal to be highly correlated. It may be that positive reappraisal facilitates problem-focused coping, or that individuals choose problem-focused coping when they see a potential for positive change, which leads to positive appraisal. This may be a particular issue in families where a false appraisal leads to a maladaptive coping style (high EE) and increases stress. Whether it is the personality traits of the appraiser, the other's behaviour or inaccurate appraisal through lack of knowledge, or misinformation about the illness and related behaviour that contributes most to inaccurate appraisal is important in the provision of education groups to relatives. Education and increased knowledge of the illness may enable families to understand the nature of the illness, the potential outcome, and ways of helping the person avoid relapse. Thus their appraisal of the stressor may enable them to assess their coping resources better, reduce their emotional tensions, and use more effective problem-focused coping. Such views are supported by Toner (1987), who looked at effective information for carers of dementia patients that may help them to cope. There are limitations in this approach, however, since these models focus on single events rather than an on-going stress such as caring for someone with a chronic illness, and thus may not be applicable to carers. We clearly need to consider coping as an on-going process.

Coping and Caring—An Ongoing Situation

Although several studies have looked at spouses living with someone who has chronic illness and identified stress in relation to maladaptive coping, more similar to coping with a relative with schizophrenia may be those studies looking at how carers cope with a dependant with dementia. Gilhooly (1987) adapted Pearlin and Schooler's model and found that those carers who used behavioural strategies had higher morale than those using only psychological ones. A mixture of psychological (internal) and behavioural (external) techniques proved to be the best. Levine *et al.* (1983) found that those carers with an internal locus of control tended to cope better. A larger study by Pratt *et al.* (1985) of carers of Alzheimer patients defined internal and external coping strategies.

Internal strategies were:

- reframing or redefining a stressful experience in a way that makes it more understandable and manageable,

- problem solving,

- passivity.

The first two were associated with significantly less carer burden. External coping resources were:

- spiritual support,

- extended families,

- friends,

- neighbours and community resources.

Spiritual support and support from extended families correlated with lower levels of burden.

Whittick (1993) found high levels of hostility and frustration in many carers of the dementing elderly, and also found evidence that coping techniques changed over time. She cautioned against any general prescription for good coping as each situation is unique, constantly changing, and with differing communication and interaction patterns.

Coping and Expressed Emotion

Interest in how carers cope with psychiatric illness has arisen in conjunction with the search to define and seek causal explanations for the concept of expressed emotion. Although there is little work relating coping style to EE, Birchwood and Smith (1987) suggest that EE is a 'state' which measures the temperature of the developing interaction between the person with schizophrenia and the relative whilst attempting to cope with schizophrenia. Does maladaptive coping by the relative produce high expressed emotion? Does the patient's behaviour influence the relative's coping style? Since expressed emotion is known to vary over time in a substantial minority of families, perhaps EE levels and relatives' coping efficacy interact to determine the stability of EE. Perhaps the first step in understanding or finding answers to these complex questions is to consider a coping model related to EE.

As described earlier, EE is a response and a fluctuating state. It can also be seen as a measure of relatives' stress when it is regarded as a maladaptive coping response or mediating variable which increases the risk of relapse through increasing stress on the person with schizophrenia. There is, however, an inherent danger in defining EE as a maladaptive coping response without asking maladaptive to whom, because if there are no other measures that indicate that relatives have high levels of stress, maybe it is an adaptive coping response for the relative in a complex situation. Attempting to alter such a coping response by the relative without taking into account individual characteristics in the person with schizophrenia that have precipitated the response, or other resources, may in fact lead to increased stress in the relative. Also, relatives may cope better at one time than another because of their own personal, external, independent life stresses. Reducing 'problem' behaviour in the person with schizophrenia may break the cycle more effectively by reducing the trigger and stimulus that cause high EE as a response. Reducing high EE by reducing time in face-to-face contact would fit into this model. This may also involve putting in more resources. Our understanding of coping theory and its relationship to EE should lead us to tread warily in giving advice during family interventions about the repertoire of skills and techniques that may help solve family problems through adaptive coping.

Goldstein *et al.* (1989) support this caution through looking at patterns of expressed emotion and patient coping styles. They point out that in the literature, EE attitudes appear to be independent of patients' behaviour. Their own study, however, shows three quite distinctive family interaction patterns associated with three different EE profiles over time. Families who retain high EE have high rates of reciprocal criticism by both patient and relative. Those families who move from high EE to low EE have patients more critical of relatives. Those families who retain low EE have minimal criticism and frequent statements of autonomous interests or wishes by the patient. Thus patient behaviour does appear to influence the genesis of EE.

Coping and Carers of People with Schizophrenia

Birchwood and Cochrane (1990) set out to identify the repertoire of coping styles or strategies adopted by relatives, and attempted to relate them to particular behaviours of the person with schizophrenia. The behavioural disturbance which led to initial family burden (stress in relatives) resulted in the relatives developing coping strategies/styles that either modified or exacerbated disturbed behaviour and social impairment. In turn, the altered behaviour of the person with schizophrenia would then feed back into the process. This was similar to Folkman and Lazarus's model of primary appraisal, coping, and secondary appraisal of the altered situation. Expressed emotion may in some way measure this interaction, although the relationship of EE to coping style is not explored in this study.

Eight broad coping styles which applied across all areas of behaviour change were identified:

- coercion (with criticism),
- avoidance,

- ignore/accept,

- collusion,

- constructive,

- resignation,

- reassurance,

- disorganisation.

Coping styles for aggressive behaviour, which was only found in a small proportion of the sample (5%), were quite different and thus excluded. Perceived control and less burden were associated with ignore/accept, collusion and constructive styles, whilst less control and more stress was associated with avoidance and disorganised styles. Birchwood and Cochrane advise against simplistic interpretation of these results and their translation into advice to relatives to alter maladaptive coping styles. They suggest that coping style may be more related to the behaviour of the person with schizophrenia at the time, rather than to an innate, permanently fixed style derived from the carers' personality. They appear to be suggesting that coping style is a more interactionist process resulting from particular behaviours or points in time. They also suggest that it is not possible to determine whether coping style is a cause or a consequence of the behaviour. Coercion, for example, was more likely to be adopted by relatives of people with low social functioning and social withdrawal, while ignore/accept was adopted by relatives of patients with high social functioning. In relation to positive symptoms, some relatives were more likely to become disorganised, whilst coercion was more probable when the person with schizophrenia was more withdrawn or inactive. It is important to note it was the behavioural disturbance arising out of symptoms which decided the relatives' coping style, not the symptoms in themselves. Coercive strategies were used by relatives of people with a large number of relapses or re-admissions. As Birchwood and Cochrane point out, it is unclear whether coercion increases as a coping style with chronicity, or if the constant use of coercion increases the rate of relapse.

Thus relatives' coping style appears to be adopted in response to particular individual behaviours arising mainly as a result of the illness process, rather than the interaction of the personalities of the relatives and the person with schizophrenia. How the patient's behaviour is perceived is also affected by the relative's own perception of stress and burden. For these reasons, offering a group intervention aimed at altering coping style may be less effective than altering the patient's symptom profile, or social functioning, or the relative's perception of burden. Similarly, limiting the carer's coping repertoire to what is perceived as adaptive or good coping, emphasising a particular coping strategy in particular situations, could be unfortunate.

Another confounding factor frequently ignored is the patient's coping style. Since schizophrenia fluctuates, it may be that people with schizophrenia employ internal auto-protective coping strategies to avoid or reduce their vulnerability to breakdown (Brenner *et al.* 1987). At a more external level, Lee *et al.* (1993) attempted to ascertain what coping tactics were perceived as helpful by patients themselves. Their study differed from others in not only looking at self-coping, but also including external factors that related to illness outcome. They excluded chronic or recovered patients from the study, and most patients did not have florid psychotic symptoms. Interestingly, patients and doctors were in close agreement as to what they regarded as helpful. This included drugs, hospital admissions to reduce stress, social support and guidance (including emotional and material support), and a meaningful daily routine. They also felt that it would be helpful to change one's perception of things (cognitive coping effort). This study also established a need for services. Whilst drugs were available, day care, occupational training and social activities were lacking. They argue that if patients were given support to improve their living, social and problem-solving skills, they could augment their self-coping skills, generate further social support, and reduce their vulnerability to relapse. This would lead us to conclude that for both people with schizophrenia and their relatives, too much reliance on a general coping prescription will not produce the best outcomes for either group.

6

SELF-HELP GROUPS
FOR RELATIVES

For well over a hundred years patients have sought to protect their rights. The 'user movement' is strong throughout the world, seeking to protect patients and potential patients against inappropriate detention, as well as campaigning for rights on many different levels. Many of the groups take a psychosocial approach to the aetiology of schizophrenia, sometimes seeing the condition as political labelling rather than an illness. The denial of an 'illness', or a biological basis to the illness, clearly leads to demands for services and management often at odds with a traditional medical model.

Over the last 20 years or so there has grown, in parallel, a relatives' movement. The National Schizophrenia Fellowship (NSF) was founded in Britain in 1972. Although usually seen as the beginning of the movement, an association of friends and relatives existed in France as early as 1963, under the name Unité Nationale des Amis et des Familles des Malades Mentaux (UNAFAM). Groups sprang up in Europe and North America following the British model.

The relatives' movement is often more accepting of the biological basis of schizophrenia, and thus the medical model, than the users' movement. Although rooted in a membership of carers, many have extended their franchise to include people with schizophrenia which, on occasions, highlights the dilemmas between the rights of patients and the rights of carers. From a solid self-help base, they have often extended their work first into education and then into service provision, most commonly day centres or drop-in centres and, to a lesser extent, accommodation projects.

Self-help groups and voluntary groups are often used synonymously, although differences exist. Different definitions of self-help also exist, but it can be broadly defined in the following ways (Levy 1978).

1. Having a primary aim to help and support members in dealing with problems and in improving coping skills.

2. Its origin is 'spontaneous', coming from group members themselves and not from external agencies.

3. Help comes from members through peer support and the belief that personal participation and face-to-face interactions are extremely important.

4. Members share a common 'problem' and agree a course of action.

5. Control of the group remains in the hands of lay members although advice may be sought from professionals.

6. The group usually starts from a position of powerlessness.

7. The group is a reference point through which members are able to identify with others for both action and definitions.

Voluntary organisations are predominantly service providers and are reliant on paid staff. They are frequently larger than the self-help groups and organised nationally or even internationally. Like the self-help groups, they enjoy charity status.

The benefits of self-help groups come particularly from the involvement of the individual with peers. Members offer advice and support; acting as a role model and giving help to others is seen as a positive experience, as well as receiving help. All self-help groups engage in education. Invited professionals are usually involved in the educational aspects of the group, which are balanced by what have been called ' "woe" nights' (Weal 1980) when members share their common experiences.

It has been noted that 'One of the most striking characteristics of self-help adherents is distrust of professionals' (Back and Taylor 1976), but this may be more true of the user movement than of relatives. Although carers' groups developed out of a sense of dissatisfaction with the system and the help received, they usually wanted to increase professional involvement and concern. In many countries they are now mainstream, being consulted by local and central government, and health and social services, as speaking on behalf of carers. While this is welcomed, it must be remembered that members are a biased sample of the whole population of relatives. They are more likely to feel that both professionals and society have failed them (Hurvitz 1976). This may reflect the nature of the illness their relative has, (e.g. unremitting psychotic symptoms or difficult-to-live-with behaviour) and the inability of treatment to manage this, as much as neglect by services. Like much of the self-help movement, there is a tendency for members to be middle class, middle aged, likely to be parents and predominantly female (Hatfield 1979a; Levy 1981).

Comparatively little research has been carried out with these groups, so exactly what they do, what members gain from them and why.they are successful remains unclear. Research that has been done describes both the burdens on the relatives, services used by relatives and what they think would help them (Hatfield 1979b; Atkinson 1986; Williams *et al.* 1986).

Galanter (1990) uses the model of the 'charismatic group' to describe 'modern cults and zealous self-help movements'. Characterised by high levels of social cohesiveness, an intensely held belief system and a profound influence on the behaviour of members, he suggests that such groups can have both positive and negative effects on psychopathology. It would probably surprise members of groups such as the National Alliance of the Mentally Ill to find themselves linked to the Unification Church (Moonies), but Galanter sees similarities. Families

'have bonded together in zealous peer-groups . . . Like modern religious sects in their early phases, the National Alliance is currently undergoing a phase of aggressive recruitment . . . Its zealously held philosophy . . . espouses that mental illness is biologically grounded; in particular it eschews a family-based view of etiology. The ideology of biologically based illness provides the members of the National Alliance who are parents of psychiatrically disabled patients with relief from the distress associated with guilt over their children's illnesses. In addition, like the belief system of the charismatic religious groups and other zealous self-help programs it also serves to organise the behaviours of members.'

This seems an overly harsh assessment of relatives' groups, and even those who oppose some of their ideology are unlikely to view them as controlling their members as effectively as do the Moonies.

Professional attitudes will depend as much on the nature of the group and its activities as on the orientation of the professionals. Levy (1978) found that about half his respondents from staff at psychiatric out-pa-tient facilities

> 'acknowledged that self-help groups may have an important or very important role to play in a comprehensive mental health delivery sys-tem.'

Common concerns of relatives' organisations are support groups and the provision of information. This includes both providing information to relatives and members about the illness through talks, conferences and information leaflets, and educating a wider audience, including professionals, about the needs of carers, also through conferences, publications and, not infrequently, talking to students in training. Education is also aimed at the general public to heighten the awareness of the problems of people with mental illness and their relatives, and to reduce the stigma, misconceptions and misinformation that sur-rounds mental illness, in particular schizophrenia.

For all groups funding is a major issue. It comes from a variety of sources including central and local government, grants from other charitable organisations and businesses, donations, membership sub-scriptions and fund-raising events.

Moving around the world it is interesting that, by and large, the relatives' groups have more similarities than differences. Although some groups are led by laypersons and others by professionals, some have a fairly rigid format and others are more flexible, some have paid staff and some do not, they are held together by what Borkman (1976) describes as 'experiential knowledge'. There is a 'core belief that people who have the shared experience of a common problem have unique resources to offer one another' (Medvene 1992). There is belief that by helping others people help themselves (Reismann 1965).

RELATIVES' ORGANISATIONS

The National Schizophrenia Fellowship, Great Britain

The National Schizophrenia Fellowship (NSF) was founded in Novem-ber 1972 as a charity. It was the culmination of over two years hard work following a letter by John Pringle published in *The Times* on 9

May 1970 under the heading 'A case of schizophrenia'. In this, Mr. Pringle outlined the problems of living with a person with schizophrenia. The correspondence which followed resulted in the setting up of a committee of relatives under the title Schizophrenia Action Group. From this simple beginning, the organisation has grown to 161 branches throughout Britain today. Of the membership, over 90% are carers.

During the 1980s there was a move towards strong regional development, leading not just to regional offices, but to independent, although usually allied, groups being set up. The organisation in Scotland formally separated in 1984 (National Schizophrenia Fellowship (Scotland)), through a mixture of nationalism and the need to represent the membership adequately in a country where the NHS and Social Services are organised differently and there are also differences in the Mental Health Laws. Groups in the north of England also went their own way, becoming the Northern Fellowship and the North-West Fellowship.

The NSF now has a variety of roles. As well as the monthly meetings for relatives held by most local groups

> 'the NSF has an advisory service which deals with requests for advice and information and provides some advocacy support. The service is open to professionals and non-members as well as members'. (Mental Illness and the Services People Need: Mike Took, NSF Southern Region)

Training courses for professionals also feature strongly, 'where users and family carers outline their experiences'. The NSF has always been a 'campaigning organisation' and it sees itself as having two roles here.

> 'We both campaign actively, e.g. for the pace of mental hospital closures to not exceed the rate of replacement community services, and respond to Central Government consultation documents and draft community care plans and NHS Trust applications.'

The NSF has moved firmly into the service provision arena.

The growth of the NSF as a service provider is demonstrated most dramatically if we consider its financial position. The year 1988–89 showed a turnover of £769 143 which, by 1992–93 had increased eightfold to £6.1 million. This is clearly in response to the guidelines set, and opportunities made, by government. The position of the NSF is, however, by no means straightforward. An interview with Martin Ede,

Director of NSF, who describes the voluntary sector as being at 'the crossroads', gives his perspective.

> 'We've seen the NSF attempting to provide services and at the same time to retain its roots, which is as a carers' organisation. It's a difficult balancing act . . . It creates tensions because some members will want us to be a greater campaigning force and worry that we may compromise our ability to campaign if we are receiving money from government and other local authorities. I don't believe that is a legitimate argument . . . because we provide about 100 different services and projects around the country we are far better informed about what is needed and that is the view that the majority of . . . NSF take.

> 'I think the question for the voluntary sector is should we become not-for-profit organisations or simply self-help groups. I think the idea of a not-for-profit organisation is one that is nearer to the majority of the work that the NSF is doing. I think that if one is setting up services for carers it is important to make sure it is properly supported, properly financed, properly run, so that the standards that we set are very high ones.'

Asked who makes decisions about the types of services provided, he replied,

> 'I think that the services that are provided should come from the carers, and the users, rather than be imposed upon them . . . It is totally wrong where people come along and say this is what we are going to provide for you and that's why many of the services are better provided by voluntary organisations because people have a sense of ownership.'

Asked about the problem of the NSF being a predominantly white, middle class organisation, he said,

> 'That is a danger of the voluntary sector because "volunteerism" as a concept is very much white, middle class. We're attempting to address that by taking positive action in a number of areas. For example . . . we've co-hosted a major conference . . . on the needs of black people with mental health problems. We are . . . working with the Bangladeshi community in Tower Hamlets. We've run a programme with the Asian community in Southall . . . So when you put those things together NSF is changing fairly positively in the sense that we are reaching far greater numbers of people from ethnic minorities.'

Looking to the future:

> 'I like to think we can break new ground, that we can be innovative, whereas statutory authorities can't be. We're examining the possibility

of a national respite care home . . . that doesn't exist in England and
Wales, although I know that you have something in Scotland . . . We are
examining, along with NACRO (National Association for the Care and
Resettlement of Offenders) and MIND, the development of psychiatric
bail hostels, as an alternative to putting people inside. We can break new
ground and I think that it is a vital role that the voluntary sector can play.'

The NSF can thus be seen to have moved a very long way from its
origins. Does the carers' group structure have any relevance today?

'The group structure is a very important one . . . one has to be very careful
about setting too high a demand on what a group can achieve. I think
that you have to have something positive otherwise the feeling of the
group can become very negative; it can become terribly inward looking,
a rehashing of personal problems. If you give them something positive
to become involved with (a project) then it can take on a whole different
outlook . . . Having a group in itself is insufficient, and that's why . . . so
many hospitals set up carers' groups and they're like shooting stars.
They start, but they soon die.'

The NSF is a successful self-help group which has gone beyond its
original bounds to become something few would have envisaged 20
years ago. Whether its strength is still, strictly, self-help probably
depends on whether you are a relative getting your only support from
a local group or not.

ENOSH: The Israel Mental Health Association

Founded in the early 1980s by the mother of a mentally ill girl, ENOSH

'is a volunteer organisation dedicated to the promotion of mental health,
the re-integration of the mentally ill into the community and creating
greater awareness of the problems faced by the mentally ill and their
families. The Biblical name ENOSH (Genesis 4, 26), meaning "Human
being", encapsulates the aims and needs of the Israel Mental Health
Association.' (ENOSH leaflet)

There are currently 50 branches throughout Israel, encompassing every
community in Israeli society, including Jews, Arabs, Druses and others.
Four of the branches have drop-in centres which provide counselling
to families, people with mental illness and professionals. This encompasses legal advice and also acts as a referral service. A number of

support groups are run, mostly supervised by a professional. It is hoped that gradually the groups will move to a self-help status as has already happened with a few. Meetings and conferences form part of the work of ENOSH. A National Centre includes a library and runs both education programmes and public relations activities.

The organisation is currently planning a major project, ENOSH village, which

> 'will consist of a residential community that provides a protected, yet productive framework for those suffering from mental illness, as an innovative alternative to life-long institutionalisation.' (ENOSH leaflet)

The village will provide housing, employment and/or vocational training and recreation, social, sport and cultural activities. A plot has been designated in the Sharon area for the village and it will eventually be home to 400 residents.

ENOSH explicitly acknowledges the psycho-educational approach.

> 'The families feel they are no longer alone, that there is someone to turn to who understands their plight and pays attention to their problem. They are able to support and help each other and this in turn gives them the strength needed to influence the rehabilitation process of their children (or any member of the family), as well as the basic principles connected with their family member's treatment.' (All information supplied by personal communication with Shmuel Cohen, Chairman, and Naomi Bruck-Shafir, Family Counselling Co-Ordinator, ENOSH.)

Association of Relatives and Friends of the Mentally Ill (Inc.): Australia

This generic organisation began in Sydney in 1974 when a social worker wrote a letter to several newspapers about the problems of families. A small group of relatives got together

> 'to explore the situation, to look at the questions, "Is there really a problem area? and, if so, what is it and why?" and "What can we do about it" ' (M. Lukes, *The ARAFMI Story. A Decade of Support 1975–1985*).

As a result a seminar, 'Mental Illness and the Distress of the Family' was held in February 1975, and in March the Association was formally founded. It now has branches in all States.

As well as the usual publications, seminars and support groups, since 1979 ARAFMI has

> 'provided a 24 hour support line which is listed in the Help page of the phone book and is a service to the wider community provided by the relatives as volunteer counsellors'. (personal communication, Anne Newham, Executive Officer)

Branches in the regions provide a range of services, including group meetings, a telephone support line, educational programmes for families and the community, respite care for families and drop-in centres. The emphasis of the Association is, however,

> 'on mutual support among relatives and friends of the mentally ill, through group meetings to share concerns and relieve isolation due to the stigma of mental illness'.

It also aims to

> 'increase self-confidence for relatives in communication with health professionals to enable better outcomes in care and rehabilitation for the affected mentally ill family member.'

An interesting and innovative move came in 1981 when Young ARAFMI was started

> 'responding to the needs in the community and recognising that education and support of younger relatives was vital. This development included visits to schools by a committed ARAFMI member which subsequently led to a pilot education programme being introduced into schools in the inner city to help erase the stigma of mental illness and create a climate of understanding and acceptance in the community. Recently, the value of this unique programme was recognised by a grant over 3 years from the Bicentennial Youth Foundation to establish a National ARAFMI School Education Programme.'

The programme

> 'operates on three levels in High Schools, Years 7–10, and is now listed by the Department of Education as a resource for the new H.S.C. subject "Science for life" in the module "the Human Body" '. (Schools Education Programme leaflet)

The Association's approach to mental illness is summed up in the introductory paragraph of the Young ARAFMI leaflet, *Is there Mental Illness in your Family? How do you cope?*:

'Many factors combine to cause mental illness. These include genetic inheritance, drug abuse, diet, family environment, social and cultural background, life stresses and physical illness. No one person is to blame. You are not to blame.'

The medical model is emphasised, however, in the list of their aims, the first of which is to

'seek to improve quality of life for patient through better medication'. (personal communication Anne Newham)

Schizophrenia Society of Canada

Previously known as the 'Friends of Schizophrenics', the Society changed its name in 1990 for a number of reasons.

'At the start . . . "Friend" in our name was an integral part of our Founding President, Bill Jefferies', concept for a new association. Look back more than a dozen years and remember how things were. Before the modern advances in medication and psychotherapy, those seriously afflicted with schizophrenia could look forward to a future which was grim at best. Apart from family members they had few friends . . .'

'Deinstitutionalisation in the 60s and 70s meant severe curtailment of social life for most family members thrust into the role . . . of the primary care giver . . . For them the word "Friend" came to symbolise the spirit of camaraderie which developed among them, as well.' (Peter McGibbon, Newsletter 1992)

Times change, and McGibbon goes on to say that

'In its own way, our new name, the Schizophrenia Society of Canada, symbolizes the growing maturity of our association. Inward preoccupations have become less important. We, too, seek to move ahead with the times and improve the effectiveness of our public awareness, advocacy and other activities . . . '

The 1992 Annual Report gives some indication of the Society's activities. The work of the Advocacy Committee included presenting a brief to a Committee of the House of Commons in respect of the first amendments to be made to the Criminal Code for Mental Disorder for 100 years, and organising a postcard campaign as a 'national lobbying effort on behalf of research funding for schizophrenia'. The Society cooperated with the department of National Health and Welfare to produce a very informative 68-page booklet on schizophrenia.

An interesting development has been the Canadian Alliance for Research on Schizophrenia (CAROS), which is 'a new organisation within the research, family and consumer/survivor communities' (CAROS leaflet). It has been

> 'established to coordinate the development and promotion of a comprehensive National Research Plan . . . Although not designed to function as a funding agency itself, CAROS advocated strongly for increased funding for schizophrenia research.'

Its goals, as well as promoting a National Research Plan and fostering, supporting and coordinating research, extend to cultivating 'a realistic, viable, and enduring funding base for schizophrenia research', developing 'a comprehensive and appropriate system of case finding and tracking' and developing a network of shared information.

ZENKAREN: National Federation of Families with the Mentally Ill in Japan

Another generic organisation, ZENKAREN, was founded in 1965 as an organisation to represent the families of people with mental illness. The organisation has local families' associations throughout the country, and in 1992 had 1200 groups with approximately 100 000 members (personal communication, Mr. Takehison Takizawa, Director). Its main aim is to increase public awareness and reduce stigma, to support local associations, and to 'develop social rehabilitation plans all through the country, such as managing workshops'. A monthly newsletter is published, conferences held, representations are made to central government and surveys have looked at family situations.

In 1988 a revision to the Mental Health Law was carried through the Japanese Diet which both improved patient's rights and established a Social Rehabilitation Facility. ZENKAREN had been campaigning long and hard for this. There is a shortage of rehabilitation facilities, but local associations are showing the way.

In March 1991, ZENKAREN opened a Mental Health and Welfare Centre (KEIYU Memorial Hall). This was made possible by a donation of four hundred million yen from Mr. and Mrs. Nakamura in memory of their daughter. It is an eight-storey building with facilities for meetings of up to 50 people, consulting and counselling rooms, offices for several other voluntary groups, a library and publishing room, an 'Industrial Plaza' for pre-vocational work for consumers (packing and mailing the monthly newsletter, for example), a sheltered workshop, a tearoom used for relaxation and a restroom complete with showers.

Alliance for the Mentally Ill of Dane County, USA

'The Alliance for the Mentally Ill of Dane County in Wisconsin was first brought together by a group of 12 people in 1977 here in Madison, WI, by people who had found each other mostly by chance, due to mental illness in their families'. (Annual Report 1992)

In the same year it was founded as a non-profit organisation and in the following year produced a newsletter. In 1979 a national conference was held in Madison, and this saw the formation of the National Alliance for the Mentally Ill, an organisation which now covers the whole of the United States with 1000 affiliates and 140 000 members. In 1980 the original Dane County Alliance became an agency of United Way of Dane County, and through community funding was able to develop office accommodation and staff support, although the 'entire organisation is staffed by our own volunteer members' (personal communication, Robert Beilman, President).

The aims of the Alliance are summed up in the Annual report:

'We believe it is our mission to provide our membership with current information about serious mental illnesses and to provide emotional support to families whose loved ones are experiencing serious mental illness. We must advocate for more and better housing, better medications and support programmes. Finally we must help our people negotiate their way through the commitment process and through the various federal entitlement programmes'.

The Alliance deals not just with schizophrenia, but also with serious depression and affective disorders, and runs special groups for parents, siblings, adult children and spouses. They have been involved in the development of, and setting standards for, a number of Community Support Programmes, including an interesting 'jail diversion program, Community Treatment Alternatives'. A number of leaflets are produced in Spanish.

The Alliance's view of mental illness and its biological basis is described in the Annual Report.

'Please note that we try to consistently use the words "mental illness" rather than "mental health". This is because we have fought long and hard to put mental illness on the national agenda. To us, mental health is something else altogether and is usually not possible on a long-term basis for someone who has an enduring, persistent mental illness. During the years that the nation talked about mental health, nothing was done about mental illness. We feel that we have made great strides, not only locally, but on a national level, in terms of priorities. Currently there is work being done to move the research portion of the National Institute of Mental Health under the umbrella of the National Institute of Health in an effort to promote the fact the mental illnesses are biologically based illnesses and should be part of the organisation that researches such illnesses.'

Cape Support for Mental Health: South Africa

The Cape Support for Mental Health is a family support group which has been in existence since 1981.

'At the end of 1980 four or five families met after finding that their dependents had been discharged from the local mental hospital with no clear picture of what could be done for them . . . and in desperation we decided to meet to see what could be done about this, essentially to help ourselves.' (personal communication, Graham Louw)

This group has grown to about 50 families in 1992, and since 1989 they have had an office in the middle of Cape Town.

The focus of the group is the monthly support meetings and, as elsewhere, the aims revolve around support, education, raising awareness and working for the development of improved facilities. In conjunction with the Cape Mental Health Society (to whom they are affiliated), Fountain House, 'a psycho-social rehabilitation centre for discharged patients', was set up. It is 'a non-racial facility that concentrates on the vocational and social needs of its members'. Accommodation is of major concern, and at the end of 1992 the group was in the process of setting up a new charitable trust, COMCARE, to enable them to establish a comprehensive housing programme.

They report support from their local hospitals and

'in a changing South Africa, we see the possibility of galvanising the activity of private and public enterprises to provide necessary services within the community'.

World Schizophrenia Fellowship

'The World Schizophrenia Fellowship is the only international organisation dedicated to lightening the burden of schizophrenia for sufferers and their families and to creating public awareness of this disease.' (Information about the WSF Leaflet 1991)

The WSF is an incorporated charity in Canada, having been formed in Toronto in May 1982 by representatives of the Schizophrenia Association of Ireland, the National Alliance for the Mentally Ill, the National Schizophrenia Fellowship, Union Nationale des Familles des Maux Mentales, the Canadian Friends of Schizophrenics, the Schizophrenia Fellowship (New Zealand) Inc., Schizophrenia Foundation Australia, ENOSH and ZENKAREN. Today the WSF has added to its membership organisations in Austria, Germany, Sweden, The Netherlands, Columbia, Uruguay, India, South Africa, Indonesia and Malaysia, and has contacts in many other countries.

The WSF functions predominantly as a coordinating and enabling organisation. Work is supported by membership fees and it has no paid staff. A 50-page book, *Schizophrenia: Information for Families*, was produced by the WSF and published by the WHO in 1992. They have also produced 21 information pamphlets which are constantly updated, and an international newsletter is published three times a year.

Its stance on the status of schizophrenia as an organic illness is clear, and it represents groups who have the same beliefs and objectives.

'All member organisations are concerned about the humane treatment of people with schizophrenia and about their primary care, which falls most frequently upon parents and lasts many years. There is much work to be done in providing housing, rehabilitation, recreation and a decent life for those with this incurable brain disease. Support and education is also necessary for families who have an enormous and continuing burden to shoulder.' (Information about the WSF leaflet 1991)

WHY DID A RELATIVES' MOVEMENT EMERGE?

From the foregoing descriptions, we see that most national organisations grew out of a number of local groups coming together. When we consider the self-help movement, a distinction must be made between groups which are local, and more essentially what is meant by self-help, and associations which are national and have a wider remit.

The groups arose first out of a deep need within relatives, a need to share their burden with an unknowing and unconcerned world, and by coming together gain support and understanding. We have already discussed the burden on relatives and will not reiterate it here except to point out that this was, to clinicians and service providers, very much an 'unexpected' consequence of the move from institutions to community. That with hindsight we wonder how such consequences could be overlooked does little to alter the situation. It is not surprising that relatives wanted help and information. What is more surprising is why it took so long (comparatively) for the movement to start. Bed numbers had dropped in Western countries since the mid-1950s: why did it take until 1970 for John Pringle to write his letter to *The Times*?

Mental illness has always been stigmatised, and both people with the condition and their relatives have been isolated. This stigmatisation came, and still comes, from a largely ill-informed public. The popularity, and misinterpretation in some cases, of the family theories of schizophrenia contributed to both the stigma and the shame, but also to resentment towards the services and professionals they thought should have been helping them. It is maybe testimony to the despair felt by relatives that they would brave this stigma to meet others in the same position.

The self-help movement in mental health followed a more general movement in medicine for patients to learn about, and to take greater responsibility for, and management of, their condition. Health education was finding its feet and delivering the message against the so-called 'lifestyle' diseases, most notably heart disease and lung cancer. Alcoholics Anonymous was hailed as a major success. Even if families or relatives were involved in some of these organisations, the main focus was still the 'patient'. Although these groups may have inspired some of those relatives who founded local groups, it still required a shift in thinking to emphasise relatives not patients. It was as clear a statement as could be made at the time; relatives were saying that they too had problems, that they too could legitimately be considered clients.

Another change which affected the relatives' movement during the 1970s was the work on expressed emotion and the influence of the family on the course of schizophrenia. This changed the relationship between relatives and professionals in dramatic ways. Previously, relatives had been passive: when patients were hospitalised they were passive recounters of past history, when patients moved back home in the first community care initiative they were seen as passive carers. Now they could be viewed as active. Not active in the 'cause-of-the-illness' blaming way of many clinicians of the 1960s but, as a result of their impact on the course of the illness, active as carers. If the way families behaved contributed to the problem, then they could be taught ways to behave differently and improve the problem. Thus the ideas of professionals and the demands of families that they be acknowledged as carers began to merge.

Relatives were also demanding more services, both for the person with schizophrenia and for themselves. Many of these demands could not, and for the foreseeable future will not, be met for financial reasons. Self-help groups were encouraged to fill the gaps themselves.

The conservative governments in the West were, as part of seeking to reduce public spending, emphasising the responsibilities of families to care for their members, which fitted the self-help movement. Coupled with this was the economic philosophy of allowing the market to set price levels and lead demand. Thus patients and relatives have been redefined as consumers, and relatives' organisations have found a ready-made contact point for health and social services wanting a 'consumer view'.

Local groups can, and do, fulfil these roles. In most countries, however, as groups became more numerous, a number of factors acted to bring them together. There is nearly always a general feeling that, eventually, a national organisation is the natural progression. This stems from a belief that there is 'strength in numbers', whether this is greater support for fund-raising, publicity or advocacy. National committees were formed, to look at wider issues. Campaigning could now be addressed at a national level, on national issues. Bearing in mind the major caring role of the relatives involved, it is remarkable how much many of them were able to give to the organisations. In a number of cases the relatives who were able to devote considerable time and energy to the organisation were no longer caring for an ill relative at home, sometimes because the person remained so ill that they were permanently hospitalised, but not infrequently because their child had died, usually through suicide. Although sometimes their involvement is described as a way of them working through their grief, or even coming to terms with their inability to save their child, this should not detract from the impact of the work they do.

However, most organisations reach a point where the administrative burden is beyond the capacity of volunteers. Coupled with ideas which no-one has time to put into operation, an awareness that serious fund-raising is necessary, and a desire to have a 'permanent address' or headquarters for people to contact, the next step is inevitable: staff and premises.

It is from this point that the national organisation and the local groups begin to diverge. Local groups are primarily concerned with providing support for other relatives, local education and lobbying for better services. National organisations quickly become involved in the provision of services. One of the main reasons for this is funding. Every organisation says that fund-raising is a problem. This is not simply that the meteoric rise of 'the charity business' in the 1980s means there is less to go round, but that funding for certain parts of the organisation is more difficult to obtain than others. Not unnaturally people who give money to charity want to know where it goes, and administration is not a popular answer. To survive in the fund-raising stakes, the organisation usually has to grow fairly rapidly. Success tends to be measured in number of projects, numbers of patients/clients/users involved, and through-put of users: all the usual measures of evaluating services. Membership is also important; the more 'fully paid-up' (fee-waived or not) members the better.

Sadly, the roots of the organisation, local support groups for relatives, although seen as worthy, often count for little in this process. They can run without staff, their only costs are hire of a room and mailing members, they do not deal with a numerically identified client population and, in most cases, people can avail themselves of their support, advice and educational opportunities without formally becoming members. The magnitude and importance of the support which comes from these groups is difficult to comprehend for people who are not themselves involved. The release from isolation, and from the stigma of having a relative with schizophrenia, is not something which can easily be put in a graph and presented to trustees when applying for money. It was not for nothing that the British organisation first designated itself a 'Fellowship', something followed by many other countries, and copied by the sister organisation for people with manic depression.

The changes in the approach to, and delivery of, services since the mid-1980s, coupled with the coming together of local groups into national organisations, has created some of the current tensions within the self-help movement which must be resolved for the movement to continue to flourish.

THE FUTURE OF THE RELATIVES' SELF-HELP MOVEMENT

For the relatives' self-help movement to continue to develop, organisations will have to make some very difficult decisions and go through what will be, no doubt, painful growing pains. Some of the early national organisations have already done this and others can learn from them.

Service Provision

Service provision almost certainly has to be at the centre of any national organisation planning for the future. Increasingly health and social services, as purchasers of services, are looking towards the voluntary sector to be providers of services. Since lack of appropriate services contributed to the growth of self-help groups, it is not surprising that relatives are keen to develop local services. Local groups can underestimate the amount of time and effort, and also the frustration, involved in applying for grants and developing services, and wonder at uneven development throughout a country or region. Local jealousies are not the only problems, however.

Both staff employed to work in projects and the people who use the project will have views about it, and these might not conform to those of relatives. Here lies a central dilemma. The majority of services that relatives' organisations are developing are for users. In which case, should not such people be involved in the planning of the services they will use?

Some people with schizophrenia are members of these organisations and have, in some cases, formed subsections or breakaway groups of their own, such as 'Voices' in Britain. Their presence on national management committees, however, is usually minimal. Many constitutions make provision for a certain number of nonrelatives on committees (usually reserved for professionals), but rarely make provision for people with schizophrenia, although this is changing.

We have already noted that in many places a tension exists between relatives' and users' organisations, and this will grow if relatives insist on the right to provide the services *they* think people with schizophrenia need without involving the user groups. This strikes at the very heart of the relatives' self-help movement. Its central tenet is to provide support for carers. Part of this support, it is argued, comes from providing services which are lacking, thus relieving some of the burden of care. User groups can argue that they are better placed to provide such services. Both organisations are competing for the same funding. Whilst on one level it should not matter who provides the service as long as users get what they need/want, on another it matters very much to the organisations in terms of their own continued viability.

A consequence of relatives' organisations moving into service provision is that relatives (as members of national management committees) will become employers and will have to learn to see themselves as such. This does not only mean looking at long-term planning and funding, but also making decisions about conditions of employment. We have noted how the development of some services has been described as exploitation of a vulnerable workforce. In their desire to be competitive in the market place and to provide services at all costs, it is to be hoped that relatives' organisations are able to set standards as good employers as well as standards for service provision.

Campaigning

National groups have in all cases become involved in campaigning, lobbying local and national government, and acting as the 'voice' of relatives to influence decision making and policy, usually with considerable success. Again, relatives' views can bring them into conflict with the users' movement. In a number of countries, the message of relatives' groups seems to be that hospitals should not be closed and that bed numbers should not be decreased. Often this is only part of the story, and the full message is 'not until community services are in place'. Even so, relatives are still more likely to want to see easier hospital admission than are user-based groups. They are also more likely to support making compulsory hospital detention 'easier', that is, extending the definition of 'harm to self' to include becoming vagrant and refusal to take medication.

The effect on policy can be quite extensive. It has been suggested, for example, that one of the reasons for less interest being shown in expressed emotion in the United States compared with Britain is the influence of the powerful NAMI and their reading of the work as blaming families.

Campaigning and advocacy work is an important part of the self-help movement, and most people agree that it should continue to be so. Some concern is expressed, however, about how strongly this will be able to continue if organisations are being funded by grants from agencies that they then criticise. As funding becomes ever tighter, this may become more of an issue. For now, most associations seem able both to develop service provision and retain their critical, campaigning analysis of the *status quo*.

Decentralisation

Inevitably as national organisations grow and become more powerful they tend to lose touch with the people who started them. Work previously carried out by relatives is now carried out by paid staff, and new developments and activities only occur as there are staff to take on such responsibilities. Political lobbying often remains the remit of a management committee rather than staff.

The success and strength at the centre can leave local groups feeling isolated, and the move towards regionalisation may go beyond simple regional loyalty. It may be a further reflection that the 'new' aims of the organisation have moved a long way from the original aims, which were essentially peer support for relatives and education. Relatives are uniquely placed to share the burden and offer advice to other relatives, and it would be a shame if this important role was lost, or accorded secondary status in the drive by associations to grow ever larger and become little more than service providers.

A re-emphasis on local groups also ensures that it is the relatives who retain control of the organisation, and that all decision making does not shift to staff. This in itself will cause tensions with staff, who have their own agenda. Differences of opinion will occur, and it is not usually a question of who is 'right', but of perspective. One example, which has occurred in several countries, is that of taking money from drug companies. Hard-pressed fund-raisers see drug companies as potential sources of income. Staff often object, usually because they have a more psychosocial approach to schizophrenia and may be negative about the widespread use of medication. Balloting of members of the organisation results in both relatives and users being in favour of approaching drug companies for support. This may be provisional (no 'promotion' of the company or the drug), but laws and guidelines usually prohibit it anyway. The feeling can be summed up by a user who said 'they've made enough out of me in the past, this is a way of getting some of it back'.

Not only may we see the diversification of organisations through geography, but also through function. The service provision part of the organisation may, eventually, find itself becoming a separate organisation.

Diversification of Groups

There are organisations which do not fit neatly into the self-help category; they are more 'campaigning groups' and may develop through supporting an unorthodox approach to schizophrenia. A newer venture is exemplified by the British organisation SANE (Schizophrenia: A National Emergency). The brainchild of Marjorie Wallace, a former journalist who won a Campaigning Journalism award for a series of articles on schizophrenia in *The Times*, SANE is predominantly a campaigning organisation and successful fund-raiser to support small research and other projects. Ms Wallace appears regularly in the news media and on television with the message that hospitals should not be closed, that there is a need for asylum, that the burden born by relatives should be understood and, apparently secondarily, for the development of community services. Although not a service provider, SANE now runs a very successful helpline. As well as providing someone to talk to and to listen to problems, a very extensive computer-based database means that whoever telephones can quickly be given details of services and support groups in their area. In its desire to convey the tragedy of schizophrenia, SANE has been accused of concentrating on the 'worst' aspects of the disease, portraying unremittingly negative messages. A poster campaign in and around London led to a legal battle with MIND and resulted in the removal of the posters.

This is yet one more example of the tensions which exist, and which will continue to exist, between the different groups who try to claim 'ownership' of schizophrenia. Some of these differences are so fundamental that there is little likelihood of resolution in the near future. This does not mean that all do not have their place, their strengths and their weaknesses. It would be more than a pity if internecine fighting decreased the strength and effectiveness of all parts of the self-help movement.

THE ROLE OF PROFESSIONALS IN RELATIVES' ORGANISATIONS

All relatives' organisations report the involvement of 'sympathetic' professionals. This relationship ranges from being willing to go along to speak occasionally to a local group, to being a member of a national management committee or acting as a formal adviser. Thus, the first role of the professional can be seen as that of expert. As advisers, their role might be to comment on particular circumstances or issues as they arise, or it might include making sure that up-to-date information is disseminated. At a local level, dialogue with a professional can do a great deal to foster good relations and remove some of the relatives' sense that they are being denied (deliberately or otherwise) access to information or services.

Professionals can also add a 'legitimacy' that can be vital when groups are new and in the early stages of making contact with others and seeking funds. A new, and possibly complicated, role for the professional is emerging as organisations become service providers and they are asked to act as consultants in the development and delivery of services. To date, professionals have been happy to give their time and services freely, and this is helped by their involvement usually being out of normal 'office hours'. However, the new help being asked for is more likely to be during the working day and can involve a considerable amount of time. As professionals are increasingly expected to be accountable for every minute of their time, as the costs of services are calculated more closely, employers may not see attending meetings of a self-help organisation as part of the person's 'job description'. Also, in acting as consultants in planning services, professionals may find themselves involved in developing competing services for limited funding with services provided by their own agency.

Groups wanting to use professionals in this way may find themselves being asked to pay for their 'expertise'. Although many within the self-help and voluntary movements may be horrified by this move, they are applying for external funding to run services, and to get this 'expertise' for 'nothing' means that the true cost of developing or running the service is underestimated, which could be important in setting precedents for funding levels.

The most delicate area of the relationship between professionals and relatives is probably when there is disagreement about the status of information. Differences about policy and the direction of the organisation are about opinion and ownership, this is about 'fact'. Professionals have a duty to exchange information to enable relatives of all educational levels to assimilate as much as they can. However, this can be viewed as brainwashing by some people who have different views about schizophrenia. The professionals' role here is to explain their position, explain why they do not accept certain theories or approaches, and explain the process by which they reached their own conclusions, thus enabling the relatives to assess the information for themselves. Whether the professional can or should go further than this is debatable. Katschnig and Konieczna (1987) do go further, saying that it is a function of the professional to recognise 'possible undesirable developments and counteracting them in good time; this may prevent a self-help organisation from losing credibility because it adheres to an erroneous or even eccentric theory'. This view is heavily paternalistic and its appropriateness is a matter for personal opinion.

Lastly, the involvement of professionals in relatives' groups should be seen very much as a link between the lay and professional systems. Wherever possible relatives should speak for themselves, and it might be that the professional has to point out that the relatives' views should be sought.

On an individual level the professional involved in relatives' organisations will find out much more about the reality of living with a person with schizophrenia, the day-to-day problems, the unrelenting pressure, the practical effects of feelings of isolation and stigma, than will ever come from reading research papers.

7

EDUCATION GROUPS

In this chapter we describe both the content and the practical aspects of the day-to-day running of education groups. In the next chapter, we describe the logistics of setting up the whole service. What we describe in these two chapters is based on our own clinical experience of running groups over the past few years within a routine NHS service.

THE GROUPS

Education and support was provided in the form of a relatives' group which met fortnightly for 10 sessions at a place and time convenient to relatives. Fourteen groups were eventually established to meet the needs of the catchment area which had not formerly had such a service.

The number of sessions was kept fairly low for several reasons. Their remit was solely to provide education and the low-key support which we have argued is a basic right of all relatives. They were designed to deal with relatives' issues and not to achieve change within the person with schizophrenia. Finally, all researchers report that it is difficult to get relatives to engage in such interventions, even over short periods of time. We felt that 20 weeks was the optimum period both to cover a substantial amount of ground in respect of education and to maintain contact with relatives.

This intervention should be seen in the context of a hierarchy of services as providing a baseline service, which may later include intensive work with individual families, including those with high EE levels. These groups are not, however, about affecting patient management as such, but about supporting relatives by encouraging them to be more informed, feel more involved and possibly reducing their stress.

THE STYLE OF THE GROUPS

The two components of the groups were education and support, and it is important to understand the difference between these if both are to be provided within one group, as has been discussed in Chapter 4. Accepting that both relatives and staff see information about the illness as a high priority, how is it to be delivered? Professionals and relatives often hold different models of schizophrenia. Professionals commonly have a medical model, while relatives may have a personalised lay model that relates back, both in terms of cause and of current behaviour, to past family events and circumstances. This personalised subjective model may have been established for many years and allowed the family to cope in their own way with the illness. It may be fruitless for professionals to attempt to impose their own medical model onto this, and may only lead to friction. A more interactive style of presenting information allows for these two models, negotiates the transfer of information, and is thus more effective, particularly if personalised to individual families. Throughout education we know that abstract information is more effective when applied to individual problems, and this is just as true when dealing with individual patients or relatives.

The group sessions lasted one-and-a-half hours, with a break in the middle for tea or coffee. The first half of the session was given over to the presentation of information on the topic for the session (see Table 1). Flip-charts were used when available, and relatives were provided in the first session with a booklet which described the sessions. Questions were encouraged when something was not understood, but general discussion was left until the second half, which was more informal with general questions, discussion about what had been learnt, the relating of this to individual problems and circumstances, sharing additional information, advice and solutions, and what may be termed 'general support'. Problem solving and goal setting were used, and relatives were encouraged to use their own practical experiences to help each other. As the groups progressed, relatives provided more support to each other and were able to deal with more emotional issues, thus reducing their own stress.

In dealing with a catchment-wide population of relatives with varying intellectual ability, from different social backgrounds, and at different stages in the course of their relatives' illness, the therapist had to use

Table 1   Group sessions

1. What does schizophrenia mean to you?

2. What is schizophrenia?

3. Why?

4. Treatment of schizophrenia

5. Relatives' problems

6. The family and schizophrenia

7. Creating a low-stress environment

8. Managing disturbed behaviour

9. Using services and dealing with crises

10. Where do we go from here?

their own judgement as to the level of information presented. In their programme, emphasis was placed on being well prepared and severely limiting the number of items of information per session; information 'bites' perhaps being more useful for those with a short attention span. We expected that much information would be passed on to other family members at home. Indeed, within these groups we found that 44% of group members said they passed on all or most information to other family members and only 11% passed on no information. Thirty per cent of relatives passed on all or most information to the person with schizophrenia, with only 15% not passing on any information. Inevitably information gains, or loses, something in its passage, so it is particularly important to ensure that information is accurate and presented as simply and straightforwardly as possible. Some people have been concerned that relatives might be upset by some of the information they are given. We asked relatives if they were told anything that upset them and 8% said 'yes'. We then asked if they wished they had not been given the information and only one person said yes to this.

RELATIVES' BOOKLET

This was given to relatives in Session 1 (see Appendix 1) so that they had a clear outline of the course of the group and had some information to hand. We hoped that it would help group leaders to maintain the structure of the group by encouraging relatives to stick to the topic under discussion and not keep reiterating the same point week after week. We also hoped it would help relatives see how their knowledge would build up, and that what was covered later depended to some extent on information dealt with in earlier sessions. Questions were included at the end to act as prompts should discussion prove to be slow starting. They were seen very much as a 'safety factor' for group leaders and, although the issues in the questions were raised, were not needed explicitly to prompt discussion.

THE CONTENT OF THE GROUPS

Rather than outline the actual information covered, which needs constant updating, here we discuss briefly the key issues covered in each session and some of the points raised by relatives. This should be read in conjunction with Chapter 9 on training.

The first four sessions deal with background information about schizophrenia as an illness, but these may still be emotionally charged issues. The next three sessions deal with more practical issues, as by now the group should be more trusting and supportive of each other and thus able to explore more difficult areas, i.e. relating to themselves and their problems rather than to the person with schizophrenia. The next two sessions deal with the management issues that are most commonly raised by relatives, namely disturbed behaviour and its management, and using services and dealing with crises. The last session sums up what has been learnt and looks forward.

Session 1: What does Schizophrenia mean to You?

This is an introductory session, since we knew that relatives would be keen to air their views. If they were prevented from having their say at the beginning, they might not feel so committed to attending and believing that they genuinely had a part to play in the group. On the other hand, if the session is nothing more than 'one long moan', then they might feel there is nothing to be gained from the group. The balance between encouraging the relatives to have full involvement but imparting a structure and an agenda is never more important than in this first session.

There were three main aims:

1. To discuss the concept of mental illness, in particular schizophrenia, and allow families to feel comfortable with the diagnosis.

2. To identify their personalised subjective model of the illness.

3. To maintain the family in the group.

To achieve this the session first presents a basic overview of what is understood by the terms mental illness and schizophrenia. Second, it describes lay and professional models of schizophrenia, highlighting similarities and differences. Third, it encourages relatives to describe their emotional reactions to the illness. A key element in this session is to avoid being over-ambitious in presenting information. To this end, the points raised are grouped into five key areas, with the understanding that they will be elaborated in future sessions. These key areas are:

- Defining mental illness and schizophrenia. What is it? How common is it? What are the chances of developing it?

- An explanation that there are many reasons put forward about its origins.

- An explanation that presentation, severity and outcome vary considerably.

- An explanation that people use different models to describe schizophrenia: biological; psychological; biopsychosocial.

- The importance of individualising the problem to the relatives' own family.

To start the session relatives are asked to comment on why they have come and their expectations of the group. These are compared, discussed between members, and help break the ice and introduce people to one another.

The session then explores the personal meaning of schizophrenia. Individual group members are encouraged to discuss their perception of their relative's problems and what explanations they have for their relative's behaviour. Depending on how relatives view schizophrenia, an illness model can gradually be introduced and related to what relatives have been saying.

The most frequent theme to emerge was criticism of services, although group leaders did not think it was all justified in that it displayed inappropriate or unrealistic expectations of services. This is not to discount the relatives' genuine distress at what they saw as a lack, and was the first of many times the group leaders would have to balance both sides of an argument and try to explain 'the reality' of the NHS or social work while not being seen to be 'too defensive' or rejecting the relatives' views out of hand.

Relatives are then encouraged to think realistically about what they can expect from the group, and this leads into a discussion of the group, how it will be run, what the sessions will cover and other administrative points. Standard group rules are set: allowing all group members space to speak, confidentiality (what they learnt of other families was to remain confidential to the group), and the vital arrangements for tea and coffee.

Since it is important that the group is seen as something more than a 'moaning session' the leader should end the session by giving some information about diagnosis, prevalence and risk factors. That schizophrenia is 'a common illness' was, in particular, greeted with relief and borne out in several groups when relatives met people they had seen about locally or known in the past, in one case at school.

This session was found by all leaders to take considerably longer than the one-and-a-half hours allotted to it and all let it run over. Most relatives had received little opportunity to vent their feelings to professionals before, and were determined to make the most of it. Their outpourings of anger, grief and hostility were initially perceived by the group leaders as stressful, but they all accepted the need for it. Group leaders found that by 'clearing the air' in the first session the majority of relatives then accepted the organised structure of the sessions topic by topic and were able to use them constructively. With hindsight, it is probably worth allocating a longer time for this session, say two hours.

This is perhaps the most important session as it engages the relatives in the group and encourages them to keep attending. Most relatives who attend Session 1 come back to attend subsequent sessions.

Session 2: What is Schizophrenia?

Having allowed the first session to be fairly free and to overrun, in this one it is necessary to restate the structure of the sessions and to hold to this. The group is encouraged to think that the time has come to settle down to some work. This session discusses the symptoms of schizophrenia and diagnosis. It is important to describe all the symptoms that may occur, and a list is provided in the relatives' handbook. The variation in symptoms over the course of the illness must be emphasised. Whilst some of the more severe symptoms of schizophrenia, such as 'voices', may be well known, less obvious but potentially more distressing symptoms such as sleep disturbance are often not related to the illness. The relationship of symptoms to behaviour can be discussed. The mythology of schizophrenia and its symptoms, such as split personality, should be discussed and, where appropriate, dismissed.

An explanation is given on how diagnosis is made; how symptoms and behaviours are grouped together to classify an illness and produce a diagnosis. The value of diagnosis can be discussed, but emphasis is placed on the importance of meeting individual needs rather than treating a diagnosis.

We found it helpful to use the positive/negative divide when discussing symptoms. Most relatives were only too well aware of positive symptomatology, and behaviour arising from these appears understandable in the light of illness. Behaviour arising from negative symptoms, however, is often interpreted differently. The interactionist approach and discovering what relatives believe while presenting the more 'orthodox' view is vital here. Negative symptoms often produce behaviour which is interpreted by relatives as laziness, fear of work, personality problems or indifference, and is generally not related to schizophrenia as an illness. It is important to explore with relatives their understanding of such behaviours and to offer alternative explanations within an illness model.

Whilst it is important to share common symptoms, it is also important to emphasise that not all patients will have the same symptoms or the same severity of illness.

The second major issue within this session is that of diagnosis. Some relatives feel that a diagnosis is vital to obtain information and services and plan for the future. Others are upset by the finality and lack of hope they feel such a diagnosis may convey. Nevertheless, half our group members said they felt they had been given their relative's diagnosis 'too late'. A discussion of what is involved when a psychiatrist makes a diagnosis, how it is arrived at, and why it may take longer than the family, or patient, would have wished may aid understanding, as will an exploration of relatives' feelings about the diagnosis, how it is viewed by the person with schizophrenia, and whether both relative and patient accept it or seek further opinions.

This can lead to exploring why having a diagnosis does not mean there is a 'cure' or solution to the problem. A commonly heard complaint, particularly from those who dispute the diagnosis, is 'how can they say I have (he/she has) schizophrenia and then not be able to cure it?' The value of dealing with an individual's symptoms and behaviour rather than treating a diagnosis can be explained.

Since most people have heard words like 'paranoid', the complexity of categorisation and the rapid changes in redefining subgroups can briefly be touched on. It may help to look for common symptoms that aid relatives to 'normalise' the illness to something that has been experienced by many members of the group. This, in turn, may lead to varying solutions being produced to difficult symptom-related behaviour.

Session 3: Why?

We spent what might seem a disproportionately large amount of time discussing the causes of schizophrenia and why it had happened to their particular family rather than on some other important issues. This was a consequence of prior discussions with families, our awareness of the importance with which families regarded cause, and the great deal of time and effort expended in searching for the reasons why schizophrenia had happened in their family. This can be connected to the belief that if a 'cause' is found then so will a 'cure'. Causal beliefs held by relatives are also likely to affect the way they view the symptoms and behaviour of their ill relative, and how they treat him or her.

No one knows what causes schizophrenia, and this is one of the central messages of this session. The most we have are 'best guesses'. A number of factors may contribute to the cause of what we know as schizophrenia, or it may be a number of illnesses of differing aetiology. This session discusses genetic, biochemical, neurological, environmental, psychological and family factors.

The description of current theories should be limited, yet constantly updated. An explanation of each theory containing no more than five key facts should be given, avoiding technical expressions and jargon that can lead to confusion. Theories which carry no credence within the scientific community may be discussed, for example, maternal child-rearing practices or vitamin deficiency. It is more important to understand the concept of the theory, such as biochemical, viral and so forth, than it is the actual chemical or viral process. However, the group leader needs to understand enough to answer questions as they arise. A brief description of modern scanning techniques is often of interest to families, along with how they are used in current research. It needs to be made clear, however, that their use is not routine and not receiving a scan does not imply negligence.

Genetic issues usually interest families and are commonly, if misrepresentedly, reported in the media. It is challenging to present the complex genetic argument in a clear, understandable format. Families are often reassured by the complexity of the inheritance story and that it is unlikely that they are passing down a single gene causing schizophrenia. Questions arise over the risk that siblings or offspring may develop the illness or pass it on, and a simple table of the very slight risks can be useful (Table 2). Biochemical and neurological explanations are often popular, as they allow relatives to 'medicalise' the illness and become more understanding of behavioural problems whilst relieving guilt as to whether they have caused or contributed to the illness.

A strong statement on the lack of evidence to support the family causing schizophrenia is important. Equally the importance of the environment, especially stress, has to be emphasised. It may be difficult to get relatives to accept the concept of stress within the family, particularly as it is often accompanied by denial. A general discussion on stress can be helpful, relating it to problems that all families experience. Relatives may then share with the group examples of stressful situations within their own home which relate to the person with schizophrenia, and should be encouraged to review options that may relieve the situation.

Table 2 Genetic risks for schizophrenia

Lifetime risk:	
General public	1%
For a person with a 2nd-degree relative, i.e. aunts, uncles, nieces, nephews, grandchildren	3%
For a person with a 1st-degree relative, i.e. mother, father, siblings	10%
Child of one parent with schizophrenia	15%
Child of both parents with schizophrenia	40%

This session ends with the question 'why me?' Families often tend to search endlessly for a cause, and since it is unlikely that one single factor caused the illness, searching and blaming something or someone is not helpful. The session should end by encouraging families to look forward to what can be achieved rather than back.

Session 4: Treatment of Schizophrenia

Often group members want to discuss their relatives' treatment on a more individual basis and this can usually be accommodated without breaching confidentiality. A number of general principles of treatment should be conveyed, not least that treatment not only involves medication, but also psychotherapy, social therapy, behaviour therapy, occupational therapy and so forth. Medication does not equal treatment but is only a component of the treatment process, a factor often forgotten in our health service provision. The result of this has been ignorance of what else constitutes treatment, and how and where to obtain these services. This session sets out to inform relatives about these wider aspects.

Often families voice concern over drug therapy whilst being unaware of the importance of social interventions that may improve functioning for the person with schizophrenia. A full review of the drugs currently available and the rationale for their usage should be provided. The side effects, which can be substantial, should be covered. How long should patients be on medication? What happens when, against medical advice, the person with schizophrenia takes themself off drugs? Since these questions can have implications not only for the patient but also for relatives and even the society in which they live, relatives will want to know their rights regarding influencing medication decisions. Many relatives are unaware that the drugs are most useful in reducing the positive symptoms of schizophrenia whilst the negative symptoms can respond to social therapies. The lack of effect of traditional drugs on *some* patients must be discussed, but a note of optimism can be sounded regarding some of the newer drugs.

This session also introduces the range of social therapies available and the rationale for their use. Therapies to improve social functioning, quality of life, occupational status and the activities of daily living are now well established. What can appear fairly trivial to the onlooker may involve sophisticated techniques and requires clear explanation. The role of the occupational therapist, psychologist or nurse is important to the success of these techniques and should be described. By understanding the aims of such activities, families often become extremely supportive of maintaining programmes at home. Issues of stress can again be raised. Rehabilitation is a long-term process and to discuss it as such may help relatives establish long-term aims for themselves in relation to the person with schizophrenia.

The discussion usually raises individual issues of what helps, what doesn't, fears about treatment and a review of 'alternative' therapies. The main alternative therapies presented to us by relatives were those of food allergies and mega-vitamin therapy, although hypnosis was also fairly frequently raised. Such theories have to be calmly discussed and not dismissed out of hand, as that lays the group leader open to the challenge that 'you haven't done much for my son' or of being a hide-bound traditionalist. The dangers of some alternative therapies should be clearly identified, but hard dogma that the medical model of schizophrenia is the only useful one can be counterproductive to the development of a good working relationship within the group. One word of warning to be issued in relation to some of the 'alternative' approaches is the cost implications, which can be considerable. This is especially important for low-income families who might feel guilty if they cannot afford to pay for something someone else is telling them is 'the answer'.

Session 5: Relatives' Problems

This session explores how living with someone who has schizophrenia affects the rest of the family, and how these problems might be managed. Taking on the role of carer is difficult. This session must acknowledge these difficulties and point out that problems with this role are common, and indeed 'normal'. Relatives may find such a role 'burdensome'. The concept of, and differences between, subjective and objective burden is introduced using lists and common examples. It needs to be explained that subjective burden, or the way relatives perceive the problem, can often be more troublesome than objective burden, or the reality of the problem. It is not them being difficult or 'weak'. Relatives should focus on listing their own problems in these terms and focus on those that *they* perceive as most stressful.

A description of the principles of problem-solving and goal-setting should be given, along with encouragement to use these techniques in relation to individual burden and examples of coping techniques which may reduce burden. Practical examples work best to illustrate these points. Relatives should be encouraged to try such techniques and report back to the group on their success or failure. In order to obtain examples of burden rather than simply provide information, relatives were encouraged to be more interactive from the outset and to make full use of the whole session to list problems, discuss them and seek solutions. Common problems tended to be anxiety, fear for the future, family friction, blame and guilt, embarrassment, personal health, and lack of privacy or time to themselves. Group members were able to help each other through problem-solving and goal-setting techniques, facilitated by the group leader, and look at how they could reduce their particular problems. Again relatives often found it useful to have their individual problems acknowledged and normalised. In some cases there may be services available of which they are unaware or are too embarrassed to ask for.

The whole issue of being a carer should be covered: how they have been selected or selected themselves to be primary carers, what this means to them in terms of burden, neglect of themselves or other family members, how they cope with these issues, resentment at being left to cope alone, not being valued or supported in the carer role, and being increasingly pressurised to take on extra care are common themes to be explored.

The exploitation of carers is now acknowledged, but little positive help is offered by the authorities. This session is specifically designed to be for the relative and their problems rather than for the person with schizophrenia, who is involved only in terms of their effect on the family. Most social interventions are aimed at reducing patient relapse and improving relatives' functioning so they can carry out their caring job better. It must be made clear to the relatives that the groups are aimed solely at giving them information and maybe reducing their personal stress, that is, it is a service for *them*.

Session 6: The Family and Schizophrenia

This session looks at the effect living with the family has on someone who has schizophrenia. The family has in some way always affected the person with schizophrenia and been affected by them. This session must avoid blaming the family for the illness or implying any causal relationship. Indeed it must be strongly reiterated that this is not the case. The session merely explores the relationship between the carer and the cared for. The important issue of stress is once again raised, and the fact that people with schizophrenia handle stress badly is examined. The main focus of the session is to discuss the mediating factor of stress between the relative and the person with schizophrenia; how they may both either contribute towards, or negate, high levels of stress. It can be surprisingly difficult to get the concept of stress over to families, and this is perhaps best accomplished by practical examples of family stress that may precipitate relapse or reduce the functioning of the person with schizophrenia. This is again put from the relative's viewpoint—the creating of a low-stress environment may make caring less stressful, reduce household friction and ease personal burden.

This session introduces some concepts relating to high EE; criticism, over-protectiveness and over-involvement. We discuss how these can be natural reactions by someone who cares in a pressurised situation. A more low-key, non-confrontational atmosphere, where support and encouragement are given without putting on too much pressure, will reduce stress on both family and the person with schizophrenia. Over-protectiveness and over-involvement are hard to see in oneself, but reducing them can lead to increased autonomy for the person with schizophrenia and a reduction in feelings of responsibility for the relative. Changes in criticism, over-protectiveness and over-involvement through time need recognition, and may be paramount during acute stages of the illness when the person with schizophrenia is difficult to manage/live with or in people with marked negative symptomatology. That such responses might validly be related to difficult circumstances has to be recognised, but so also does the fact that they often extend into periods when the person with schizophrenia is reasonably well. It is during these periods that it may be helpful to persuade relatives to offer more 'arms length' support.

Although EE has been the main focus of family interventions, it is useful to widen the discussion to other aspects of relatives' interactions, especially positive aspects of family relationships. Relatives often raise management issues in this session, and it is useful to go back over aspects of coping techniques. Since the literature has shown that most individuals adopt a wide repertoire of coping techniques that can be equally successful, this should be acknowledged, along with explaining the lack of information on what constitutes *definitively* successful coping. Relatives should be encouraged to contribute suggestions on how they have coped in similar situations. Maladaptive coping, that is action that appears to be making the situation worse, may arise from misinformation or misinterpretation of circumstances. Relatives sharing solutions to problems can lead to an improvement in coping techniques.

Session 7: Creating a Low-stress Environment

This session picks up on points raised in the last two sessions, looking at using the knowledge gained about stress and its effect on schizophrenia to maximise family functioning for the benefit of each family member. Strategies are offered for reducing stress within the household, and relatives are invited to contribute their own ideas. The need for both psychological/emotional *and* behavioural strategies should be covered. An advantage of having all types of relatives in the group was that strategies suggested by apparently low-EE relatives were more readily picked up by high-EE relatives than they would have been if offered by the group leader. This session thus focuses very specifically on the concept of stress, but the relationship of high EE to stress must be carefully explained. Often, describing expressed emotion as a thermometer measuring the emotional temperature of family interactions is useful, and then stress can be seen as something that raises that temperature to a possibly unacceptably high level.

The concept of expressed emotion is extremely complex and should not be gone into in great depth. Group leaders report that it is almost impossible to explain EE to families without some criticism of their handling of the person with schizophrenia being implied or inferred. Overall, it is more important to focus on practical suggestions to reduce stress supplied by all the group. We asked families to design a low-stress (quiet) environment that may help the person with schizophrenia to cope more easily with the family situation.

Session 8: Managing Disturbed Behaviour

The overall aim of this session is to provide positive, practical guidelines to help the relative cope with disturbed behaviour within the home. Despite the articulated demand by relatives for advice on managing disturbed behaviour, there has been little response from professionals. This lack of help often leads relatives to feel angry and frustrated. The group can offer suggestions on setting limits, responding to delusions or hallucinations, managing suicide attempts, and dealing with verbal and physical aggression. What aggravates such behaviour? What improves it? Is it situational or generalised? Lists of individual behavioural difficulties and precipitating factors can be helpful. Again there is a varied successful and unsuccessful coping repertoire, including avoidance, collusion and confrontation. Each relative has to find what works best in their situation, so there can be no set rules. Frequently, other relatives provide the most helpful suggestions to reduce behavioural difficulties. The group leader can offer guidelines on coping with difficult behaviour and discuss how health professionals would tackle these in a health-care setting. It has to be remembered, however, that relatives may have more experience than staff in this. Relatives should be encouraged to have confidence in their own expertise and to expand upon years of knowledge, prior to the illness as well as after, of how their ill relative best responds when upset or under stress.

Relatives also have to consider how they manage their own distress and the effect that severely disturbed behaviour has on their own well-being.

Distress to themselves has to be minimised, and techniques to alleviate the problem should be discussed in the group. Using a flip-chart to write up other group members' suggestions regarding the management of disturbed behaviour in relation to a particular person can give that relative a more individualised approach to their problem. They can also take the notes away as a reminder.

Session 9: Using Services and Dealing with Crises

This session provides a comprehensive overview of services available to people with schizophrenia, what they do and what services are missing. Relatives can describe their problems in dealing with services, including availability. It is helpful to discuss what can reasonably be expected of services and what they can and cannot provide. Families may go to the wrong person for the wrong thing, and a description of the role of individual health professionals is useful, particularly the duty hospital doctor. In addition, much support and guidance can be found outside the health-care system and should be explored in relation to the local situation.

Dealing with health-care professionals can be intimidating, and guidelines are provided for getting the most out of the doctor or other health worker. Role-play can be used in this session, if relatives are comfortable with this, to practise dealing with professionals. This can help find the best manner in which to articulate their requests or overcome feelings of intimidation.

This topic leads on to how, having established routine channels of contact with the service, the service will respond in a crisis. The main form of emergency contact remains through the GP contacting the hospital duty doctor. Crisis intervention services, now currently in vogue, are seldom seen in practice apart from in demonstration services. The system remains fraught with difficulties, both in obtaining access to appropriate staff and in the time involved in trying to get help. It is often felt by relatives, justifiably, that the system conspires against them and is oblivious to either their needs or those of the person with schizophrenia. Relatives should be helped to plan the best route through the system in times of crisis in order to achieve effective help.

A list of telephone numbers, and a prior arrangement with the GP or the patient's consultant to contact them in times of relapse, may speed up the process.

Sadly, dealing with services may be about making the best of a bad job. Often deciding what is most appropriate from what is available, and ensuring that it is effectively delivered, may be seen as success. Listing problems that are encountered when seeking services can encourage group discussion on realistic or unrealistic expectations. Lack of identified services, where there is a demonstrated need by relatives in the group, may lead them (and staff) to have more confidence in making their demands heard more loudly. Finally, it seems important that families recognise and come to terms with their frustration over difficulties in dealing with services. This may also lead them into the more useful channel of demanding services rather than allowing such frustration to damage their own health.

Session 10: Where Do We Go from Here?

The overall message of this session is to get relatives to think positively about the future. In closing, relatives can go through what they have covered in the previous weeks. They can bring up new or previously covered issues, or discuss changes that the group has helped them make and how successful these have been. In this session there is an opportunity to discuss follow-up, and what sort of on-going support they would like, and comment on the usefulness of the group.

Goal-setting may help relatives to consider how they plan to manage their relationship with the person with schizophrenia and reduce their own personal stress in response to the caring role. A list of support groups available within the area should be provided. Relatives vary in what support they find useful. For some, continuing in their current group but with a self-help format may be the answer. Since self-help groups can founder due to lack of structure and support we suggest describing the setting-up of such a group and offering the support of a professional at 'arms length'. Other options for continuing support may include existing groups provided by the voluntary agencies. A clear description and handouts of all the voluntary organisations in the area can be provided. In our area the National Schizophrenia

Fellowship (Scotland) expressed a willingness to contact individual families (with their permission) and to introduce them to an existing group. Relatives who wanted no further contact with the service were still encouraged to describe what they felt they had gained from the group (if anything), and how they could see their relationship with the person with schizophrenia moving forward. The telephone number of their local CPN was provided to all relatives in case they wanted to discuss problems in the future, and this was much appreciated.

INTERPRETING THE MEDIA

One issue which developed as a theme running through sessions was the way mental illness, and schizophrenia in particular, is reported in the media. Relatives often see 'public education' as a service which is missing, and 'a change in the public's attitude' as one of the things which would most help them, and the person with schizophrenia, to cope with the ramifications of the illness. Group leaders should thus be aware of current media stories, whether on television or in the newspapers, fiction or non-fiction. Documentary programmes and major articles may be a source of much good information, but can also present a one-sided picture. Unfortunately, this 'one side' is likely to be negative, concentrating on violence, aggression or suicide, and on the lack of services leading to people being abandoned in the community. Although some of this 'investigative' journalism highlights real problems and may stem from a genuine sense of concern at neglect or lack of justice, it is realistically tempered by the awareness that it is bad news, tragedy, pathos and fear that sells newspapers and raises viewing figures. Many relatives in the groups reported being troubled by things they had seen or read in the media, and the impact of this 'worst scenario' on a misinformed public, as well as on people with schizophrenia themselves. Some relatives reported 'worst scenario' media reports triggering depressive episodes in the person with schizophrenia or themselves. Many wanted reassurance over some of the information, particularly that their relative would not inevitably become violent or aggressive.

Fiction can be as useful or disquieting as documentary reporting, can spark discussions and need not present a negative or sensationalised view. In recent years a number of British soap operas have portrayed mental illness reasonably sympathetically, and have been accompanied by interest in the newspapers. A recent study of the tabloid press and television (Glasgow University Media Group 1993a), however, indicated that by far the greatest category of representations of mental illness, both fictional and non-fictional, refer to the identified person harming others. What is most worrying about the biased and sometimes misleading reporting of mental illness is that this is accepted by the public and 'can overwhelm experience'. This last fact is described in the report of an audience reception study of media images (Glasgow University Media Group 1993b). Even when people had (positive, if limited) experience of someone with mental illness, this could be discounted in the face of media messages. Possibly even more alarming is that this was also reported by a number of relatives in our groups, who lived in fear that their child (often quiet, passive, apathetic, displaying mainly negative symptoms) would turn into 'the maniac' beloved of the tabloids. These fears must be discussed, along with the reality, throughout the sessions. Although some images live on (and on) in the collective awareness of mental illness, this will also need to be tailored to the specific memories of relatives in the group, and current stories in the national and local media.

8

ORGANISING
RELATIVES' GROUPS

This chapter looks at the development of the service from a practical point of view, working through the stages from selling the idea of relatives' groups to management, and finding staff and accommodation, to contacting relatives and encouraging them to attend the groups. We describe the methods used in south Glasgow, their advantages and disadvantages, and also draw on the experiences of other researchers and clinicians.

Introducing a new service, whether across a catchment area or as a single entity, requires the organisation to change to accommodate this, and change in organisations is never easy. The 'management guru', Tom Peters (1988), points out that

> 'No skill is more important than the corporate capacity to change per se. The company's most urgent task, then, is to learn to welcome—beg for, demand—innovation from everyone.' [his underlining]

Introducing a new service means tackling the organisation, and although many are superficially open to change and innovation this often hides a rigid, unyielding framework of the 'this-is-the-way-it's-always-been-done' school. As statutory and voluntary agencies become more caught up in the 'enterprise culture', it takes skill to juggle the twin demands of economics and service delivery. Introducing a new service requires more than just a good idea and good luck. It requires a clear strategy to influence the organisation to accept and deliver the service. It also means you have to understand the organisation and how to influence it. Barrowclough and Tarrier (1992) also describe managing change in the organisation, highlighting the work of Georgiades and Phillimore (1975).

SELLING THE SERVICE

Any new service has to be sold, and as a service innovator this is your first task. You need to be clear *why* you think the relatives' groups are a 'good idea', *what* you expect them to achieve and *how* you intend to do this. You have to sell the service to a number of different groups of people, the management, the staff who will run the groups, and the patients and relatives themselves. The first half of this book has given you a rationale for introducing relatives' support and education groups, and this can be distilled into a brief argument to present your case, tailoring the specifics to meet local needs and the interests and expectations of the people to whom you are speaking.

What case can be put forward for a 'carer service'? Any outline on advocating a service for relatives can usefully begin by reiterating government policy, particularly the recent White Paper which strongly advocates service provision (Secretaries of State for Health, Social Security, Wales and Scotland 1989). A second 'selling point' to a management who are attempting to appease the demands of our consumer society is that customers wish such a service and have frequently vocalised this wish (National Schizophrenia Fellowship 1974). Financially it may reduce the burden on other health services utilised by relatives who show higher levels of psychological problems than the average population (Fadden *et al.* 1987a, b). With the move towards community care, relatives who function as carers are increasingly part of the community care package with its more holistic approach towards mental health service provision.

We live in financially constrained times and new services must compete with each other for funding. Services for carers are important, but may be seen as 'low priority'. The comparatively high profile of voluntary self-help groups in this area may encourage managers and others to view this as something which can be established 'on the cheap'. This is something which has to be resisted. Carers' services should not be established on a 'good will' basis. They deserve official funding rather than being seen as a 'creeping development' occurring out of someone's 'good idea'. This cannot be emphasised enough, and from our own experience a great deal of time and effort is needed to establish these principles of the service. This effort will not be wasted.

Services should not be set up on a good-will basis for two reasons, which relate to personal values and service values. Personal values imply the exploitation of staff through their enthusiasms. Such enthusiasm can rapidly wane as the reality of work pressures builds up. Also, staff may leave and not be replaced by others equally motivated. 'Enthusiasm services' are difficult to evaluate appropriately, making replication difficult. This is a problem seen in demonstration services in academic centres. Research staff often bolster the original service and may work long hours, motivated by being in a centre of excellence and the production of research papers. 'Average' service provision must be provided by 'average' people. Simply expecting 'more' of staff is not the way to establish a new service. People have families, they have a home and a personal and social life, all of which take time and energy. Nevertheless, they are frequently expected to do 'more' at work (defined as 'demonstrating commitment') while at the same time maintaining the other side of their lives.

Service values are also important. To provide a service for nothing yet again hides the true cost of community care. It also implies that carers' services are secondary to, or less important than, other service provision. This is not to always to insist that carers' services must attract 'new money' which, realistically, may not be around, but to advocate competition with other services on an equal footing.

It is useful to have an awareness of consumer demand when trying to sell a new product. Managers and service purchasers will be more attracted to your ideas if, in addition to background and research literature, you have a good working knowledge of the local situation. The new service will need to be sold to groups already existing in the area, such as self-help groups, so as not to be seen to be in competition and not to provide something which already exists. Apart from increasing links with other agencies and not duplicating work, it saves embarrassment when no clients appear to make use of the 'new' service.

Other information which will be needed when 'selling the service' will be a clear, realistic description of the service offered with all resource implications, including budget, all of which is described in later sections.

A 'new service' should always be subject to monitoring and evaluation to assess its effectiveness and value for money. A particular advantage for relatives' services in undergoing this process is in ascertaining what level and type of service is actually required in a particular area. Regions, and even districts, will vary considerably in their requirements. We have noted the number of relatives' groups which have been established in Scotland in response to articulated demand but are then poorly attended by relatives, leading to demoralised staff and sceptical management. There is an implicit danger in then assuming that services are not required. Far more work is required to evaluate the exact needs of carers in this area.

An assurance that feedback from the service will be available and that modifications can be made in the light of this (including, if necessary, scrapping the service) is usually taken as positive reassurance.

MEETING MANAGEMENT

To introduce a new service on a catchment-wide basis means meeting, and persuading, senior management and then heads of all departments: psychiatry, nursing, social work and occupational therapy. Convincing senior staff of the usefulness of a carers' service, particularly if it involves redeploying resources, is often a problem. Used to dealing with major crises and problems in individual patients, it is difficult for them to prioritise a carer service. However, over the years we have seen a shift in attitude as our service has been seen to offer effective support and value for money. Carers' services are still not routinely offered in ordinary health-care provision, but awareness is growing regarding their needs, and increasingly more 'off the shelf' packages describing the running of groups are available (Barrow-clough and Tarrier 1992; Kuipers *et al.* 1992).

This raises the question of who should 'front' the project or be seen as its leader. We will discuss the staffing of the service later, but for now it is enough to say that it needs to be someone sufficiently senior, with enough 'clout' to meet with senior management, be taken seriously, and be able to effect change. In Britain this very often means a medic, and a consultant psychiatrist may be needed to present the service, even if they are not the person who will actually organise and run the groups.

Before meeting management, two documents should be prepared: the first setting out the case for a carer service; the second an operational policy on how the service will run and resource implications. These documents should only be in rough draft. Rough draft does not, however, mean scrappy and badly presented. It does mean that options are left open for other team members to contribute ideas and for further testing of the market to be carried out. These documents should be short (one side of A4 paper for the first and two sides of A4 for the second, to include a projected budget and staff requirements). Busy people will not stop to read anything longer than that, and you will impress them with your efficiency and professionalism if you are clear, concise and take up as little of their time as possible.

Handling meetings well is a skill. You must be clear in your own mind about what the aims of the meeting are before you start, or you may find yourself sent away 'to think again' or 'set up a working party to investigate the idea', which effectively means it will never again see the light of day. If you have any doubts about your ability to handle meetings and negotiate in them, then *The Strategy of Meetings* (Kieffer 1988) is an excellent guide. Ultimately you will need the agreement of management to specific resource allocation (money and staff), not simply a vague approval of a good idea.

Go over your presentation with colleagues and make sure you have answers for the questions which are most likely to be asked. At the same time do not appear to be too rigid, everything may not be possible in quite the way you planned but there might be other alternatives. Above all, do not promise more than you can deliver.

When seeking to introduce change into an organisation you will be met with one of three responses, which will fall into a normal distribution curve. At one extreme will be those who are enthusiastic, who support the idea and who do not require any persuasion. They may even be asking you what they can do to help. These people need rewarding and enough nurturing to maintain their enthusiasm, but not a massive investment of time. Keeping them feeling involved is important and may, in some instances, be achieved by allocating them concrete tasks. This also has the advantage of sorting out, at an earlier stage, active supporters, who will actually *do* something and passive supporters who will simply be vocal. At the other extreme are those who are unequivocally against the new service (or possibly just against change of any kind). There is often a mistaken tendency to invest time and energy in trying to change these people, particularly if they are senior.

Usually this is a waste of time. Cut your losses and invest the time and effort into persuading the large undecided middle group. You need to carry as many people with you as possible, and in most bureaucratic organisations one person cannot block a new development if a substantial number of other senior people are for it.

MEETINGS WITH OTHER STAFF

It is not enough to get the approval of management. Other staff have to be carried along too, and not just those who will run the groups. Talk to staff of all disciplines at all levels. Take advantage of local seminars, journal clubs or teaching sessions to promote the service. Bottom-up enthusiasm is not enough on its own to generate a new service, but top-down imposition is rarely successful either. Researchers or clinicians already running groups can be invited, if necessary as part of a small local conference to promote the idea. This can usefully be supplemented by also inviting someone from a relatives' support group run by a voluntary organisation to speak and give the consumers' perspective.

Have prepared a short handout and a concise reading list for those who want further information. The more of this you have prepared in advance, the more committed, and efficient, you appear to be. The development of the service is not just about convincing people that it is a good idea, but also that it is 'do-able' and that you are capable of doing it.

BUDGET

Every new service requires funding, and this is likely to be the area where most questions and most negative views arise. We have already discussed why the service needs adequate funding and should not be run on goodwill. It probably helps to keep things in perspective if discussions about *why* money is needed (the principle of the service) are kept separate from *how much* is needed (running the service).

The requirements of the service must be clearly identified and agreed prior to the service starting. Resources must be allocated either through identifying 'new monies' or by resource transfer. In Britain, with the increasing move to establish community services as a priority, it may be possible to negotiate a transfer of money or build the service into a general psychiatry sector service commitment. This money should ideally be clearly identified and ring-fenced. It has been our experience that it is sometimes easier to negotiate money in separate blocks, for example, accommodation, staff, stationery and so on, through different managers. People commonly underestimate the true cost of a service, failing to take into account many of the smaller incidental costs which rapidly mount up over a period of several years.

Another option is to look at shared costs between agencies: one providing staff, the other perhaps a building or rent costs. In an era when health and social agencies are asked to work together to provide support in the community, this may be the ideal service to test their commitment to this principle.

The main headings for the budget will be staff, accommodation, travel (for staff), group running costs, incidentals, evaluation and training.

Staff. Details of recruiting staff are discussed below. Staff time will account for the vast majority of the budget. This may be high initially if multiple groups are running, but decreases over the years as key areas of need are identified and groups are only required for new families. For groups which run in the evenings, overtime or out-of-hours costs must be negotiated.

A vital cost must include employing a group coordinator. This is usually someone within the service (clerk) with one session per week freed to organise contacting relatives, the setting up and running of the groups, ordering tea and coffee, paying the rent and so on. The service falls apart without this coordination, which can be incredibly time consuming. Someone is also required to bring together some sort of case register of all the people with schizophrenia, and time/costs must be allocated for this.

Accommodation. The details of finding suitable accommodation are discussed below. In the budget, all that is needed is rent costs, including payment for a caretaker and insurance.

Travel. Staff travel costs are required not just for the groups, but to interview relatives at home before they join the group (see setting up the service).

Groups running costs. The major cost is the production of the manual for each relative. This will need to be photocopied or printed, although you may be able to get outside funding to support this. Smith and Birchwood had booklets printed in conjunction with Health Education.

Tea and coffee for relatives at groups is an important part of the session, and although costs are apparently modest they add up over time and require budgeting for. Alternatively, a charge can be made to relatives.

Incidentals. Patients and relatives have to be written to, other staff contacted, records kept and so on. Stationery, postage and telephone costs must be included in the budget.

Evaluation. If the service is to be evaluated, these costs should be indicated separately although they will come under similar headings, e.g. staff and incidentals.

Training. Staff to run groups must be trained. Costs for this will range from sending people to specialist courses to in-house training. Money will then be needed for the production of training manuals, photocopying references and the purchase of a few basic books. Staff time/costs must be allocated for training.

RECRUITING STAFF TO RUN GROUPS

What staff are best involved in running relatives' groups? This depends mainly upon what type of group is being run. The early intervention studies aimed at reducing expressed emotion in families used very specialised research staff. A training programme and manual has now been designed from these interventions (Kuipers *et al.* 1992). Similarly, other groups of research workers in intervention studies in EE have now turned specialised research programmes into commercial packages and training courses, such as that run by Falloon and colleagues. Most local service groups which aim only to support relatives rather than alter patient outcome use a variety of disciplines and staff. Often these are people who have been directly involved with the patient whose relatives now attend the group.

Common guidelines are involved in the selection, training and support of group leaders, irrespective of their background. In many cases there is great initial enthusiasm shown by staff to become involved in a new type of service. This will only be turned into genuine commitment if a number of factors are addressed. Time must be specially 'ring-fenced' to provide the service and money, particularly overtime and out-of-hours payments, properly organised and agreed with management. Staff must commit themselves to the training, and a full explanation of this needs to be given along with a broad outline of the groups and the material to be presented. Supervision sessions have to be organised and a commitment made to attend these. It must be made clear that this is not a service to be squeezed into an already overfull working day because it is thought to be a good idea, but is a particular remit with sessional commitments. It is often the case that one interested consultant may initiate the service. This may be useful, as they may act as a powerful advocate for resources, but such a commitment must again be allocated sufficient time.

We used a variety of disciplines to run our groups, namely community psychiatric nurses (CPNs), occupational therapists (OTs), social workers (SWs) and junior doctors. By and large our experience in running a clinical service appears to mirror that of the original intervention studies from the academic centres. CPNs appear to be particularly well placed in terms of expertise and local community knowledge to run such groups. With their commitment to families they often find it easier to allocate time to run groups and frequently carry out the initial interviews with relatives while making routine visits.

Should the group leader know the patient and/or their family? CPNs have visited many families over the years, are trusted by them, and are not generally perceived as threatening or invading privacy. This can help in gaining access to relatives and persuading them to take part in the groups, but problems can arise. In education groups not aimed at therapy or reducing EE, it may be more difficult for the group leader to avoid attempts by relatives within the group to focus on the person with schizophrenia who is known to all, or find out information about the individual rather than more general education. Focusing on education and relatives' problems may be better achieved by staff not known to individual family members.

Barrowclough and Tarrier (1992) discuss whether family interventions should be a specialised service from a specialised team, or a general service delivered by any personnel within the service, assuming family intervention to be a core skill, and come down in favour of specialised services.

Whilst we feel that all services should be able to offer relatives' groups, in terms of coordination, expertise and maintaining family contact they are more easily delivered by one team working part-time in this area. A generalist service often fades away leaving staff isolated and lacking support, and may deteriorate to the lowest common denominator of expertise. A specialist service is more likely to develop a team identity. Regular meetings and supervision avoid stress, low morale and 'burn-out'; in addition they improve the quality of the service through an exchange of information and experience.

ACCOMMODATION

A common assumption of where to site groups is that relatives are most likely to want to attend a group in a local facility such as a community centre or church hall near where they live. This is not always the case. Many factors come into play when deciding where to run groups, ranging from relatives' choices to service practicalities.

Relatives vary in where they want groups, not least depending on how they view the illness, and this must be taken into account when planning a service. Although making service provision more difficult in terms of operational costs and planning, it is important in achieving an effective service.

If relatives perceive schizophrenia or mental illness as stigmatising, they often do not want the group to be held round the corner from where they live, and are prepared, and prefer, to travel further afield. As we have seen, viewing schizophrenia within a medical model makes coping easier for some families. If this is the case their expectation and choice may be that their group will be held in a hospital environment, preferably a general hospital. Locating groups for these families in a local non-health care facility can be seen by them as devaluing both their problems and their role in managing the illness. Another aspect of relatives' choice is that for many families faced with increasing social isolation and alienation, the group is seen as a 'night out'. In our Glasgow study, groups located 'up the town' were infinitely more popular than those on peripheral housing estates as families took advantage of local pubs and restaurants.

Service practicalities also dictate where to locate groups. Whilst health care facilities are free of charge to health care professionals, other buildings are not and have to be rented and insured. If this money is not forthcoming, it may be necessary to make a small charge to families for the sessions. This is likely to be met with resistance, not just by families with a low income but by everyone who supports a health service free at point of delivery. Another alternative may be to seek donations from charitable organisations, although this again turns it into a peripheral, 'optional' service. A valid argument can be put forward that community mental health care should have a clearly identified budget for what are known as 'hotel services'. Whether this budget should come under health (NHS) or social (Social Services) care is debatable.

Groups tend to run most effectively and maintain their clientele best when refreshments are provided. Although tea/coffee/biscuits will only amount to a small sum, it is important to include all sundries in the overall estimated cost of the service and check that the facilities for this exist in the accommodation acquired. Time taken to ensure a group is in the right place at the right time with properly organised sundry facilities is invaluable. Relatives feel they are being offered a profes-sional service, and respond by valuing the service and maintaining their attendance.

Place interacts with the timing of groups, and is important as they have to cater both for unemployed and employed relatives who may be able to attend only at particular times, such as in the evenings. Evening groups may pose particular problems both in obtaining accommoda-tion and the staff to run them, and then in ensuring safety in 'difficult' areas of the city. Here caretakers perform an important function in maintaining the service, and in some cases 'escorts' may be provided or relatives encouraged to travel together. Some locations may only be suitable for out-of-hours groups in the summer, with long, light eve-nings, and may need to be postponed during the winter.

Whilst cities have their own problems of danger, rural areas can be disadvantaged in terms of access and availability of services and rela-tives may have to travel considerable distances.

PERSONNEL IN THE SERVICE CATCHMENT AREA

An area often ignored in developing new services is that of gaining the confidence and support of other workers, not just in the parent service but also those outside it. Contact must be made with local voluntary organisations and users' groups. These contacts are invaluable in promoting the service, encouraging relatives to attend, and developing the format and content of the groups' material to make it more relevant to the local population. For us, starting up groups in a deprived inner-city area with a limited budget, voluntary organisations and local community services proved exceptionally helpful. The National Schizophrenia Fellowship (Scotland) provided a project leader to talk to groups about follow-up support and also ran a follow-up support group. The Salvation Army donated free premises for evening groups, and provided a caretaker in what was an extremely 'difficult' area. Many community centres were provided free of charge for group sessions, and offered well- furnished surroundings with many other people using the buildings and cafes available for recreational purposes.

We continue to be surprised and delighted at how local communities respond so well to specific services offered to relatives, and help and support the work. It may often be difficult for them to initiate such groups themselves, but they appear to welcome support to families of the mentally ill in the community. A cautionary note must be sounded in that this community support can hide the true cost of the service, and this should be budgeted for at the outset. 'Free' accommodation, and so forth, should always appear in cost statements for the service as donations.

SETTING UP THE GROUPS

Approaching and engaging relatives in groups is an important process which, if mismanaged, may lead to rejection of the service. Most researchers have reported difficulties in getting relatives to attend groups. This is despite repeated requests for such a service from families and organisations that represent them to professionals. Since practical examples can be more useful than general theories of service provision, we describe how contact was made with relatives from a Health Service perspective in south Glasgow. We describe problems we encountered which led us to consider the issues and other options in contacting and engaging relatives in groups.

Patient Register

First find your clients. If the hospital does not have a register of everyone with a diagnosis of schizophrenia, then one will need to be set up to trace all eligible people with schizophrenia and their families. There are various ways of developing a register, and it is worth considering what other uses it might be put to before you begin.

We established an out-patient register which provided information on all patients with schizophrenia who had been admitted to hospital in south Glasgow in the last 10 years. Other information recorded included date of birth, address, and name of family members if available. Care should be taken when setting up a register that access to it is restricted and that registration of data held conforms with requirements under the Data Protection Act. Inevitably a number of patients will not be able to be contacted, having died or moved away. A major concern was in the area of misdiagnosis, since patients were diagnosed on admission rather than on discharge from hospital. This led to acute confusional states, drug-induced psychosis and organic disorders being misdiagnosed as schizophrenia. After it was 'cleaned up', our register was reduced by nearly one-third, and this highlights worries over using routinely collected health board data as an avenue to access a specific group of patients and their families.

A register is not a necessity for all service development. Many studies have used diagnosis on discharge as their point of entry to their target population, and this is most suitable if the service is only to be offered to relatives of recently discharged patients. From an out-patient register with just over 500 names, we ended up with about one-fifth of patients having a relative in a group.

Medical Permission

Since educational groups offer a medically orientated approach to schizophrenia, and if organised within the health service take place under the umbrella of 'medical services', permission to approach a patient and their family should be sought from their doctor prior to contact. Although this might simply be seen as clinical etiquette, there are two other important reasons for seeking this approval. First, to ensure that the proposed service would not be detrimental to the family, and second, to obtain personal patient information that their doctor felt may be pertinent. A drawback to this approach may be that doctors can refuse permission and block contact with their patients and relatives. We encountered no such difficulties. In fact, additional information was helpful in alerting us to difficult relationships between patients and their families, and home visits that were more appropriately done by two staff in daylight or by more senior staff. Referrals were accepted from other staff for patients on the register, but always referred back to their original consultant.

Contacting Patients

Since the role and responsibility of health services is primarily to the patient, we contacted relatives through the patient. This involved all patients being seen by a psychiatrist, when the purpose of the relatives' group was explained to them and permission was sought to contact relatives. This approach protected both patient confidentiality and the patient's right not to involve their relative in their illness. It also avoided the problem of the patient feeling excluded from the service even though it is aimed at the relatives.

Another important feature was that it ensured that patients knew their diagnosis before anything was said to relatives. Although a few patients did say that they had never formally been told their diagnosis, they had worked it out for themselves and none expressed surprise (which does not mean to say that they agreed with the diagnosis).

This strategy also means, that patients can block their relatives' access to services designed specifically for relatives. In our group of patients, 16% refused us permission to contact their relatives. (A further 12% had previously refused any contact with us regarding the project.) Some of these families heard of our service and approached us directly to request access to the groups. This posed an ethical dilemma. In the light of the patients' views, these requests were refused. Yet this service was not aimed at patients, it was primarily for relatives and their problems in coping with, and caring for, an ill relative.

Not everyone agrees that patients' permission need be obtained before contacting relatives, believing that relatives have a right to the service and that patient confidentiality is not an issue. This debate is discussed in more detail in Chapter 10.

Contacting Relatives

It is essential when approaching relatives that staff are clear what it is they are offering. They should follow a standard procedure of initial contact and the information they give about the group itself. Since rejection by the family can be common, a strategy should be devised for dealing with this, particularly as many families take up the offer of a group on re-contact.

After patient permission was obtained, a letter was sent to their relatives asking if it would be possible to visit them at home to discuss their interest in attending the planned support group. A time was suggested in the letter, with the names of the professionals who would call, a telephone number and a contact name to speak to if this time was inconvenient. It was suggested that we would prefer to meet the whole family or as many members as possible, including the patient. A tear-off slip was also provided to be sent back if they wished no further contact or were not interested in us calling. In our study we contacted 302 relatives, of whom 109 took up a place in a group. Of those who did not, a small number were too ill or infirm to travel. Nearly half, however, said they were interested, but despite follow-up did not appear at a group.

First Interview with Relatives

Our initial contact always took place at the patient's home, as previous experience within our catchment area has indicated that both patients and their families are unreliable in attending appointments in any of our health-care facilities. The need to contact relatives at home has been emphasised by other researchers (Kuipers *et al.* 1992). Most home visits took place in the evenings, when families were able to have more members there and staff felt they were not trying to cram the interview in between other activities in their working day. We cannot emphasise strongly enough that such extra work must be paid for by an appropriately funded service, as described earlier. The interview, by necessity, was long and took up two hours or more as families often included an 'advisor' such as a trusted friend or even a parish priest. Another notable addition to these meetings was the family's dog, who often required careful handling. Advice on this is beyond the scope of this book!

For many families these interviews provided the first opportunity they had been given in years to 'sound off' about services, their own fears and anxieties regarding the illness, and the future of their relative. The importance of allowing families to do this cannot be emphasised enough, although it can be stressful for the interviewer who, in most cases, had had no previous involvement with their care. Guidelines were set for interviewers and had been discussed extensively during training. The guidelines included allowing and supporting each member of the family to have an equal share in the discussion, listening sympathetically to criticisms of the service, either justified or unjustified, but not involving themselves in critical comments, and moving the discussion forward to offering a relatives' support group whilst not promising it would offer an instant solution to their current problems.

Issues about the importance of tea and hospitality in relatives' homes have been discussed elsewhere (Kuipers *et al.* 1992). This requires sensitive cultural handling. Suffice it to say that in the west of Scotland, not to partake of tea would seem excessively rude but our most famous national beverage should be avoided at all cost.

It was explained to relatives that whilst the service was being established it would be monitored and evaluated. We were also interested in obtaining information on whether it would ultimately best be targeted at specific groups of families. To do this we asked them to complete questionnaires at home, one before and two after the group. We arranged a further visit some weeks later during which we would also discuss practical arrangements and a starting date for the group. All families were given a choice of starting dates, times to attend and venue.

Not all families are at home when they say they will be. We have all experienced families not being home despite a time being agreed for us to call, or finding only one family member where several had promised to attend. In a few families this may represent a chaotic lifestyle, but more commonly it can be a reflection of their ambivalence to often chaotic, distant or uninterested professional services over the years. A missed appointment often allows the family to feel some degree of control over the professionals, or is an indirect expression of anger towards previous services that they may feel have failed them. With this group of families, perseverance is often rewarded with a later fruitful relationship.

Families that Refused to Attend

Some families did reject our offer of an education and support group. There appear to be many reasons for this. Often it may be related to the current mental state of the patient, or to the length and chronicity of the illness. When families want help varies immensely. For some it is during acute exacerbations of the illness, at hospital admission or immediately upon discharge. For others the more chronic phase, when negative symptoms are more prominent, is more stressful and support is welcome. Similarly, some relatives feel that help is vital at an early stage of the illness and later on is, as several said 'far too late'.

There is considerable variation in how families react to the first contact. It is important to remain patient, polite and tolerant throughout, and to continue to offer contact if it is felt to be appropriate. Equally, many families wish for privacy to cope alone, and this wish must be respected. Staff must remain sensitive and attuned both to the wishes of the family and to the person with schizophrenia.

Group Membership

Whilst we thought it important to involve the whole family in the initial discussion and make an offer of a group to all members, we stipulated that not more than two members could attend any one group. This was to avoid 'swamping' other group members with issues about one family. The numbers of relatives from each family who were interested in attending varied considerably.

In most cases our initial contact with families was organised through the mother of the patient, often the most effective person in persuading other family members to attend. This was reflected in group sessions, where mothers accounted for 43% of all attenders, fathers 18%, spouses/partners 18%, siblings 14% and offspring 3%. The other 4% were a niece, a nephew and friends. The relatives who came to the groups tended to be older. Although one might expect a middle-aged group (and 77% of our groups were were over 40), nearly one-third were over 60 years and 19% were retired. Eighty-one per cent of the relatives in our groups lived with the person with schizophrenia.

The offer of transport to and from the group made little difference to those who attended, failed to attend or refused the group.

Maintaining Relatives in Groups

Setting up a relatives' service requires a great deal of effort, both in terms of staff enthusiasm and obtaining resources. Yet many relatives fail to either start or stay in the group. If this is the case we must ask whether the effort involved in establishing such a service is justified. Several authors have put forward a good argument for service provision in relation to interventions aimed at reducing relapse. Families who are difficult to engage and maintain in therapy appear to have an elevated risk of recurrent relapse and be financially burdensome on the service (Smith and Birchwood 1990; Tarrier 1991). If this is the case, can we both maximise the families initially engaging in treatment and minimise the number of relatives dropping out of the service?

Several researchers (Meichenbaum and Turk 1987; Barrowclough and Tarrier 1992) have attempted to identify factors that make it difficult to engage and maintain families in therapy. The subject is complex, with factors ranging from the personalities of the clients themselves to how the service is set up and operated—factors which we have discussed at length earlier in this chapter and in previous chapters. In addition, relatives who have different expectations from those which are being provided may be difficult to maintain in a group. Yet within our programme, research showed that relatives' expectations were substantially met. We asked relatives to rate their expectations both before and after the groups on a seven-point scale where seven is the highest score. Taking four and above as generally having 'high' expectations, 88% expected the group to be useful, 95% informative, 87% supportive and 94% to give advice. This is, of course, a biased sample, as those not interested in the groups did not get this far in the assessment procedures. After the groups, 91% said the groups were useful, 96% informative, 79% supportive and 86% that they had provided advice. On the same seven-point scale, the two sessions with the most ratings of six and seven were 'relatives' problems' and 'the family and schizophrenia', which would seem to indicate that we were right in aiming the content at the relatives themselves and their problems.

One explanation for the general satisfaction may be due to cultural congruence—families and staff appeared to have similar conceptualisations of the illness, and similar views on what knowledge and help they required. Our previous involvement with voluntary organisations and self-help groups had given us a good grounding in the questions and concerns most likely to be raised. However, the issue of cultural attitudes and expectations in minority and ethnic groups is an important one which is seldom raised and deserves more attention.

CONTACTING RELATIVES OUTSIDE THE HEALTH-CARE SETTING

Some people with schizophrenia were very unhappy about us contacting their relatives and they refused permission for us to do this. This problem led us to seek solutions as to how a service to relatives might be offered independently of the person with schizophrenia. One solution may be to 'demedicalise' the service, offering it outside a routine health-care setting. There may be some merit in making such a service the remit of the social services or voluntary agencies. This would certainly get round the problem of contacting the family through the patient, although social services may need to go through the client. On the other hand, they may find it easier to designate relatives as 'clients' than the health service does. How would contact be made? Perhaps by referral from hospital or community health-care professionals, GPs, social workers, or self-referral, with general advertising through posters and leaflets in hospitals, GP surgeries, social work departments, libraries, churches and other public places. Problems may arise if the person with schizophrenia is unhappy with their relative attending a group and discussing issues involving their care. Problems may also occur if different approaches to the illness are taken by agencies and conflicting messages given with no help in integrating them or choosing between them. A criticism of health-care groups is often that they are training families to be more 'compliant' and 'fit into services'. Different organisations often have different agendas and ideologies.

MAINTAINING OTHERS' ENTHUSIASM

Some of your time will need to be spent maintaining the enthusiasm of other staff, not least group leaders, during the protracted setting-up stage and once the groups are underway. Supervision of group leaders is an important aspect of this and is discussed in Chapter 9. We have already mentioned that feedback to management and senior staff is important. Your reports to management need to be clear, concise and free from any jargon or abbreviations.

MAINTAINING YOUR ENTHUSIASM

You might be lucky and find setting up relatives' groups a simple, straightforward and quick operation. Then again, if you are developing groups as a whole new service you might find the process slow, frustrating and more complicated than you would have thought possible. You need, during this long process, to make sure that you are able to maintain your own enthusiasm as well as everybody else's.

From our own experience we found that it is helpful to have two people doing this job. At one level this was because of the 'skill mix' (to use the current jargon). One of us is a consultant psychiatrist and the other an academic psychologist. Not only did we bring different skills to the task, but having different settings there was both access to the health service and distance from it when necessary. At different times and with different people, one or other of us was more appropriate to present plans, persuade others or generally 'front' the project. At different times and to different people clinical, research, administrative and planning skills took priority.

It also meant that we were able to support one another through the long planning and negotiating procedure, dealing with management and, it has to be said, some psychiatrists and other staff. Support from other colleagues is helpful, general support from family is welcome and comforting, but having someone who has as much invested in the project as you have means that you can talk about it to them in more detail and at greater length.

CHECKLIST OF STAGES IN SETTING UP GROUPS

Note that some of these stages will run concurrently.

1. *Background* —*research literature: why is this a good idea?*

   —interventions: what are you going to do?

   —local situation: anything relevant, e.g. are there
   local voluntary groups already in existence?

2. *Plan strategy* —How does the organisation run?

   —Who do you have to influence?

   —Whose support is necessary?

   —Desirable?

   Support of immediate superiors is an advantage at this stage.

3. *Prepare* plans/discussion documents.

4. Lay *groundwork* with staff at all levels in all disciplines.

5. *Identify people* at all levels who are supportive and willing to be involved.

   Develop a 'team' if this is appropriate.

   Some of these people may be at a distance but can still provide support.

6. Meet *management*—obtain commitment to service.

   —obtain resources where necessary.

7. Meet *senior staff* of different disciplines
   —obtain commitment to service.

   —obtain resources where necessary.

8. Plan *intervention* in detail, with team members.

9. Identify *staff* who will be group leaders; start training pro-gramme.

continues

10. Find suitable *accommodation* for groups.

11. Contact *patients*, then relatives.

12. Start *groups*, possibly at pilot level.

13. Maintain close *contact* with group leaders, particularly in the early stages.

    Offer support and supervision.

14. *Monitor* groups and provide feedback at all levels within the organisation, and, if appropriate, outside the organisation.

15. If appropriate, seek *publicity* to make services known to as many relatives as possible.

16. Continue to *monitor* groups to maintain optimal service.

17. Using sound behavioural principles, remember to build in *feedback* at all levels and, where appropriate, *rewards*, particularly for yourself!

9

TRAINING STAFF

Most studies have used dedicated research staff to run groups. Other staff may also be highly motivated to run groups but need assistance in developing the appropriate skills. Our groups were run by CPNs, social workers, occupational therapists and junior doctors. We provided eight one-and-a-half hour training sessions to familiarise them with both background information and the practical skills needed to run groups. Clearly staff bring a wide variety of skills to their role as group leader, and the advantage of multidisciplinary training was not just the exchange of information between individuals, but also the appreciation of different disciplines skills. There were three basic parts to the training. The first session described the service and gave an evaluation of the project, and can be reduced if an evaluation is not planned. Four sessions covered background information about schizophrenia and research on family involvement and education. The last three sessions covered the running of the groups, both content and more general aspects.

BACKGROUND INFORMATION

It is easy to think of groups for relatives as 'low key' and that only superficial information is required. Some relatives are, in fact, very knowledgeable and want discussion in considerable detail, particularly regarding aetiology and drugs. Group leaders must judge the level of the group and how much information is wanted or can be assimilated.

These sessions bring staff up to date, confirm their knowledge and give an opportunity to discuss issues. Most people report that it is the things that they themselves understand least well which are hardest to explain

to others. It was constantly emphasised that group leaders must consider the impact of information on relatives, so these sessions encouraged staff to think about how sensitive material might best be put
across. For education to be effective, group leaders have to engage in
dialogue and discussion with relatives, which means listening to them
and understanding their perspective. Thus, it is also important to
consider what 'lay' views are held.

One particularly sensitive session is that on the relationship between
the family and schizophrenia. Staff who want to run groups for relatives are, almost by definition, going to be interested in relatives and
believe that they require information and support. Nevertheless, there
are often resonances of the 'old' family theories echoing in their views.
It is important to establish the difference between discredited theories
of causality and the development of interactionist theories. The role of
expressed emotion in particular needs to be discussed in relation to
potential 'blame' of families and how information on EE will be received by them.

Most staff know little about the role of relatives as carers beyond their
day-to-day clinical experience, and it is helpful to clarify this. Groups
have a different emphasis if relatives are seen as clients or co-workers,
the latter might lead to a more 'therapeutic' approach.

Handouts can be given and some basic books and review articles
should be available. Once basic information has been covered, training
moves on to look at each group session, and discusses what should be
covered and what issues might be raised by group members. There are
also a number of general points which are not specific to individual
sessions.

GROUPS AS EDUCATION

The purpose of the groups needs very careful explanation, and the
difference between education groups and other kinds of family interventions should be discussed. Some staff may be trained in group or
family therapy, and these in particular will need to be aware of the
limits of education groups.

The use of illustration and example in the learning process is important,
and group leaders need to understand how to make use of relatives'

experiences without turning the sessions into 'therapy'. The basic format of the session, a didactic presentation and group discussion, provides a structure to prevent the group becoming 'therapeutic'. Group leaders should be prepared with examples to illustrate abstract concepts, and encourage relatives to find examples from their own situations. Relatives should be helped to look for links or similarities between recounted incidents, so that group members learn generalities or 'rules' which can be applied in different circumstances. Differences between individuals and families are important, and maintaining the balance between common elements and the variety of relatives' experience is a major task.

As education the groups have an agenda, are organised in a logical sequence and have goals (what relatives are expected to learn). This is set out in the first session and modified in the light of the relatives' expectations. Thus requests to cover particular topics or advice about specific issues can be accommodated. The aim of getting an individual into hospital, of securing day care, or of forcing them to take medication or forcing another relative to change can be shown not to be part of the group's purpose.

Relatives who have got as far as attending the first session will welcome the emphasis on 'education'. Those who want something more or something different will be discussed below. Group leaders can emphasise the importance of knowledge in order to make more informed decisions and reduce relatives' feelings of helplessness. However, knowledge alone will not lead to behaviour change, and this also needs to be made clear. This last point may also need to be made clear to group leaders, who otherwise may be looking for unrealistic changes in their group members, and become disappointed or frustrated when this does not happen.

Emphasising education means that group leaders have to plan each session thoroughly and not simply rely on relatives' questions to lead them through the points. Nor should the discussion simply be a 'free-for-all' without structure. Group leaders will have the basic headings, sub-headings and specific points for each session. General, comprehensive ideas are presented first, followed by more specific points and then the fine detail. A reiteration of the general points can be used in conclusion. Thus, for example, when presenting aetiology the main starting place could be the complexity of the causation of schizophrenia, that it is not due to any *one* factor, and that nobody has the total answer. From here, the general categories of types of theory can be listed before dealing with each one in turn. The detail will depend on the interests and ability of the group, before finally returning to the general issues of complexity and incompleteness.

At each stage of the process the group leader should check that members understand what is being covered. Asking if people understand or whether they have any questions can be intimidating, and only the most confident may be willing to express ignorance. Use 'what questions do you have?', which implies that questions are expected and acceptable, rather than 'do you have any questions?', which can be inhibiting. Relatives can be asked for their opinion in ways that get them to comment on what they have learnt. 'Does that make sense?' can be interpreted as it being the individual's responsibility to make sense of it. 'Does that sound reasonable or a bit far-fetched?' might bring out personal comment. Group leaders should not be frightened of saying that some of the information is difficult, or even that they have difficulty in putting it across clearly. Relatives will probably be sensitive to being 'talked down to', but will also appreciate being told that it is not their 'fault' if they find certain parts difficult to understand because the material *is* difficult,

The use of overhead projectors, flip-charts and handouts all add to the sense of 'education' rather than 'therapy' and can help to keep the group leaders, as well as relatives, on course.

Group leaders must remember that to assimilate new information people need to hear something more than once. The old adage 'tell them what you are going to tell them, tell them, tell them what you have told them,' holds true. Summaries as well as outlines are vital. So is the ability to say the same thing in a variety of different ways, using different examples. It is easy to fall into the trap, when someone says they do not understand, of simply giving them more information, more detail, in the hope that this will make things clearer. What is needed, however, is to give the same information phrased differently or from another perspective. A well-prepared variety of examples is essential. The multi-disciplinary nature of training sessions can be extremely useful, as nurses, social workers and doctors will all have different ways of viewing and presenting the same material. Their own educational, as well as clinical, experience will give them different insights into the material and examples to illustrate this.

A major problem for staff new to the role of 'teacher' is believing that 'more is better', and trying to cover too much. This can stem from believing that 'a little learning is a dangerous thing', and that something has to be understood 'properly', or the desire to show off their knowledge. This needs to be resisted. The core content of each session is established during training and that should be what the group leader aims to get over clearly. Anything beyond this is a bonus. Ultimately what is important is that relatives have gained information which they understand, which means something in the context of their lives, and which they are capable of using appropriately. They are not students who have to impress examiners with a wealth of detail.

THE STRUCTURE OF THE GROUP

Both relatives and group leaders need reminding of the overall programme and agenda for each session. Questions can be asked during the first 'lecture' part of the session, but substantive discussion points are left for the second half. The time available for the mid-session break is spelt out and a clear starting and finishing time adhered to. Insisting on this might be seen as rigid and formal, but there are good reasons, not least to emphasise that relatives are there to 'work' and it is not a social group. Setting a time limit is fair to everyone and helps keep people to the point and discourages wandering.

Some groups develop a very social 'feel' to them, and leaders need to establish the 'start' of the group both at the beginning and after the break to distinguish this from relatives' socialising. If the accommodation allows, time before or afterwards in which relatives *can* socialise can be a positive addition, but it must be emphasised as that: an *addition*, not part of the group. Some relatives go for a drink after groups and invite the group leader. This should be politely declined, although Christmas (and other major events which are being celebrated) can be exceptions. Even then, group leaders should not stay long. The groups are not social clubs, and despite some relatives' attempts to turn them into this the two aspects must be kept separate.

COMMUNICATION IN THE GROUP

Staff should already have an understanding of communication skills through their professional training. Basic interviewing skills can be used to draw relatives out, including the use of open-ended questions and leaving sufficient time for people to respond. A question-and-answer history-taking mode should be avoided.

Staff should discuss how they will handle questions to which they do not have the answer. This will depend on the nature of the 'ignorance'. For matters of fact, we would advocate a straightforward approach, admitting you do not know. This should, however, be followed with 'but I will find out'. The answer, if there is one, can then be presented the following week. Where it is a matter of opinion regarding interpretation of 'fact' or advice about management issues, then there is nothing wrong with saying that there are a number of views and then stating your preferred option. Where the question has no answer the sensitivity of response is particularly important, and the relative has to be helped to understand not just that there is not an answer, but *why* there is no answer. These questions occur most commonly in relation to the cause of schizophrenia ('why my son?'), or when someone is not responding to medication or other treatment ('there must be something else that can be done'). Acknowledging the emotion which lies behind such questions or statements is the most important part of responding to them.

People are divided in whether jargon should be used in groups. Certainly it should never be used without explanation. Words in common usage in a profession should be explained, as the relatives will almost certainly come across them. A general comment along the lines that everything has its own language and that 'it is easy to forget and slip into this so just ask me if I use a word which is unfamiliar' can help relatives feel more comfortable about asking for an explanation. Relatives should not be overloaded with unnecessary jargon, but an understanding of the language of professionals is another step in reducing feelings of helplessness and powerlessness.

The general level and style of language should suit the educational level of the group. This does not mean 'talking down' or being patronising, but sometimes using shorter rather than longer words and sentences.

Care needs to be taken over the use of certain words and concepts. Relatives are likely to be particularly sensitive to any hint of 'blame'. Group leaders should use the training sessions to discuss how to phrase sensitive ideas and discuss what words should be avoided. The relatives themselves can be included in the process in some instances, for example, how is the person with schizophrenia to be referred to in the group? Relatives will most commonly use 'patient', or 'sufferer', and where they adhere strongly to a medical model may be very reluctant to give up the label 'patient'. The implications of this may need to be discussed; for example, that it labels the whole of the person's existence and puts them in a dependent role. This could be compared, for example, with the objection of some people with schizophrenia to the use of the word 'burden' when this is discussed in the family session. Most relatives seem to be happy with the word 'sufferer', although we have reservations (Atkinson 1993).

Therapists are usually expected to present an emotionally 'neutral' face to clients, and while some responses are inappropriate, to be seen as unresponsive is unhelpful. Group leaders have to cope with some emotionally charged sessions and some very upset people. Whilst leaders should avoid expressing their own distress, it must be made clear that they are aware of, and accept, the distress of others. Statements such as 'I know how you feel . . . ' should be avoided, as relatives are likely to point out, rightly, that the group leader *does not* know how they feel unless they have been in a similar situation. The distinction between sympathy and empathy must be kept in mind. What may be thought of by the group leader as 'neutral' may be viewed by very involved group members as 'uninterested'. Clear statements, verbal and non-verbal, acknowledging acceptance of the relatives' views must be given, and for some groups this may need to be more overtly 'emotional' than others. Cultural (including class) nuances must be understood.

Other aspects of communication are best discussed under the heading of group interactions.

INTERACTIONS WITHIN THE GROUP

A background knowledge of group dynamics is helpful for group leaders, but some topics can be dealt with in training.

Group Discussion

The success of the groups lies, to a large extent, in the quality of the group discussion, and staff must decide on the best way of stimulating this. This means thinking about the purpose of the discussion, including:

- making sure that relatives have understood the content of the session;
- allowing relatives to clarify what has been said;
- giving relatives the opportunity to disagree with what has been said;
- allowing relatives to raise issues that have not been dealt with so far;
- helping relatives to put information in the context of their own circumstances;
- helping relatives to correlate new information with (possibly contradictory) previously held views;
- encouraging relatives to see the practical implications of the information;
- reassuring relatives who might be upset about what they have heard;
- allowing relatives emotional expression about what they have learnt.

Such a list makes it clear that a simple 'free-for-all' or asking 'has anyone got any questions?' and hoping for the best is unlikely to produce the best results.

Relatives should be encouraged to relate the material to their own experiences. This demonstrates the level of their understanding, helps them assimilate it into their personal situation, and also taps into their own beliefs and models of illness. Their experiences, shared among the group, also aid generalisation and are a source of ideas and advice on management which may not have occurred to staff.

Asking relatives to make judgements or evaluations also helps assess how well something has been understood as well as giving the relatives' frame of reference. For example:

- 'On balance, do you think cutting down on medication is worth the risk?'

- 'Is it better to be over-protective and have no independence yourself than to risk your son doing something dangerous/unpleasant/bizarre?'

Since relatives will have different views on these and similar points, a lively discussion is almost guaranteed.

When trying to stimulate discussion, questions that simply require a factual answer and sound as though the leader is setting a test should be avoided. Nor is it enough to simply get back 'parrot-fashion' what has been presented; the discussion must take the information beyond that. This means avoiding the discussion turning into a simple question-and-answer session between the leader and relatives, but encouraging the relatives to talk to one another and ask questions of each other. The break for tea in the middle of the session is an aid to this in the early sessions when some relatives may be reticent. They will speak to one person when they might not speak to the whole group.

Relatives who say little need to be encouraged to take a more active part in discussions. If they seem unduly anxious when invited to contribute, it might be wise to ease back a little or you risk losing them from the group altogether. Some people need a couple of sessions before they feel comfortable about contributing.

Difficult Group Members

Although we must be wary of negatively labelling group members, it would be unrealistic to pretend that some relatives do not cause problems. Probably the most common problem is the person who talks too much. These people often get labelled, at least covertly, high EE. Although this is sometimes the case, it is by no means always so. Some may talk too much at first out of nervousness, but others simply want to tell *their* story, *in full*, and get help, and apparently have little interest in listening to others, learning about things they believe have no relevance to them, or complying with the group's programme. Other people are simply talkative and need dealing with firmly, politely and kindly but, above all, quickly. Group leaders have to learn how to interrupt long monologues to keep the rest of the group involved. They also have to keep the group to the agenda. Pointing out that the topic of the week is diagnosis and details of treatment will be discussed in two weeks time is one ploy. If the story is long and involved the leader can politely interrupt, highlight the problems already mentioned, and suggest that they return to the story later (next week?) so that everyone has a chance to speak. Most members will accept that everyone should have a chance to speak at each session. One time when it may not be appropriate to silence someone is when a relative who has said very little suddenly finds the confidence to speak. This may come out as one long story. The majority of relatives understand that to stop the person talking then may mean they will not speak again, or will leave the group.

Arguments may break out between relatives, but the group leader should prevent these from developing. This is not to say that disagreements are to be avoided. A distinction should be made between differences of opinion, where neither person is really 'right', and disagreements over fact, where one person is definitely wrong. Factual inaccuracies or misinterpretations must be corrected, as tactfully as possible, to prevent other members accepting them. However, it is helpful to try to find out why someone believes what they do, and questions like 'where did you hear that?' can demonstrate how easily something can be misinterpreted. A few relatives may strongly believe a theory thought by others to be erroneous (usually vitamin deficiency), and this can be more of a problem. Spending time arguing with them will be unproductive; they are unlikely to change their mind, a great deal of time can be wasted, and other group members can be left in some confusion as to both the status of that information and also of other information presented by the group leader.

Although differences of opinion are to be expected and can mean that all aspects of an issue are debated, group leaders should prevent disagreement from becoming personal. It is one thing for relatives to disagree about, for example, whether the person with schizophrenia should live at home with the family, on their own or in a hostel, and quite another to say, or even imply, that someone is a bad parent, or uncaring, or not doing their duty because they take a different view. When discussing family responses and EE, relatives should avoid labelling another group member 'hostile' or 'over-protective' in a judgmental fashion.

Disagreements will be heightened if some of the relatives do not like each other, and group leaders will need to stop animosity taking over.

If the group are sitting in a circle or horseshoe, 'confrontational pairs' should not sit opposite each other. To have them on the same side means there is much less opportunity for eye contact, which reduces the expression of hostility.

Some relatives may have health or social service backgrounds. This is not usually a problem unless they choose to set themselves up as an alternative authority to the group leader. The group can then become divided and lack cohesion. Particular difficulties arise when someone with contentious beliefs uses their background to lend weight to their argument. On the other hand, people with health or social work experience can add a great deal to the group.

Although group leaders have to take major responsibility for the style and interaction of the group, this does not rest entirely with them. In a well-functioning group, members will also seek to influence its running and may themselves act to limit the disruptive influence of one group member

GROUP LEADERS' RESPONSE TO THE GROUP

Despite many group leaders having considerable experience of families, working with relatives in a group can bring some surprises and will undoubtedly contribute to their understanding. Professionals should have learnt not to express value judgments, but this can prove more difficult in the apparently informal group situation. A not uncommon expression of despair from relatives is the revelation that they wish their ill relative were dead. This is usually expressed as 'then he/she would be at peace' or even 'We'd all be at peace'. A few relatives may express shock at such feelings, but many more will understand the utter despair which lies behind them. Even if shocked, the group leader has to allow group members to express such feelings and then handle them. The guilt which is likely to accompany them will not be helped by responses of shock or any form of judging.

Group leaders must be vigilant against judging group members against their own value system. Where a value system is introduced, as it may be with hostility or over-protectiveness, this must be made explicit. The value systems surrounding 'normal' family life can be particularly insidious unless monitored. It is helpful if group leaders have some background understanding of family theories and family interactions in general. Class influences what is seen as 'normal' as much as it does communication patterns.

One trap for group leaders is that of being on the defensive. They may to have to bear the brunt of years of accumulated dissatisfaction with the health and social services, and deal with a variety of (possibly unrealistic) demands for 'something to be done'. Leaders may find themselves wanting to defend colleagues/services which they feel 'have done their best'. An overly defensive stand will not only undermine the authority of the group leader, but will be viewed by relatives as not listening to them, or not being interested in their views or experiences, or only being there to maintain the *status quo* and make excuses. In some cases it might be that an explanation of *why* something did or did not happen is appropriate, or why relatives' demands are unlikely to be met, but this follows acknowledgement and understanding of the relatives' views and emotions. Although some relatives might be persuaded to another point of view, most will be unwilling to relinquish their long-, and strongly held, beliefs and leaders must respect this and not persistently argue their point.

This can be difficult, and we reiterate our observation that group leaders should have realistic expectations of what relatives (as well as themselves) will get out of the group. It is not going to convert all relatives to 'right thinking', nor should it aim to. The group is, after all, about education and not brainwashing. It is unlikely to transform people's lives dramatically and instantly, despite some positive effects. Unless a strong sense of realism is maintained, group leaders may find themselves frustrated and angered by the litany of problems, despair and sense of hopelessness they hear from relatives. If they give in to this not only will they suffer, but the group will lose its power and momentum. The leader has to keep the group on course, examine what can be learnt and used positively from the negative stories, and move the group into new areas. Anger at injustice can be channelled into appropriate action to change the system, but this will lie outside the group sessions.

Most group leaders find working in the group a positive and rewarding, if tiring, experience. Support sessions should pick up anyone who is being 'dragged down' by the experience, and steps should be taken to remedy this. Already hard-working, pressurised staff do not need accelerating into burnout through empathy with the relatives' frustration and anger.

MAINTAINING RELATIVES IN GROUPS

Research shows that it can be difficult to get relatives to both engage and remain in a group. Relatives will be more likely to attend if they feel they are getting something they want out of the group. If for no other reason, leaders should be attuned to the needs of relatives; not blindly following their lead, but incorporating their wishes, as far as possible. One question, for example, is whether relatives are allowed to discuss issues as and when they want. If this happens the logical sequencing of the sessions is lost and the group can deteriorate into little more than moaning sessions. Despite relatives being happy to have this freedom for a while, it can quickly pall. They will start to feel that the group is going nowhere, they are getting nothing out of it, and that it is, ultimately, a dispiriting and disheartening experience. Group leaders must, therefore, lead the discussion onto more positive and practical matters and make sure that the sessions always end on a positive note. It can be helpful to ask, towards the end of the session, 'does anyone feel worse than when they arrived?' If someone is particularly upset, this gives the opportunity of dealing with this before they leave.

It goes without saying that leaders should be on time, and be well organised, consistent and generally positive. Relatives who feel they have been badly treated in the past may be particularly sensitive to being 'messed about' in poorly run groups. A well-organised service is not just efficient, but demonstrates respect for the members.

Some relatives may find travelling to the group difficult and, where practical, lifts can be arranged between members. If the group leader offers lifts they need to take care that this is not seen as 'favouritism', and that the member involved does not use it as an opportunity for individual 'therapy'.

THE GROUP SESSIONS

We now outline issues and common problems for each session. The handouts in Appendix 2 should be read in conjunction with the following comments. At the end of each session we give some problem scenarios from past groups which can be worked through as preparation.

Session 1: What Does Schizophrenia Mean to You?

This is an introductory session to remind relatives of the purpose of the groups, and let them express their feelings and outline their problems. It can seem informal and 'free-and easy', but for that very reason needs careful planning. The leader must ensure that the aims of the group are conveyed to members and the group rules set and accepted. Relatives need to understand that the group is not about solving their individual problems, or providing them with new clinical services. Relatives must be encouraged to be realistic from the outset, not just insofar as the goals of the group are concerned, but also in what they can expect from themselves, from other family members, and from the person with schizophrenia. Relatives' response to this, what they might interpret as 'taking away hope', will depend on a number of factors, including their coping style and the extent to which they have adapted to their relative's illness.

The confidential nature of the group must be stressed. Relatives have been known to pass on information about individuals/families to other involved parties, believing they were being helpful. It must be clear that repeating anything outside the group is unacceptable.

Establishing the 'work' atmosphere can be difficult in this first session, but leaders who have problems with this at the beginning find the group difficult from then on. Everyone should be encouraged to speak, but in order to prevent the session ending on a negative note, with everyone depressed not just by their own stories but also by the stories of others, the group leader should, as a summary, highlight the positive aspects of the group, explain where it is going, and confirm the agenda for the next session.

Problem scenarios

1. As the group is about to start a mother arrives, and joins the circle of relatives placing a large wok on the ground in front of her. She announces in a loud voice, directed to the group leader, 'I've got to

leave 15 minutes early, love, to get to my Chinese cookery evening class'.

2. The group has been very talkative, to the extent that the group leader has had difficulty even explaining the purpose of the group. The discussion has ranged wide, covering not just the problems of living with someone with schizophrenia, but other family and local problems. As the group is packing up, a number of women are talking together. One of them turns to the group leader and says 'You bring the coffee next week, son, and we'll bake the cakes.'

Session 2: What is Schizophrenia?

The first task of this session is to restate (or regain control of) the structure of the group. After the 'free-for-all' of the previous session, relatives may be reluctant to be kept to a specific topic and group leaders must be firm, but sympathetic, in maintaining this.

The aims of this session are to help relatives understand the nature, complexity and variability of symptoms. Group members will describe their relatives' behaviour and symptoms, and this must be related both to a global picture of schizophrenia and to the relatives of other group members. Violence and aggression will almost certainly be raised, and questions asked about whether everyone with schizophrenia becomes violent. If there has been anything in the media recently about 'a schizophrenic' (sic) attacking someone, this could take over the discussion. The distinction between laziness and apathy usually brings forth a lot of comments about disagreements in the family over this.

A secondary aim is to explore the need for diagnosis, its procedure, complexity, fallibility and relationship to treatment. Some relatives will complain that they were never given a diagnosis or they were not given one soon enough. Less common is the complaint of being given a diagnosis too quickly; usually related to seeing a diagnosis of schizophrenia as 'taking away any hope'.

Problem scenarios

1. Despite your best endeavours to describe the process of diagnosis, one mother still insists that her son has never been properly diagnosed.

2. A father refuses to accept that his son does not have control over all his behaviour and that he would be alright 'if he got off his backside and found himself a job'.

Session 3: Why?

This is a popular session as relatives struggle to make sense of what has happened. Even if they have talked through treatment with professionals in the past, most have not had the opportunity to discuss causes. It is the wider issues of 'why has this happened?' which should take up most of the discussion, rather than details of brain imaging technology or neurotransmitters. In their search after meaning, relatives will go back in their child's history to discover things that happened to him or her and not to siblings to explain 'why this child' and not another. These explanations might be straightforward, if misguided: 'he fell out of tree when he was eight. Could that have anything to do with it?'; or things that hint at wider family problems: 'his father has never believed that he was his son. He's always ignored him. Could that have been it?'

The genetics of schizophrenia will usually bring forth two types of response and the group may focus on either. The first is the 'risk' element, the likelihood of other siblings developing the illness or the risk of siblings, or possibly the person with schizophrenia, having offspring who might develop schizophrenia. Relatives must be helped to assess the risks involved realistically, particularly in the light of some media reporting. Reassurance can come in a variety of guises. One example, used by the person involved, is a psychiatrist who has a parent with schizophrenia but who also has a young family. This person's willingness 'to take the risk', as it is seen, is especially comforting and reassuring.

The second, less common, scenario finds the group getting bogged down in blame: the 'it's not my side of the family' argument. Such comments are unhelpful, and leaders should avoid getting caught up in them. As in the search-after-meaning explanations which describe long-standing family problems, leaders must avoid getting into 'therapeutic-type' discussions, or even too much personal history.

Environmental and family factors will be raised, but much of the discussion can be left for later sessions.

The biggest problem is not the complexity of the information (relatives will make explicit how much detail they actually want), but the spectre of 'alternative' theories. Often someone knows something about vitamin deficiency or food allergies and will advocate diet and megavitamins. They may be using this with their own relative or know of someone who does, apparently successfully. Simply pointing out that the session is about cause and not treatment will not be enough to squash discussion, but may give the leader time to find out more information and marshal their arguments if this has not been done before.

Problem scenarios

1. A parent becomes agitated at what they see as possible signs of schizophrenia in a younger child. There is at least one person with schizophrenia in an older generation and the genetic arguments seem compelling. They become very upset at the thought of another child developing schizophrenia and express doubts about their ability to cope.

2. A group member launches into a description of the work on vitamins. As group leader you express some doubts about the veracity of this work. The group member then challenges you, very personally, suggesting that you have a closed mind, are bigoted and prejudiced, and have a vested interest in keeping to the traditional medical model to keep your job.

Session 4: Treatment of Schizophrenia

Drugs will be the major topic of this session, and relatives appreciate a clear and undramatic account of the different drugs, what they do, what the side effects are, and the pros and cons of long-term medication. This inevitably means discussing prognosis in general, and other forms of social and behavioural therapies. It is useful to outline these before a discussion of the details of medication, as treatment needs to be looked at as a whole. Group members will want to discuss relatives who refuse medication and to know what can be done. 'Compelling' people to take medication will be raised, along with concerns about lack of services in the community and the decline in hospital beds. The latter issues may contribute to a more general discussion on community care and the pressures put on relatives to be carers. This is best left to the following session. Compulsory treatment may also require discussion, and can be returned to in Session 9 along with crisis management.

People who are unhappy with diagnosis and/or treatment are entitled to a second opinion. Why this might be appropriate and how to get one are explained. However, it is worth exploring whether second opinions have been sought before, and whether, at the heart of this, is an unrealistic quest for a 'cure', or at least 'an answer'.

If diet and vitamins came up in the previous session they will come up again now. Hopefully, the leader has done the appropriate homework.

Hypnosis is also raised reasonably often, usually in connection with delusions, with the argument 'why can't they be hypnotised not to believe this?' This requires going back to the explanation about delusions and then describing the limitations of hypnosis. The availability of psychotherapy and psychoanalysis may be raised. Allied to this might be mentioned courses which offer to 'improve your self-confidence'. The pros and cons of private treatment should be discussed *in general* before moving on to specific therapies. Do relatives believe they will see 'better' therapists privately, or are they looking for therapies which are not available on the NHS? The financial implications must be made explicit, and it is important that those with financial constraints do not feel they are denying their relative something which might be of benefit through lack of money.

Problem scenarios

1. A mother expresses concern that her daughter does not take her medication regularly and relapses as a consequence. The mother has resorted to crushing tablets and adding them to her daughter's food. She wants confirmation that this is acceptable. Others express an interest in this method of dealing with similar problems. Ideally she would like her daughter to be legally forced to accept medication.

2. A father says he 'doesn't hold with all these drugs' and accepts continuing symptoms and the risk of relapse. He is at work all day

and it is his wife (who does not come to the group because they don't like to leave their son alone) who bears the brunt of their son's behaviour.

3. A mother complains about Dr. MacX who only sees her son for 10 minutes every few months, does not see him at his worst, will not believe her descriptions of her son's unacceptable behaviour, avoids meeting her and has told her she is 'hysterical' and 'adding to the problem'.

Session 5: Relatives' Problems

The group leader's aim for this session, modified in the light of relatives' wishes, should, nevertheless, prevent it becoming a moaning session. One aim might be to get relatives to move from simply recounting to considering their and others' coping strategies and what they might do to improve their situation. The group leader must keep relatives talking about *their* problems rather than the problems of the person with schizophrenia. Since spouses/partners, siblings or offspring of people with schizophrenia will be in a small minority, if any are in the group it is particularly important that their different perspective is addressed, and not ignored in favour of the more numerous parental view.

This session does not usually cause any major problems for leaders as previous discussion makes it unlikely that anything completely unexpected will be raised, although it is this session in which relatives may admit to wishing their child dead. It is helpful, however, if group leaders open the discussion by mentioning the distinction between objective and subjective burden, and that the latter does not depend on the former. This can legitimise feelings which relatives may otherwise be reluctant to express. The 'normalising' of emotions is vital to this session.

The areas to watch are one person taking over the discussion, or a relative becoming very upset as they describe their situation, and finding it difficult to regain control. Where family friction is described, care should be taken not to lay the blame at the door of whoever is absent, nor to start developing the discussion along the lines of family therapy.

Problem scenarios

1. Group members seem to be trying to out-do each other to describe how 'self-sacrificing' they are and how bad the problems are at home.

2. The group seems to be pushing one member into the role of scape-goat for 'not caring enough'.

Session 6: The Family and Schizophrenia

This is potentially one of the more difficult sessions as the group leader moves into the area of family dynamics and the potential role of relatives in relapse. Emotions will run high, particularly if relatives feel they are in any way being blamed. Although the main thrust of the session is to explain expressed emotion and possible changes in family functioning which might contribute to lower relapse rates, it might be necessary to refer to some of the earlier family theories if only to refute them or put them in context. Neither the leader nor members should become over-defensive, and everyone should contribute. Relatives should not be put in a position where they have to justify their behaviour as a way of justifying themselves. This does not mean, however, that different coping strategies will not be addressed and some be seen as more appropriate than others. Over-protectiveness, in particular, needs to be seen through the eyes of the relatives who display it if they are to be encouraged to see how it may be less than helpful.

The focus of the session, however, is what sort of response family members have to the person with schizophrenia, rather than how this can be changed, which comes in the following session. Relatives may see problematic behaviours in others but not in themselves, and sufficient time needs to be given to exploring both the behaviour and the reasons people give when justifying it. The possibly fluctuating nature of EE means that relatives must consider their behaviour over time and in relation to different situations. Asking the group to respond to a member's description of problem behaviour, ('what would you have done?', 'how would you handle that?') can encourage them to think about their behaviour outside their own setting, and bring out different responses.

Group leaders will be tempted (privately) to label relatives low or high EE. It should be remembered that only a small percentage will be high EE. Pre-judging relatives on this topic is to be avoided. It is easy to label what may be seen as less desirable traits, for example, over-talkativeness, as high EE.

Problem scenarios

1. You have privately identified a mother as high EE and showing signs of over-protectiveness. There appears to be some justification for this, as in the past the person with schizophrenia has been unable to manage money and ran up a number of debts which the family had to pay and could not easily afford. She uses this as a reason for her continuing overprotectiveness and is unwilling to see any other point of view.

2. The group becomes very hostile to you as leader, and accuses you of blaming them for causing schizophrenia (or at least perpetuating it), not understanding their position, and speaking from ignorance because 'you are not a relative and don't live with it'.

Session 7: Creating a Low-stress Environment

This session should move beyond EE to look at other expressions of stress-related behaviours and coping skills. The group leader needs a fairly comprehensive view of stress and management techniques, and to be able to distinguish the appropriateness of a problem-solving or cognitive–emotional approach. Managing stress is about creating a low-stress environment, not just for the person with schizophrenia, but also for other family members. Included in this is exploring relatives' responses and helping them see where they have choices. The limitations as well as the possible unfairness of the 'you made me . . . ' approach need analysing, along with how relatives might move to taking responsibility for their behaviour and emotions. Again it is important not to make this sound like one more thing relatives are being blamed for. Nor should it be seen as saying that relatives do not have a right to be angry, bitter or frustrated, but that what they do with these feelings is up to them. Along with this will come a discussion of *whose* problem certain behaviours are. This may spark a discussion on the comparative rights of relatives/carers versus people with schizophrenia/ patients. Aspects of this discussion will be continued in the following session.

Problem scenarios

1. Group members have very different views on how much latitude having schizophrenia allows someone, and what should be tolerated and what is unacceptable. The group looks as though it might become polarised into two factions and feelings are getting out of hand.

2. One mother has been identified by the group as being very overprotective but she cannot see it. The group seems determined to make her see the 'error of her ways'.

Session 8: Managing Disturbed Behaviour

This session deals with specific issues raised by the relatives, particularly problems which have not been covered elsewhere. Most common are violence and aggression, the use of alcohol and 'street drugs', the management of acute symptoms ('when he talks to the voices, what should we do?'; 'should we try and talk her out of her delusions?'), and the more chronic, negative symptoms, including apathy, lack of motivation, day–night reversal, isolation and loneliness.

Relatives have been demanding advice for specific management issues for some time, and the group leader may have to acknowledge that this has not been forthcoming. Group leaders have often built up considerable expertise in managing disturbed, difficult behaviour. These skills need to be translated into working in the community and helping relatives deal with such problems. This may not happen if staff do not see the community, specifically the home, as their responsibility, or do not see their strategies as appropriate for relatives. If this is the case, leaders should ask themselves why.

There is the possibility of relatives hearing about very difficult and distressing problems from others, and worrying about their relative developing similar problems. The realistic possibility of this happening, or not, must be addressed.

Sexuality and its expression is less likely to be discussed in the group than other problems. The group leader will need to decide how, or if, this topic is to be raised, or whether they are prepared to speak to people individually about it where there seems to be a problem.

Problem scenarios

1. A mother describes her son's behaviour which led to him being detained in a State Hospital for some time. He is now at home, although his behaviour causes some problems. Another mother, whose son has not shown any similar tendencies, becomes very upset, both at the story and at the possibility that her son will develop similar violent behaviours.

2. Certain group members insist on having 'answers' or solutions to management problems to which the group leader can see no solution.

Session 9: Using Services and Dealing with Crises

The aim is to help relatives understand the system and to make better use of services. Relatives will describe problems in getting help when they need it, especially at times of acute crisis or in the early stages of relapse. The discussion may produce novel ideas of how to engage local services. This session needs to be tailored to the local situation, not least in respect to crisis management and intervention services. It is also another of the sessions where the leader needs to guard against becoming over-defensive.

If the group is interested, rights under the Mental Health Act as well as the different types of sections which can be used to hold and treat patients can be outlined. They should also be given information about the various statutory bodies which are there to protect patients' rights and how these can be accessed. Mention of various voluntary organisations and details of local contacts should also be given.

Problem scenarios

1. Everyone in the group agrees that getting appropriate help at time of crisis is impossible. Everything the group leader suggests is

refuted or laughed at as unrealistic, seen as impossible, or told simply does not work.

Session 10: Where Do We Go from Here?

This session summarises the main points, deals with anything new and, hopefully, leaves the relatives feeling more positive. It is important that the end of the group is handled sensitively, and that relatives do not feel they have been abandoned. If the leader is to remain a contact point for relatives, the practicalities of this, including exactly what the remit is, should be explained.

Problem scenarios

1. The group strongly resists the idea of stopping and tries to persuade the group leader to continue.

10

THE ETHICS, VALUES AND POLITICS OF CARING

Setting up educational groups for people with schizophrenia does not happen in isolation, nor separate from other services, nor apart from the needs and views of both people with schizophrenia and their relatives, nor apart from the attitudes and constraints of a wider society. There are no value-free policy makers, no value-free staff, no value-free interventions. As we have seen throughout this book, the development of services for relatives, of which education groups are only a small part, involves different clinical views of causation and correlation, different social policy views of relatives' duty, and different philosophical views about the utility of knowledge.

There are ethical and political issues which frequently get side-stepped as people under pressure tackle practical, day-to-day provision of care. The awareness that decisions are influenced by political, ethical and value judgments is, if not ignored, allowed to take a back seat. Although we are predominantly concerned with groups for relatives, many of the issues in this chapter are of relevance to the wider development of services and inter-agency relationships. Very often the consideration of services and the treatment (in the broadest sense) of those who use such services (also in the broadest sense) starts from the position of the individual's rights, and this is where we, too, will begin.

RIGHTS VERSUS ENTITLEMENTS

Issues surrounding rights are raised at many different levels. Legal safeguards to protect patients are enshrined in the Mental Health Laws of different countries, there are independent, statutory organisations such as the Mental Health Act Commission and the Mental Welfare Commission, and there are various independent voluntary organisations which promote rights and advocacy, such as MIND. Such concerns have a substantial history.

It was the report of the Metropolitan Commissioners in Lunacy in 1844, chaired by Lord Ashley (later Earl of Shaftesbury), that led to the first comprehensive mental health law in Britain: the Lunatics Act of 1845. One provision of the Act was the setting up of a powerful national body, the Lunacy Commission. It was made up of five lay members (who included Lord Ashley in the chair), three medical commissioners and three legal commissioners. The commission had jurisdiction over the whole country, their remit extending to private madhouses as well as the county asylums.

However, during the 1860s and 1870s there was concern among the general public about the lunacy laws and asylums. Shaftesbury and the asylum doctors argued, then as now, that what was most important was not changes in the law, but greater public support, as well as better staff and training for them. The spread of the disquiet was aided by the popularity of the first cheap newspapers and the desire, again then as now, for the reporting of sensational stories. Amid this unease was founded the Alleged Lunatics' Friend Society. The group counted among its members former asylum patients as well as members of the establishment. The Society was less concerned with the welfare of lunatics who were incarcerated, than with preventing people being committed to asylums. Their particular campaign was for the mandatory two medical certificates to be supplemented by a magistrate's order before a patient could be detained (Jones 1991).

It was not until the Lunacy Acts Amendment Bill of 1889 (five years after the death of Lord Shaftesbury) that the safeguards wanted by the legal profession were introduced, against medical opinion. The doctors believed that such measures would delay treatment and deter patients from seeking treatment. Their preferred option was to move to greater informality, so that treatment could be given earlier and on an informal (i.e. not legally detained) basis. It was not until the law of 1930 that the mass of legal technicalities and red tape was swept away, allowing most patients to enter hospital on a voluntary basis.

Although a gap between legal rights and moral rights can lead to a variety of interpretations about the way people should be treated and services delivered, there is general agreement that patient autonomy is central and interacts with precepts such as paternalism, confidentiality, informed consent and the right to refuse treatment (Atkinson 1991). Legal rights, in many instances, are best seen as entitlements, and that is usually what is meant when either a patient or their relative says they have a 'right' to a particular treatment. The person is, in their view, entitled to it.

Relatives' rights, however, are not incorporated in law and are very vague to most professionals. The rights of individuals within a family are highlighted when considering family therapy. Who is the client? 'The family' as an entity is not the client, for the 'family cannot speak' (Carpenter 1987). Assumptions about norms in families are made, and herein lies the central dilemma. There is much greater agreement about the roles and rights of parents and children who are minors, than there is about parents and adult children.

Autonomy might be accepted as the guiding principle which applies to any person, but this often sits uneasily with what is expected of relatives as carers. It is not simply a matter of establishing what might be considered relatives' rights, but examining the relationship between the rights of the patient and the rights of the relative. Unfortunately, these are all too often in conflict—what is best for the patient may not be best for the relative, and *vice versa*. We need to look at how what are seen as the basic rights of patients affect relatives, and the provision of services to relatives.

AUTONOMY

The principle of respect for the autonomous person, whether this is oneself or another, can be seen as the overarching ethical principle upon which all others are based. To be autonomous means being able to choose for oneself, this choice operating through selfdetermination and self-government. The distinction between the two can, at times, appear subtle. To be self-determining, individuals must be able to formulate, and then carry out, their own plans, desires, wishes and policies. Through this they are able to determine their course in life. To be able to both formulate and then carry out the choices made demands a

certain mental and physical capacity. Where autonomy is valued, that
society will seek to maximise both the choices and the individual's
ability to make such choices.

Self-government means that individuals are able to govern their life,
or make their choices, within their own rules and values. Such rules
and values may proscribe certain desires held by the individual, producing conflict. This is commonly seen in the dilemma between short-
term desires and goals (and thus autonomous choices) and their
potential damage to long-term choices (or autonomy).

Clearly, in no society does any individual have full autonomy; at the
very least political and social restraints limit choice. Within such limitations, however, we do expect people to be able to exercise choice over
lifestyle, religious, philosophical and political beliefs, practices and
organisations, work, housing, travel and migration, education and
relationships. For autonomy to be genuine within a society there needs
to be equal access to resources.

The autonomy of the individual in the role of patient is upheld by,
amongst other safeguards, the principle of informed consent and the
right to refuse treatment. Such practical issues can uphold other, more
intangible, rights such as the 'right to know'. Why is the right to know
important? It assumes that knowing is, or is thought to be, 'a good
thing'. Or is it the *right* to knowledge that is a good thing? Is it because
it is in the interests of the individual to have information pertaining to
themselves and their condition, or because a society where people are
given information about themselves (that is, told the truth) is better
than one where the truth is concealed? This holds just as true for the
individual as 'carer' as for the 'patient'.

PATERNALISM

It is almost inevitable that when discussing autonomy, paternalism will
be raised since it is often invoked as a legitimate reason to breach an
individual's autonomy. The argument, used as being the principle of
beneficence when acting on another's behalf, in their best interest, to
prevent self-harm or exploitation, is clearly seen in examples of patient
care. Mental Health Laws exist to legalise paternalism, but also to limit
its use. There are those who oppose paternalism in all its forms, holding

autonomy to be of higher value. John Stuart Mill (1859), for example, believed that paternalistic behaviour could only ever be justified to prevent harm to others, not for a person's own good. He excludes from his argument, however, not only children but also 'those who are still in a state to require being taken care of'.

AUTONOMY, PATERNALISM AND CARING

It should not be surprising that carers, both professional and informal, frequently have a strong allegiance to the principles of beneficence and non-malfeasance in preference to autonomy. It has been suggested that 'an exaggerated regard' for autonomy might put at risk the doctor–patient relationship, since it is a doctor's duty to do their best for individual patients, 'not just to provide a list of alternatives from which the patient (now the consumer) select according to their needs and desires' (Baum *et al.* 1989). The aim of any treatment, however, is normally to restore the individual to health, and thus greater autonomy.

The relationship between a patient and doctor, or other professional, is very different to that between family members, even where one of them is considered to be 'ill'. Ties of kinship motivate relatives in their caring role. Thus, voluntary workers are more like professionals and fall into the formal caring group for, although not paid but motivated by altruism, this is directed to people they do not know, rather than developing from a pre-existing relationship.

Innovations in service delivery, such as brokerage, aim to maximise a patient's autonomy by putting them at the centre of the decision-making process, as does the discharge policy and the care programme approach. Despite public rhetoric regarding consumer choice, there is little evidence of this. There is no mention made of relatives' right to choose whether or not they want to take on the role of carer. As 'carers', the individuals appear to have lost their right to autonomy. The closest the British Government comes to acknowledging that there is even a choice to be made, is in the first chapter of *Caring for People*:

> 'The decision to take on a caring role is never an easy one. However, many people make that choice and it is right that they should be able to play their part in looking after those close to them.' (paragraph 1.9)

That some discharge protocols *do* include consulting relatives is to be welcomed, but it is not a legal right.

Paternalism is more likely to be seen as a problem by patients than by relatives. Most restrictions on the latter's freedom come from lack of other alternatives, in respect of lack of provision of services, rather than imposed choices 'for their own good'. This might not be the case, though, when the carer is put into the role of carer-as-client. Inevitably, the relative-as-carer is more likely to be viewed as a source of paternalistic behaviour. Although we expect parents to act in the best interests of their children, the extent to which we expect them to exert control (or even influence) will depend largely on the age of the child, but also takes into account Mill's difficult concept of those still requiring care. The more formal the role of relative-as-carer becomes, the more difficult it will be to distinguish between 'normal' paternal behaviour of parent-as-parent and extended paternal behaviour of parent-as-carer. This is important, both because it is generally assumed that we should be promoting autonomy in patients/clients, and because of the different views of 'best interest' that exist. 'Killing with kindness' is a well-understood concept except by the people who practice it. The over-protection and over-intrusiveness which can be part of high EE may be seen by the relative as acting in their 'ill' relative's best interest, although seen objectively it may contribute to relapse in that person.

This may be further complicated by gender issues. Women are more likely than men to be socialised; to value relationships in preference to autonomy (Eichenbaum and Orbach 1983). If autonomy is experienced as a rejection of others, whether this is to specific needs or a generalised sense of other, it will consequently be less valued than a caring relationship. Such a relationship, in turn, may be viewed by others as paternalistic or over-protective.

These differences in respect to autonomy and paternalism may show themselves in the positions taken by voluntary groups with a membership predominantly of users, compared to groups which are predominantly relatives. The latter more frequently want to see the law changed, or interpreted to expand the concept of self-harm, so that people who, for example, stop taking their medication can be compelled to do so, or people who apparently choose to live a nomadic, possibly vagrant, life can be compelled to live in a designated place, not necessarily hospital.

The challenge to balance paternalism against autonomy is both difficult to meet and ultimately subjective. Issues may be seen more clearly the more distanced one is from the situation, and its consequences. Thus relatives frequently complain that unless someone has lived with a person with schizophrenia, they do not fully understand how demanding, how limiting, how frustrating or how tiring this can be. While this is almost certainly true, distance may make it easier to see and develop the two sides of an issue. Although decision-making may be no more comfortable, it often helps to set out both sides in discussions with the family, and openly acknowledge that sometimes the rights of one side (or what is best for them) are seen as an infringement of the rights of the other (or limiting their choices to what they think is best).

In most instances patients' rights take, or are expected to take, precedence over carers' rights. Relatives may well voluntarily give up some of their rights, their autonomy, when they take on a caring role. This is no excuse, though, for services then acting as though they have no rights at all, or as though they are always secondary. Maybe the providers of services feel, as Kant observed, that we cannot be sure a person is acting out of a sense of duty if (considerable) benefit is to be gained from being dutiful.

CONFIDENTIALITY

The Hippocratic Oath makes the concept of confidentiality explicit, and it is accepted as fundamental, and central, to the doctor–patient relationship. Although not usually explicitly discussed with the patient, it is taken for granted that information will be shared with the multi-disciplinary therapeutic team. The rationale behind the sharing of such information is that it is 'in the patient's best interests'.

Relatives, even in a primary caring role, are not formal members of the multi-disciplinary team and their right to information about the patient is a cause of much confusion and frustration. Where relatives are primary carers, they may argue (rightly?) that to do their 'job' well they require access to information about the patient. This may include not just diagnosis, but also information on medication, current and future treatment plans, and the management of problem behaviours. The person with schizophrenia is in a 'patient' relationship (and all that implies) with team members, but is not a 'patient' to his or her relative. Although the giving, or exchange, of information often goes along with

planning treatment or aftercare, and relatives usually want to be involved in that, it would be perfectly possible to give relatives information and still not involve then in any decision-making process. It is
thus important to keep separate the issues of confidentiality and right
to knowledge, and involvement in decision-making.

Another area where relatives usually expect to be informed is when the
patient's behaviour will affect them. Patients who are harbouring
violent thoughts or feelings about their family might be construed as
dangerous, and danger to others is usually taken as the major exception
to the principle of confidentiality (Dyer 1989). This is not always the
case. Different countries and States apply different rules and at different times. Not all mental health professionals accept dangerousness as
a reason for breaching confidentiality, and see it as using psychiatry as
an agent of social control (Gurevitz 1977), or impractical as psychiatrists are not good at predicting dangerousness (Roth and Meisel 1977).
Relatives may also expect to be informed if there is any reason to believe
that the patient is a danger to themselves, particularly if they are at risk
of suicide.

The decision to disclose information to relatives is one of individual
opinion and conscience. Some clearly do not see any problem in
discussing the patient and his or her management with relatives, and,
indeed, believe that it is their duty so to do. Others are more reticent.
Although they may legitimately be concerned about breaking the trust
of the doctor–patient relationship, confidentiality may also be used as
an excuse not to confront potentially difficult or time-consuming situations (Atkinson 1989).

One practical solution is to ask the patient's permission to disclose
relevant information and discuss what this encompasses. When offering education groups to relatives, we approached the patients first to
obtain their permission. The patient may also be encouraged to share
information and take on the role of giving information. The problem
arises when either the patient refuses consent for information disclo-
sure or even to allow relatives to meet members of the multi-disciplinary team, or when relatives are suspicious (with good cause or not)
of the person with schizophrenia conveying information honestly or
accurately.

It is not enough at this point to shrug one's shoulders, point to the
binding principal of confidentiality, and say that nothing can be done

(Atkinson and Coia 1989). Professionals and services have a responsibility to carers almost as much as to patients. Ways of giving information have to be found which do not breach confidentiality. One alternative would be to remove the responsibility of care from the relative by putting other care arrangements in place, including housing.

People with long-term health problems or disabilities of any kind may have to accept that if they live with their parents, or other relatives, then these relatives will be treated as carers by the authorities, whether those involved agree or not. Also, that living with these people does give them some rights to information regarding both condition, prognosis and treatment plans. Another dilemma arises when the person with schizophrenia is living with parents because there is nowhere else to go. To insist that parents then have access to information may be viewed by a patient as adding insult to injury.

Adult children, whether living voluntarily or not with their parents, still have the right to be treated as adults. Giving information about them to parents could be seen as keeping them in a 'child' role and limiting their autonomy. Such an argument would also suggest that it might increase the person's dependency. Since most treatment/rehabilitation programmes aim to promote independence, the role of the relative as 'supervisor' must be used with extreme caution.

However, there are ways of giving information which do not breach confidentiality (Atkinson and Coia 1989). These include using staff to run groups who are not involved with the patient and who thus cannot divulge confidential information because they have none. Concentrating education on 'schizophrenia' and the relatives' personal views and understanding of this, rather than on 'your relative', may also ease the minds of people with schizophrenia who feel their rights are being denied them. Self-help groups, relatives' groups run by other organisations, and groups run as evening classes all take the giving of information away from the relationship between patient and doctor, or other professional, and thus relieve the burden of confidentiality. Relatives could refer themselves to the service, and patients need not be involved in the process at all. Even where a group is run by either the health or the social service, referral could be from relatives themselves. If they are not approached formally by the service, there would be no need to obtain the patient's permission. Of course, to be involved at all in education the relatives have to have been told the diagnosis, as does the patient (Atkinson 1989).

Although relatives themselves are most likely to point to their right to know as a reflection of their role as carer, other aspects of information may be equally important to them. One of these is where there are genetic implications of a condition. In Huntington's chorea, for example, the genetic link is undisputed, and may affect offspring's decisions about having children. In schizophrenia, our knowledge about genetic links is much less and issues are not clear cut. This does not mean that family members, siblings in particular, might not be concerned and need to explore the implications of their relative's illness for themselves and prospective offspring.

One aspect that they may be less willing to consider, but which does inform many educational packages, is the family's role in the maintenance of illness and the relapse process. It is assumed that the functional knowledge given to relatives allows them to change their way of relating to the person with schizophrenia and thus reduce 'harm'. To justify this approach, however, it needs to be demonstrated that knowledge and behaviour change are related.

The dilemma between protecting patients' rights of confidentiality and the relatives' need for information can be overcome if the desire to do so is there. The justification to breach confidentiality, when or if this happens, is usually made on the grounds that it is 'in the patient's best interest', whether the outcome for the patient is direct or indirect. Another argument would follow a broadly utilitarian approach. The care of people with schizophrenia in the community rests predominantly on relatives, and such care carries a burden. Thus, to reduce this burden, services to carers, including knowledge, must be given, and this 'good' outweighs any negative feelings patients might have about such an infringement of confidentiality.

GENDER ISSUES

A recurrent theme throughout the literature on carers is gender and care. Government rhetoric assumes that it is women who are, and who will be, carers. It is the natural order of things. Historically women have been dependants on men, and this was enshrined in the Beveridge

Report (1942) which laid down the blueprint for Britain's social welfare system based on an idealistic, possibly sentimental, view of the equal relationship of partners in a marriage.

Gender and Family Therapy

Hopefully not just those who would call themselves feminists might now take issue with some of the earlier descriptions from family therapy of the 'normal' and 'healthy' executive subsystem of a family which assumes a dominant male. It is as though family therapists had taken 'a snapshot of white middle-class family life in the '50s and mistaken it for a Platonic model of family structure' (Golder 1985). Walrond-Skynner (1987) suggests that it is 'remarkable', although we may wish to substitute 'worrying', that 'family therapists have appeared to be so untouched by the feminist movement'. The role of women needs to be addressed by clinicians as well as policy makers, and by both in the historical context of their social and economic position.

Family dynamic theories of schizophrenia have tended to focus more on mothers than on fathers, usually with the rationale that mothers are more involved in the child's upbringing. Mothers, usually the route through which families enter therapy and the mainstay of that therapy (Walrond-Skynner 1987), are still often described as 'over-involved' (Carpenter 1987). Although this is not identical with the concept of over-involvement in EE, there are similar resonances. There is a general trend for mothers to be viewed by adult children as having been warmer and more protective, both among 'normal' children (Perris *et al.* 1985) and among people with schizophrenia (Khalil and Stark 1992; McCreadie *et al.* 1994a). From both a historical and a current perspective, women (mothers) are seen as the person who, on a daily basis, keeps the family together and organises them, as well as keeping them in therapy. We were very aware of using mothers to put us in touch with other relatives and generally to persuade family members of the value of education groups.

How, then, are such people expected to deal with the paradoxical communications which demand that they are less 'over-involved' and less 'over-protective' while at the same time expecting them to attend groups, keep other family members involved, supervise medication, and generally act as a carer to the patient. That some mothers can do this *without* becoming 'over-involved', particularly if they have given up employment to take on this role, should be seen as remarkable rather than conveying covert blame to those who do not achieve this ideal. The assumptions which underlie family therapy and feminism come into conflict. Family therapists believe that it is the functioning of the family as a whole, as a *system*, which leads to family dysfunction and is thus the focus of treatment. Feminist theory, however, contends that there is an imbalance of power between men and women, in the family no less than in society. How services will be developed depends on the individual's position on these issues.

Gender and Caring

A similar dichotomy exists in relation to women as carers. On the one hand, this role is the taken-for-granted view and set against it is an approach which concentrates on the division of labour which puts women under pressure to take responsibility for others, maintains them in the private rather than the public sphere, and limits their access to resources and thus to independence.

The difference in attitudes between men and women regarding caring and family responsibilities has focused predominantly on care of the elderly. Women are expected to assume caring responsibilities, but the motivations of men and women differ (Ungerson 1987). Women, by and large, feel duty, obligation and a sense of guilt. Men are more likely to explain their motives in terms of love. Women feel they have no choice. Men, on the other hand, frequently see themselves taking on the caring role as a conscious choice, and thus can experience satisfaction from making this choice. One of the sad things about the obligation put on women is not just that the element of choice is removed, but with it the pleasure derived from willingly taking on the caring role.

Women take on the greater responsibilities for caring for all 'dependent' groups (Green 1988), but their over-representation does not stop there. Women are also over-represented in the low-paid caring jobs in statutory and private caring agencies (Finch and Groves 1980; Langan and Ostner 1991). This is not to deny that there are substantial numbers of men caring for elderly people (predominantly husbands caring for wives). However, the number of men caring for other groups is unclear, and the general picture in psychiatry is again of a predominantly female carer group.

THE DUTY OF CARE

Caring should be an active choice, but all too often is passive, the result of pressures exerted on the individual. There is an assumption that relatives *will* care for ill family members, that it is their duty. The decision *not* to act as a carer can thus be difficult in the face of a disapproving society. The decision to be a carer may never be made explicit; the role is taken for granted by services, relatives, the 'carer' and the 'cared for'. It should be noted, however, that there are no legal definitions of responsibilities between adult kin in Britain, and there have not been since the abolition of the Poor Law in 1948. Previously, there was a legal expectation that children would financially assist their parents if necessary, and that grandparents as well as parents were responsible for the support of minors.

The Conservative Government in Britain has made explicit the assumption that it is the family's responsibility to care. *Caring for People* says:

> 'The greater part of care has been, is and always will be provided by families and friends.' (Foreword)

> 'The Government acknowledges that the great bulk of community care is provided by friends, family and neighbours. The decision to take on a caring role is never an easy one. However, many people make that choice and it is right that they should be able to play their part in looking after those close to them . . . ' (paragraph 1.9)

> '...the reality is that most care is provided by family, friends and neighbours. The majority of carers take on these responsibilities willingly...' (paragraph 2.3)

> '...Decisions will need to take account of the local availability and pattern of services as well as any sources of support available in the community—whether from family, friends, neighbours or the local voluntary organisations...' (paragraph 3.3)

> ' ...GPs will be expected, under their terms of service, to ... find out whether carers and relatives are available ...' (paragraph 4.12)

> '...It is acknowledged that the bulk of care of people with disabilities, including those with considerable disabilities, falls on family, friends and neighbours. The role of the informal carer is vital ...' (paragraph 10.18)

Britain is not the only country to be facing the economic challenge of providing care to its ill and disabled members, and seeking to place the responsibility for care firmly within the family. It is a trend shared by North America and large parts of Europe. Although most people expect to care for family members and, even if it is referred to as 'duty', are happy to take on the role, there is a distinction to be made between 'appropriate' levels of care within a normal family framework and taking on the extended role of full- or part-time carer.

There are no clear norms and beliefs regarding the responsibilities of families (Finch and Mason 1993). This is indicated by the fact that although research shows that women are more likely to give help than men, this is not the result of differential norms or values attached to care and family responsibility. More important are *circumstances*, so that there are '*some circumstances* in which most people do agree that the family should take responsibility'.

These circumstances centre around what might be called 'deserving cases', when there were limits on the help needed, either in terms of time, effort or skill, or when the relationship was between parent and child. Although this relationship is the one which has fixed responsibilities most closely associated with it, it is slightly more likely to be in the direction parent to child and does not necessarily imply actual care. Although most people agree that children have a responsibility to do *something* for elderly parents in need of care, there is no clear consensus on *what* this should be.

The ideology that care in the family is best is rarely challenged. That it might have negative consequences is not considered. The responsibility or desire to care for family members can be argued to spring as much from biology and instincts as from social convention and conditioning, or from religious or moral beliefs. All play a part. What is more important here, is the perception of caring that society has, and the values implicit in the role.

The overwhelming push to give value to 'care' by families has resulted in a backlash against formal, paid care. Community care projects are notorious for their low pay, poor conditions of work, part-time, temporary or irregular hours, and the general low priority given to the health and welfare of staff, and also *by* them to the client groups, all subsumed under the heading 'community care'. Croft (1986) points out that another expression of the devaluing of this care

> 'is the way that caring for old and mentally handicapped people is seen as a suitable activity for other devalued groups, like juvenile delinquents

and adult offenders, or as part of their punishment in "community service".'

THE POLITICS OF DEPENDENCY

A challenge of involving families in care is that it can further thrust the person with schizophrenia into a dependent role. It is not easy to find a suitable word to describe the person or the relationship which does not end up being a label. In some instances 'patient' is an appropriate word to describe a relationship but not a person in their entirety. Some writers refer to 'cared-for' people, usually the elderly, as 'dependants'. Again, this might describe aspects of the relationship, but should not become a label for a person. To acknowledge the family's responsibility, or duty to care, to quantify the burden on them and to assess their needs can, if we are not careful, confirm a view that people with schizophrenia are nothing more than dependants, in need of caring. This is not helped by people with mental illness being discriminated against in the labour market (even when they can work), and thrusting them into a low-income life dependent on State benefits. Set against this is the reality that many people with schizophrenia will never be totally independent (in the everyday sense of self-supporting and self-caring). There will always be part of the person, of their life, which is dependent. 'Independence' as a goal of therapy, of rehabilitation, has been pushed so hard that we rarely question whether dependency has to be all bad, or whether having certain limitations on functioning has to equate with 'dependence' and 'caring'.

Community care is usually advanced as a way of enabling people to be more independent. Is this true? Is it simply a move from one form of dependence to another? Does it, in fact, expand the group of people who are, in some way, dependent?

One of the difficulties we have in discussing all these issues is that of moving between the individual and society. Burden is as much a reality for society to bear (usually in economic terms) as it is for the elderly parent caring for a chronically ill child. Autonomy usually takes centre stage in any discussion of ethics and values, with paternalism generally counter-opposed. It might be more appropriate to consider dependency as the alternative model, or even as a co-terminus model in which independence and dependence are two sides of a greater whole. Mendus (1991) argues that we need to 're-emphasise the role of dependence as a moral good in human life', that dependence 'far from being opposed to personal achievement, may often be the thing which gives value and meaning to our achievements.' If we take the view that dependency is not all bad, that indeed it is an essential part of our humanity, then the way in which we view the development of services, the roles of carers and those designated dependent, will be substantially altered. This is not the same as saying that deprivation or suffering is 'good for the soul' or 'character-building' (Atkinson 1993), but to suggest that among other characteristics, being needy and vulnerable are part of the human condition.

The political climate of the last 15 years has undermined dependency at every level, and was no more clearly set out than in the speech of the then Secretary of State for Social Security, John Moore, in 1987 to the Conservative Party:

> ' . . . a climate of dependence can in time corrupt the human spirit ...'

> '...The job therefore has been to change this depressing climate of dependence and revitalise the belief ... that individuals can take action to change their lives; can do things to control what happens to them...'

> '...dependence in the long run decreases human happiness and reduces human freedom . . . '

> '...the well being of individuals is best protected... when they are helped ... to achieve things on their own, which is one of the greatest satisfactions life can offer...'

Such views have surface validity when dependence is only seen as a result of deprivation, hardship, suffering or a lack of something that everyone else has. In part, they echo the old Poor Laws which dominated the provision of welfare in Britain until 1948. To some extent the 'new' models of care are a restructuring and revaluing of these old Poor Law provisions.

Community social work was welcomed by many on the political right for promoting the community's own resources and down-playing State provision. It was also welcomed by some socialists as putting 'community' at the heart of service planning and delivery. 'Community' is thus proposed as a 'good thing' by both the political right and the political left, but for very different reasons. The former see it predominantly as of economic value, whereas the latter describe community in terms of social value. Such views are current throughout much of the West, not least in the United States and Canada. We are all, however, dependent on circumstances, on constitution (the character traits and abilities we have), and on outcome (being unable to predict the exact consequences of our actions).

The 1980s saw a resurgence of the cult of the individual and self-help. Whilst this can have laudable consequences, and the self-help movement has been of immense importance, there are problems when this becomes the approach of choice, and collective responsibility is relabelled dependence, and dependence is assessed in terms of collective financial costs. It could be argued that the (verbal and minimal financial) support given to self-help groups is because this moves the focus of the problem from society to the individual. Families should be able to deal with their old, their sick and their handicapped, and if they cannot then they should only be helped to do so with the minimum of input from the State that is possible (rather than acceptable).

Mutual aid, the spreading of responsibility from individuals to the community, is one way of viewing the development of State benefits, including Social Security and the National Health Service. Assistance is then a right, not an act of charity. Dependency should not be an issue, as such schemes encompass the whole community and all are expected to contribute insofar as they can. High unemployment levels in the West mean that many chronically sick or disabled people do not have the opportunity for employment. The number of people who have life-long dependency on the State is comparatively small, and their dependency is recognised as one of constitution. Those people who *could* work if circumstances were different are the group to whom the myth of dependency and state 'handouts' applies; those people who treatment and rehabilitation have made (more) independent, trying to exercise choice within a system which still perceives them as dependent, and does not create an appropriate environment for them to exercise their independence.

The two-faced nature of government in relation to dependency is highlighted when we consider the role of women as carers. The rhetoric and the reality of community care depend heavily on women to function in the role of carers of dependants. The unfortunate outcome of this, for government no less than for the women themselves, is to turn female carers into dependants—dependent on male wage-earners or State benefits. The former is seen as positive, upholding traditional family roles, and the benefit system does little to undermine this. The latter, however, is seen as the corrupting spirit of dependence which the government seeks to discourage and is, of course, most likely in women who have been 'appropriately' dependent on their husband if the marriage breaks down or the husband dies and they have given up work. This paradoxical approach to 'good' dependency (within the family) and 'bad' dependency (on the State) leaves some women in a 'damned if you do and damned if you don't' situation.

The problems inherent in this view of dependency would be overcome, or at least challenged, if the State recognised its dependence on women, or carers in general, for the non-paid work that they do. The State cannot easily do this, however, without making payment for this task, the one thing it wants to avoid at all costs as the financial implications are overwhelming.

The maintenance of the traditional view of women as carers means that even when other alternatives are available, they may not be accepted. Scandinavia generally has better provision for care than Britain and North America, but women dominate the public-care sector (generally lower paid than other forms of private-sector employment), and still feel a sense of obligation to take on informal care responsibilities (Borchorst and Siim 1987; Langan and Ostner 1991). It may be that relinquishing responsibility and accepting formal help is experienced by the individual, or perceived by others, as being a consequence of a failure to 'cope', or of being uncaring, which may then challenge the woman's self-image in respect of what it means to be a woman (Briggs and Oliver 1985). If this is the case, then we must carefully consider how far expecting women to become informal carers, and thus causing them to be dependent, also perpetuates a further dependency in those they care for, as they seek to justify and maintain their new, socially acceptable and socially defined role.

The problem with arguing that dependency 'can corrupt the human spirit' is that it assumes that everyone has the same constitutional, circumstantial and outcome ('luck') factors to pursue enterprise and independence. A society which pretends that people do have control over their lives, that they can and should take control, denies the reality that for many people constitution, circumstances and outcome curtail this control to the extent that their independence is (temporarily) lost. To berate them for not trying is to move to a position of putting them at fault, laying the blame for their situation at their own door.

Ultimately it restricts our understanding of others, and 'the language of independence and control' may even, Mendus (1991) asserts, 'distort our understanding of moral life' for at 'the limit, it leaves no room for the tragic, nor the pathetic', as it deprives us of 'the language in which to express the misfortunes which befall us, and to understand the misfortunes of others'.

When talking to relatives and people with schizophrenia, the question 'why?' recurs. 'Why us?' 'Why my child?' 'Why schizophrenia?' 'Why me?' Such questions do not have an answer. The person is expressing existential feelings, not demanding an explanation of the current theory of genetics or the latest work on brain imaging. What they are trying to do is come to terms with the tragedy that has befallen them, or their child, with the onset of schizophrenia. They were not responsible. The person with schizophrenia was not responsible. To make this believable, it is not just they who have to come to terms with illness and dependency, but society as a whole and government as a particular reflection of that society.

There are no total solutions. There is no way of turning a person with schizophrenia into a person with schizophrenia who has no problems, is independent and enterprising and, through self-help, achieving, if for no other reason than that none of us are totally lacking in some form of dependency. The myth that just because a problem can be stated it must have a solution is common. At best there are partial solutions, partial answers, partial autonomy and partial dependency. One of the functions of education and support groups for relatives is to enable relatives to explore and, hopefully, come to terms with this. The next step must be education for policy makers and for governments, to enable them also to reach a similar understanding.

REFERENCES

Abramowitz, I. and Coursey, R. 1989. Impact of an educational support group on family participants who take care of their schizophrenic relatives. *Journal of Consulting and Clinical Psychology*, **57**, 232–6.

Ahmed, S. and Vishwanathan, P. 1984. Factor-analytical study of Nunnally's scale of popular concepts of mental health. *Psychological Reports*, **54**, 455–61.

Alanen, Y.O. and Kinnuman, P. 1975. Marriage and the development of schizophrenia. *Psychiatry*, **38**, 346–65.

Al-Khani, M.A.F., Bebbington, P.E., Watson, J.P. and House, F. 1986. Life events and schizophrenia: A Saudi Arabian study. *British Journal of Psychiatry*, **148**, 12–22.

Altorfer, A., Goldsteing, M.J., Miklowitz, D.J. and Nuechterlein, K.H. 1992. Stress-induced indicative patterns of non-verbal behaviour. Their role in family interaction. *British Journal of Psychiatry*, **161**, Suppl. 18, 103–13.

Anderson, C.M., Reiss, D.J. and Hogarty, G.E. 1986. *Schizophrenia in the Family: A Practitioner's Guide to Psychoeducation and Management.* New York: Guilford Press.

Angermeyer, M.C. 1987. Theoretical implications of psychosocial intervention studies on schizophrenia. In H. Häfner, W. Giattaz and W. Janzavik (Eds) *Search for the Causes of Schizophrenia.* Berlin: Springer-Verlag.

Appleby, L. and Dickens, C. 1993. Mothering skills of women with mental illness. *British Medical Journal*, **306**, 348–9.

Arrindell, W.A., Emmelkamp, P.M.G., Brilman, E. and Monsma, A. 1983. Psychometric evaluation of an inventory for assessment of parental rearing practices. *Acta Psychiatrica Scandinavica*, **67**, 163–77.

Arrindell, W.A., Perris, C., Eismann, M., Perris, H., Van der Ende, J., Ross, M., Benjaminsen, S., Gaszner, P. and Del Vecchio, M. 1986. Cross-national generalizability of patterns of parental rearing behaviour: Invariance of EMBU dimensions representations of healthy subjects from Australia, Denmark, Hungary, Italy and The Netherlands. *Personality and Individual Differences*, **7**, 103–11.

Atkinson, J.M. 1982. The effect of involving a relative in behavioural programmes with chronic schizophrenic patients in the home setting. *International Journal of Behavioural Social Work*, **2**, 33–40.

Atkinson, J.M. 1986. *Schizophrenia at Home. A Guide to Helping the Family.* Beckenham: Croom Helm.

Atkinson, J.M. 1989. To tell or not to tell—the diagnosis of schizophrenia. *Journal of Medical Ethics*, **15**, 21–4.

Atkinson, J.M. 1991. Autonomy and mental health. In P.J. Baker and S. Baldwin (Eds) *Ethical Issues in Mental Health*. London: Chapman and Hall.

Atkinson, J.M. 1993. The patient as sufferer. *British Journal of Medical Psychology*, **66**, 113–20.

Atkinson, J.M. and Coia, D.A. 1989. Responsibility to carers—an ethical dilemma. *Psychiatric Bulletin*, **13**, 602–4.

Atkinson, J.M. and Coia, D.A. 1991. Carers, the Community and the White Paper. *Psychiatric Bulletin*, **15**, 763–4.

Back, K.W. and Taylor, R.C. 1976. Self-help groups: Types or psychological processes. *Journal of Applied Behavioural Science*, **12**, 295–309.

Barker, J.T. 1984. Psychoeducation. In J.A. Talbot (Ed.) *The Chronic Mental Patient: Five Years Later*. New York: Guilford Press.

Barnes, M. and Berke, J. 1971. *Mary Barnes. Two Accounts of a Journey Through Madness*. London: MacGibbon and Kee.

Barrelet, L., Ferrero, F., Szigethy, L., Giddey, C. and Pellizzer, G. 1990. Expressed emotion and first admission schizophrenia: Nine-month follow-up in a French cultural environment. *British Journal of Psychiatry*, **156**, 357–62.

Barrowclough, C. and Tarrier, N. 1990. Social functioning in schizophrenic patients. I. The effects of expressed emotion and family intervention. *Social Psychiatry and Psychiatric Epidemiology*, **252**, 125–9.

Barrowclough, C. and Tarrier, N. 1992. *Families of Schizophrenic Patients. Cognitive Behavioural Intervention*. London: Chapman and Hall.

Barrowclough, C., Tarrier, N., Watts, S., Vaughn, C., Bamrah, J.S. and Freeman, H. 1987. Assessing the functional value of relatives' knowledge about schizophrenia: A preliminary report. *British Journal of Psychiatry*, **151**, 1–8.

Bateson, G., Jackson, D.D., Haley, J. *et al.* 1956. Towards a theory of schizophrenia. *Behavioural Science*, **1**, 251–64.

Baum, M., Zilkha, K. and Houghton, J. 1989. Ethics of clinical research: Lessons for the future. *British Medical Journal*, **299**, 251–3.

Bebbington, P., Wilkins, S., Jones, P., Foerster, A., Murray, R., Toone, B. and Lewis, S. 1993. Life events and psychosis. Initial results from the Camberwell Collaborative Psychosis Study. *British Journal of Psychiatry*, **162**, 72–80.

Beels, C.C. 1975. Family and social management of schizophrenia. *Schizophrenia Bulletin*, **13**, 97–118.

Berkowitz, R., Kuipers, L., Eberlein-Fries, R. and Leff, J. 1981. Lowering expressed emotion in relatives of schizophrenics. In M.J. Goldstein (Ed.) *New Developments in Interventions with Families of Schizophrenics*. San Francisco/London: Josey Bass.

Berkowitz, R., Eberlein-Fries, R., Kuipers, L. and Leff, J. 1984. Educating relatives about schizophrenia. *Schizophrenia Bulletin,* **10,** 418–29.

Berheim, K.F. and Lehman, A.F. 1985. Teaching mental health trainees to work with families of the chronic mentally ill. *Hospital and Community Psychiatry,* **36,** 1109–11.

Beveridge, W. 1942. *Report of the Interdepartmental Committee on Social Insurance and Allied Services.* CMND 6404. London: HMSO.

Billings, A.G. and Moos, R. 1981. The role of coping responses and social resources in altering the stress of life events. *Journal of Behavioural Medicine,* **4,** 139–57.

Birchwood, M. 1992. Early intervention in schizophrenia: Theoretical background and clinical strategies. *British Journal of Clinical Psychology,* **31,** 257–78.

Birchwood, M. and Cochrane, R. 1990. Families coping with schizophrenia: Coping styles, their origins and correlates. *Psychological Medicine,* **20,** 857–65.

Birchwood, M. and Smith, J. 1987. Schizophrenia and the family. In J. Orford (Ed.) *Coping with Disorder in the Family.* Beckenham: Croom Helm.

Birchwood, M., Smith, J., MacMillan, F., Hogg, B., Prasad, R., Harvey, C. and Berings, S. 1989. Predicting relapse in schizophrenia: The development and implementation of an early signs monitoring system using patients and families as observers. A preliminary investigation. *Psychological Medicine,* **19,** 649–56.

Birchwood, M., Cochrane, R., Macmillan, F., Copestake, S., Kucharsha, J. and Cariss, M. 1992a. The influence of ethnicity and family structure on relapse in first-episode schizophrenics. A comparison of Asian, Afro-Caribbean, and White patients. *British Journal of Psychiatry,* **161,** 783–90.

Birchwood, M., Smith, J. and Cochrane, R. 1992b. Specific and non-specific effects of educational interventions for families living with schizophrenia. *British Journal of Psychiatry,* **160,** 806–14.

Birley, J. and Hudson, B. 1983. The family, the social network and rehabilitation. In F.N. Watts and D.H. Bennett (Eds) *Theory and Practice of Psychiatric Rehabilitation.* Wiley: Chichester.

Birtchnell, J. 1988. Defining dependence. *British Journal of Medical Psychology,* **61,** 111–23.

Borchorst, A. and Siim, B. 1987. Women and the advanced welfare state. In A.S. Sassoon (Ed.) *Women and the State.* London: Unwin Hyman.

Borkman, T. 1976. Experiential knowledge: A new concept for the analysis of self-help groups. *Social Services Review,* **50,** 445–56.

Bowen, M. 1960. Family concept of schizophrenia. In D.D. Jackson (Ed.) *The Etiology of Schizophrenia.* New York: Basic Books.

Brenner, H.D., Böker, W., Müller, J. *et al.* 1987. On autoprotective efforts of schizophrenics, neurotics and controls. *Acta Psychiatrica Scandinavica,* **75,** 405–14.

Briggs, A. and Oliver, J. 1985. *Caring: Experiences of Looking after Disabled Relatives*. London: Routledge and Kegan Paul.

Brockingham, I.F., Hall, P., Levings, J. and Murphy, C. 1993. The community's tolerance of the mentally ill. *British Journal of Psychiatry*, **162**, 93–9.

Brown, G.W. 1959. Experiences of discharged chronic schizophrenic patients in various types of living group. *Millbank Memorial Fund Quarterly*, **37**, 105–31.

Brown, G.W. and Birley, J.L.T. 1968. Crises and life changes and the onset of schizophrenia. *Journal of Health and Social Behaviour*, **9**, 203–14.

Brown, G.W. and Rutter, M. 1966. The measurement of family activities and relationships. A methodological study. *Human Relations*, **19**, 241–65.

Brown, G.W., Birley, J.L.T. and Wing, J.K. 1972. Influence of family life on the course of schizophrenic disorders: A replication. *British Journal of Psychiatry*, **121**, 241–58.

Buchremer, G., Stricker, K., Holle, R. and Kuhs, H. 1991. The predictability of relapse in schizophrenia patients. *European Archives of Psychiatry and Clinical Neurosciences*, **240**, 292–300.

Carpenter, J. 1987. For the good of the family. In S. Walrond-Skinner and D. Watson (Eds) *Ethical Issues in Family Therapy*. London: Routledge and Kegan Paul.

Carpenter, W.T. Jr. and Heinrichs, D.W. 1983. Early intervention, time-limited, targeted pharmacotherapy of schizophrenia. *Schizophrenia Bulletin*, **9**, 533–42.

Carpenter, W.T. Jr., Hanlon, T.E., Heinrichs, D.W., Summerfelt, A.T., Kirkpatrick, B., Levine, J. and Buchanan, R.W. 1990. Continuous versus target medication in schizophrenic outpatients: Outcome results. *American Journal of Psychiatry*, **147**, 1138–48.

Cazzullo, C.L., Bertrando, C., Clerici, C., Bressi, C., Da Poute, C. and Albertini, E. 1989. The efficacy of an information group intervention on relatives of schizophrenics. *International Journal of Social Psychiatry*, **35**, 313–23.

Cheek, F.E., Laucius, J., Matiuche, M. and Beck, R. 1971. A behaviour modification training programme for parents of convalescent schizophrenics. In R.D. Rubin, H. Feisterheim, A.A. Lazarus, and C.M. Franks (Eds) *Advances in Behaviour Therapy: Proceedings of the Third Conference of the Association for the Advancement of Behaviour Therapy*. New York: Academic Press.

Chung, R.K., Langeluddecke, P. and Tennant, C. 1986. Threatening life events in the onset of schizophrenia, schizophreniform psychosis and hypomania. *British Journal of Psychiatry*, **148**, 680–6.

Clausen, J.A. and Yarrow, M.R. 1955. The impact of mental illness on the family. *Journal of Social Issues*, **11**, 3–64.

Coia, D.A. and Atkinson, J.M. 1989. Relatives' support groups in the community. Annual Meeting of the Royal College of Psychiatrists.

Cole, J.D. and Kazarian, S.S. 1988. The level of expressed emotion scale: A new measure of expressed emotion. *Journal of Clinical Psychology*, **44**, 392–7.

Cole, S.A. and Jacobs, J. 1988. The family treatment of schizophrenia: An integration of family systems and psychoeducational approaches. In T.B. Karasu (Ed.) *Psychiatric Treatment Manual*. Washington: American Psychiatric Press.

Cozolino, L.J., Goldstein, M.J., Nuechterlein, K.H., West, K.L. and Snyder, K.S. 1988. The impact of education about schizophrenia on relatives varying expressed emotion. *Schizophrenia Bulletin*, **14**, 675–87.

Creer, C. and Wing, J.K. 1974. *Schizophrenia at Home*. Surbiton: National Schizophrenia Fellowship.

Creer, C., Sturt, E. and Wykes, T. 1982. The role of relatives. In J.K. Wing (Ed.) *Long-Term Community Care Experience in a London Borough. Psychological Medicine*, Vol. 12, Monograph Suppl. No. **2**, pp. 29–39.

Croft, S. 1986. Women, caring and the recasting of need—a feminist reappraisal. *Critical Social Policy*, **16**, 23–39.

Cumming, E. and Cumming, J. 1957. *Closed Ranks. An Experiment in Mental Health*. Cambridge, MA: Howard University Press.

D'Arcy, C. and Brockman, J. 1976. Changing public recognition of psychiatric symptoms. Blackfoot revisited. *Journal of Health and Social Behaviour*, **17**, 302–10.

Dearth, N., Labenski, B.J., Mott, M.E. and Pelleorini, L.H. (Families of the Mentally Ill Collective) 1986. *Families Helping Families. Living with Schizophrenia*. New York: Wm. Norton.

Doane, J.A., West, K.L., Goldstein, M.J., Rodnick, E.H. and Jones, J.E. 1981. Parental communication deviance and affective style: Predictors of subsequent schizophrenia spectrum disorders in vulnerable adolescents. *Archives of General Psychiatry*, **38**, 679–85.

Doane, J.A, Falloon, I.R.H., Goldstein, M.J. and Mintz, J. 1985. Parental affective style and the treatment of schizophrenia: Predicting the course of illness and social functioning. *Archives of General Psychiatry*, **42**, 34–42.

Doll, W. 1976. Family coping with the mentally ill patient: An unanticipated result of deinstitutionalization. *Hospital and Community Psychiatry*, **27**, 183–5.

Downey, K.J. 1967. Public images of mental illness. A factor analytic study of causes and symptoms. *Social Science and Medicine*, **1**, 45–65.

Dulz, B. and Hand, I. 1986. Short-term relapse in young schizophrenics. In M. Goldstein, I. Hand and K. Hahlweg (Eds) *Treatment of Schizophrenia: Family Assessment and Intervention*. Berlin: Springer-Verlag.

Dyer, C. 1989. Public interest and a psychiatrist's duty of confidentiality. *British Medical Journal*, **229**, 1301.

Egeland, B. and Stroufe, L.A. 1981. Attachment and early maltreatment. *Child Development*, **49**, 547–56.

Eichenbaum, L. and Orbach, S. 1983. *Understanding Women: A Feminist Psychoanalytic Approach*. New York: Basic Books.

Esterson, A., Cooper, D.C. and Laing, R.D. 1965. Results of family-orientated therapy with hospitalised schizophrenics. *British Medical Journal*, 8 December, pp. 1462–5.

Fadden, G., Kuipers, L. and Bebbington, P. 1987a. The burden of care: The impact of functional psychiatric illness on the patient's family. *British Journal of Psychiatry*, **150**, 285–92.

Fadden, G., Bebbington, P. and Kuipers, L. 1987b. Caring and its burdens. A study of spouses of depressed patients. *British Journal of Psychiatry*, **151**, 660–7.

Falloon, I.R.H. 1985. *Family Management of Schizophrenia*. Baltimore, MD: Johns Hopkins University Press.

Falloon, I.R.H. 1992. Early intervention for first episodes of schizophrenia: A preliminary exploration. *Psychiatry*, **55**, 4–15.

Falloon, I.R.H. and Brooker, C. 1992. A critical re-evaluation of social and family interventions in schizophrenia. *Schizophrenia Monitor*, **2**, 1–4.

Falloon, I.R.H. and Liberman, R.P. 1983. Behavioural family intervention in the management of chronic schizophrenia. In W.R. McFarlane (Ed.) *Family Therapy in Schizophrenia*. New York: Guilford Press.

Falloon, I.R.H., Watt, D.C. and Shepherd, M. 1978. The social outcome of patients in a trial of long-term continuation therapy in schizophrenia: Pimozide vs. fluphenazine. *Psychological Medicine*, **8**, 265–74.

Falloon, I.R.H. Liberman, R.P., Lillie, F.J. and Vaughn, C.E. 1981. Family therapy for relapsing schizophrenics and their families: A pilot study. *Family Process*, **20**, 211–21.

Falloon, I.R.H., Boyd, J.L., McGill, C.W., Razani, J., Moss, H.B. and Gilderman, A.M. 1982. Family management in the prevention of exacerbation of schizophrenia: A controlled study. *New England Journal of Medicine*, **306**, 1437–40.

Falloon, I.R.H., Boyd, J.L., McGill, C.W., Williamson, M., Razani, J., Moss, H.B., Gilderman, A.M. and Simson, G.H. 1985. Family management in the prevention of morbidity of schizophrenia: clinical outcome of a two year longitudinal study. *Archives of General Psychiatry*, **42**, 887–96.

Falloon, I.R.H., Laporta, M., Fadden, G. and Graham-Hole, V. 1993. *Managing Stress in Families. Cognitive and Behavioural Strategies for Enhancing Coping Skills*. London: Routledge.

Finch, J. 1984. Community care: Developing non-sexist alternatives. *Critical Social Policy*, **9**, 6–18.

Finch, J. and Groves, D. 1980. Community care and the family: A case for equal opportunities? *Journal of Social Policy*, **9**, 487–514.

Finch, J. and Mason, J. 1993. *Negotiating Family Responsibilities*. London: Routledge.

Flannigan, D.A.J. and Wagner, H.L. 1991. Expressed emotion and panic–fear in the prediction of client treatment compliance. *British Journal of Clinical Psychology*, **30**, 231–40.

Folkman, S. 1984. Personal control and stress and coping processes: A theoretical analysis. *Journal of Personality and Social Psychology*, **46**, 839–52.

Folkman, S. and Lazarus, R.S. 1980. An analysis of coping in a middle-aged community sample. *Journal of Health and Social Behaviour*, **21**, 219–39.

Folkman, S., Lazarus, R.S., Gruen, R.J. and Delongis, A. 1986. Appraisal, coping, health status and psychological symptoms. *Journal of Personality and Social Psychology*, **50**, 571–9.

Freeman, H.E. and Simmons, O.G. 1958. Mental patients in the community: Family settings and performance levels. *American Sociological Review*, **23**, 147–54.

Freeman, H.E. and Simmons, O.G. 1963. *The Mental Patient Comes Home*. London: Wiley.

Fromm-Reichmann, F. 1948. Notes on the development of treatment of schizophrenics by psychoanalytic psychotherapy. *Psychiatry*, **11**, 263–73.

Galanter, M. 1990. Cults and zealous self-help movements: A psychiatric perspective. *American Journal of Psychiatry*, **147**, 543–57.

Gaskill, D. and Cooney, H. 1992. Coping with schizophrenia: What does the spouse need to know. *Australian Journal of Advanced Nursing*, **9**, 10–15.

Geiser, R., Hoche, L. and King, J. 1988. Respite care for mentally ill patients and their families. *Hospital and Community Psychiatry*, **38**, 291–5.

Georgiades, N.J. and Phillimore, L. 1975. The myth of the hero innovator and alternative strategies for organisational change. In C.C. Kiernan and F.D. Woodford (Eds) *Behaviour Modification with the Severely Retarded*. Amsterdam: Associated Scientific Publishers.

Gibbons, J.S., Horn, S.H., Powell, J.M. and Gibbons, J.L. 1984. Schizophrenic patients and their families: A survey in a psychiatric service based on a DGH Unit. *British Journal of Psychiatry*, **144**, 70–8.

Gilhooly, M.L.M. 1987. Senile dementia in the family. In J. Orford (Ed.) *Coping with Disorder in the Family*. London: Croom Helm.

Gilleard, C.J. 1984. *Living with Dementia*. London: Croom Helm.

Gillis, L.S. and Keer, M. 1965. Factors underlying the retention in the community of chronic unhospitalised schizophrenics. *British Journal of Psychiatry*, **111**, 1057–67.

Glasgow University Media Group 1993a. *Mass Media Representations of Mental Health/Illness*. Report for the Health Education Board for Scotland.

Glasgow University Media Group 1993b. *Mass Media Representations of Mental Health/Illness: Audience Participation Study*. Report for the Health Education Board for Scotland.

Glick, I.D., Clarkin, J., Spencer, J.H., Haas, G.L., Lewis, A.B., Peyser, J., De-Mane, N., Good-Ellis, M., Harris, E. and Lestelle, V. 1985. A controlled evaluation of inpatient family intervention—preliminary results of the six month follow-up. *Archives of General Psychiatry*, **42**, 882–6.

Goldberg, D.P. and Hillier, V.F. 1979. A scaled version of the General Health Questionnaire. *Psychological Medicine*, **9**, 139–45.

Golder, V. 1985. Feminism and family therapy. *Family Process*, **24**, 31–47.

Goldstein, M.J. 1987. The UCLA high risk project. *Schizophrenia Bulletin*, **13**, 505–14.

Goldstein, M.J. and Kopeiken, H. 1981. Short and long term effects of combining drug and family therapy. In M.J. Goldstein (Ed.) *New Developments in Interventions with Families of Schizophrenics*. San Francisco, CA: Jossey-Bass.

Goldstein, M.J. and Strachan, A.M. 1986. The impact of family intervention programmes on family communication and the short-term course of schizophrenia. In M.J. Goldstein, I. Hand and K. Hahlweg (Eds) *Treatment of Schizophrenia: Family Assessment and Intervention*. Heidelberg: Springer-Verlag.

Goldstein, M.J., Rodnick, E.H., Evans, J.R., May, P.R.A. and Steinberg, M.R. 1978. Drug and family therapy in the aftercare treatment of acute schizophrenia. *Archives of General Psychiatry*, **35**, 169–77.

Goldstein, M.J., Miklowitz, D.J., Strachan, A.M., Doane, J.A., Nuechterlein, K.H. and Feingold, D. 1989. Patterns of expressed emotion and patient coping styles that characterize the families of recent onset schizophrenics. *British Journal of Psychiatry*, **155**, Suppl. 5, 107–11.

Goldstein, M.J., Talovic, S.A., Nuechterlein, K.H., Fogelson, D.L., Subotnick, K.R.L. and Asarnow, R.F. 1992. Family interaction versus individual psychopathology. Do they indicate the same processes in the families of schizophrenics? *British Journal of Psychiatry*, **161**, Suppl. 18, 97–102.

Grad, J. and Sainsbury, P. 1963. Mental illness in the family. *Lancet*, **i**, 544–7.

Green, H. 1964. *I Never Promised You a Rose Garden*. London: Victor Gollancz.

Green, H. 1988. *Informal Carers. General Household Survey 1985*. London: HMSO.

Griffiths, R. 1988. *Community Care. Agenda for Action. A Report to the Secretary of State for Social Services*. London: HMSO.

Gurevitz, H. 1977. Tarasoff: Protective privilege versus public peril. *American Journal of Psychiatry*, **134**, 289–92.

Gurin, G., Veroff, V. and Feld, S. 1960. *Americans View Their Mental Health: A Nationwide Interview Survey*. New York: Basic Books.

Haas, G.L., Glick, I.D., Clarkin, J.F., Spencer, J.H., Lewis, A.B., Peyser, J., DeMane, N., Good-Ellis, M., Harris, E. and Lestelle, V. 1988. In-patient family intervention: A randomised clinical trial. *Archives of General Psychiatry*, **5**, 84–9.

Hall, J. 1990. Towards a psychology of caring. *British Journal of Clinical Psychology*, **29**, 129–44.

Hall, P., Brockington, I.F., Levings, J. and Murphy, C. 1993. A comparison of responses to the mentally ill in two countries. *American Journal of Psychiatry*, **162**, 99–108.

Hatfield, A.B. 1978. Psychological costs of schizophrenia to the family. *Social Work*, **23**, 355–9.

Hatfield, A.B. 1979a. The family as partner in the treatment of mental illness. *Hospital and Community Psychiatry*, **30**, 338–40.

Hatfield, A.B. 1979b. Help-seeking behaviour in families of schizophrenics. *American Journal of Community Psychiatry*, **7**, 563–9.

Hatfield, A.B. 1983. What families want of family therapists. In W.R. McFarlane (Ed.) *Family Therapy in Schizophrenia*. New York: Guilford Press.

Hatfield, A.B. 1988. Issues in psychoeducation for families of the mentally ill. *International Journal of Mental Health*, **17**, 48–64.

Hatfield, A.B. 1990. *Family Education in Mental Illness*. New York: Guilford Press.

Hatfield, A.B., Fierstein, R. and Johnson, D. 1982. Meeting the needs of families of the psychiatrically disabled. *Psychosocial Rehabilitation Journal*, **6**, 27–40.

Hatfield, A.B., Spaniol, L. and Zipple, A.M. 1987. Expressed emotion: A family perspective. *Schizophrenia Bulletin*, **13**, 221–35.

Higson, M. and Kavanagh, D.J. 1988. A hostel-based psychoeducational intervention for schizophrenia: Programme development and preliminary findings. *Behaviour Change*, **5**, 85–9.

Hirsch, S.R. and Leff, J.P. 1975. *Abnormalities in the Parents of Schizophrenics*. London: Oxford University Press.

Hoenig, J. and Hamilton, M.W. 1966. The schizophrenic patient in the community and his effect on the household. *International Journal of Social Psychiatry*, **12**, 165–76.

Hoenig, J. and Hamilton, M. 1967. The burden on the household in an extra-mural psychiatric service. In H. Freeman and J. Farndale (Eds) *New Aspects of the Mental Health Services*. London: Pergamon.

Hoenig, J. and Hamilton, M. 1969. *The Desegregation of the Mentally Ill*. London: Routledge and Kegan Paul.

Hogarty, G.E. 1985. Expressed emotion and schizophrenic relapse: Implications from the Pittsburgh study. In M. Alpert (Ed.) *Controversies in Schizophrenia*. New York: Guilford Press.

Hogarty, G. 1993. Treatment essentials of a health care delivery system for the severely mentally ill. Royal College of Psychiatrists Spring Meeting, Swansea.

Hogarty, G.E., Anderson, C.M., Reiss, D.J., Kornblith, S.J., Greenwald, D.P., Java, C.D., Madonia, M.J. and the EPICS Schizophrenia Research Group 1986. Family psycho-education, social skills training and maintenance chemotherapy in the aftercare treatment of schizophrenia. 1. One-year effects of a controlled study on relapse and expressed emotion. *Archives of General Psychiatry*, **43**, 633–42.

Hogarty, G.E., McEvoy, J.P., Munetz, M., DiBarry, A.L., Bartone, P., Cather, R., Cooley, S.J., Ulrich, R.F., Carter, M. and Madonia, M.J. 1988. Dose of

Fluphenazine, familial expressed emotion and outcome in schizophrenia. Results of a two-year controlled study. *Archives of General Psychiatry*, **45**, 797–805.

Hogarty, G.E., Anderson, C.M., Reiss, D.J., Kornblith, S.J., Greenwald, D.P., Ulrich, R.F. and Carter, M. 1991. Family psycho-education, social skills training and maintenance chemotherapy in the aftercare treatment of schizophrenia. II. Two-year effects of a controlled study of relapse and adjustment. *Archives of General Psychiatry*, **48**, 340–7.

Hooley, J.M., Orley, J. and Teasdale, J.D. 1986. Levels of expressed emotion and relapse in depressed patients. *British Journal of Psychiatry*, **148**, 642–7.

Hoover, C.F. and Franz, J.D. 1972. Siblings in the families of schizophrenics. *Archives of General Psychiatry*, **25**, 334–42.

Hudson, B.L. 1975. A behaviour modification project with chronic schizophrenics in the community. *Behaviour Research and Therapy*, **13**, 339–41.

Hurvitz, N. 1976. The origins of peer self-help psychotherapy group movement. *Journal of Applied Behavioural Science*, **12**, 283–94.

Illfeld, F.W. 1980. Understanding natural stressors. The importance of coping style. *Journal of Nervous and Mental Disease*, **168**, 375–81.

Jackson, H.J., Smith, N. and McGory, P. 1990. Relationship between expressed emotion and family burden in psychiatric disorders: An exploratory study. *Acta Psychiatrica Scandinavica*, **82**, 243–9.

Jacobs, S. and Myers, J. 1976. Recent life events and acute schizophrenic psychosis: A controlled study. *Journal of Nervous and Mental Disease*, **162**, 75–87.

Jenner, J.A. 1991. Crisis intervention techniques for hallucinating patients and their relatives. In N.R. Punukollu (Ed.) *Recent Advances in Crisis Intervention*. Huddersfield: Intervention and Community Psychiatry Publication.

Johnson, J.A.W. 1976. The duration of maintenance therapy in chronic schizophrenia. *Acta Psychiatrica Scandinavica*, **53**, 298–301.

Jolley, A.G., Hirsch, S.R., Norrison, G., McRink, A. and Wilson, L. 1990. Trial of brief intermittent neuroleptic prophylaxis for selected schizophrenia outpatients: Clinical and social outcome at two years. *British Medical Journal*, **301**, 837–42.

Jones, K. 1991. Law and mental health: Sticks or carrots? In G.E. Berrios and H. Freeman (Eds) *150 Years of British Psychiatry 1841–1991*. London: Gaskell/Royal College of Psychiatrists.

Kanter, J. and Lin, A. 1980. Facilitating a therapeutic milieu in the families of schizophrenics. *Psychiatry*, **43**, 106–19.

Karno, M., Jenkins, T.H., de la Selva, A., Santana, F., Telles, C., Lopez, S. and Mintz, J. 1987. Expressed emotion and schizophrenic outcome among Mexican-American families. *Journal of Nervous and Mental Disorder*, **175**, 143–51.

Käsermann, M.L. and Altorfer, A. 1989. Family discourse: Situations differing in degree of stress and their physiological correlates. *British Journal of Psychiatry*, **155**, Suppl. 5, 136–43.

Katschnig, H. and Konieczna, T. 1987. The philosophy and practise of self-help for relatives of the mentally ill. In J.S. Strauss, W. Böker and H.D. Brenner (Eds) *Psychosocial Treatment of Schizophrenia*. Toronto: Hans Huber.

Kavanagh, D.J. 1992. Recent developments in expressed emotion and schizophrenia. *British Journal of Psychiatry*, **160**, 601–20.

Keith, D.V. and Whitaker, C.A. 1980. Add craziness and stir. Psychotherapy with a psychoticogenic family. In M. Andolfi and I. Zwerling (Eds) *Dimensions of Family Therapy*. New York: Guilford Press.

Kelly, F. 1964. Relatives' attitudes and outcome in schizophrenia. *Archives of General Psychiatry*, **10**, 389–94.

Khalil, N. and Stark, F.-M. 1992. Do perceived parental rearing patterns influence social behaviour dimensions and disease severity in schizophrenia? *Acta Psychiatrica Scandinavica*, **86**, 146–52.

Kieffer, G.D. 1988. *The Strategy of Meetings*. London: Piatkus.

Kirk, S.A., 1974. The impact of labelling on rejection of the mentally ill. *Journal of Health and Social Behaviour*, **15**, 108–17.

Kirk, S.A. 1975. The psychiatric sick role and rejection. *Journal of Nervous and Mental Disease*, **161**, 318–25.

Koenigberg, H. and Handley, R. 1986. Expressed emotion: From predictive index to clinical construct. *American Journal of Psychiatry*, **143**, 1361–73.

Kottgen, C., Sonnichsen, I., Mollenhauer, K. and Jurth, R. 1984. Group therapy with the families of schizophrenic patients: Results of the Hamburg Camberwell Family Interview Study III. *International Journal Family Psychiatry*, **5**, 83–94.

Kreisman, D.E. and Joy, V.D. 1974. Family response to the mental illness of a relative: A review of the literature. *Schizophrenia Bulletin*, **10**, 34–57.

Kreisman, D.E., Simmens, S.J. and Joy, V.D. 1979. Rejecting the patient: Preliminary validation of a self report scale. *Schizophrenia Bulletin*, **5**, 220–2.

Kuipers, L. 1979. Expressed emotion: A review. *British Journal of Social and Clinical Psychology*, **18**, 237–43.

Kuipers, L. 1992a. Expressed emotion in 1991. *Social Psychiatry and Psychiatric Epidemiology*, **27**, 1–3.

Kuipers, L. 1992b. Expressed emotion research in Europe. *British Journal of Clinical Psychology*, **31**, 429–43.

Kuipers, L. and Bebbington, P. 1988. Expressed emotion in research in schizophrenia: Theoretical and clinical considerations. *Psychological Medicine*, **18**, 893–909.

Kuipers, L., Leff, J. and Lam, D. 1992. *Family Work for Schizophrenia. A Practical Guide*. London: Gaskell/RCP.

Laing, R.D. 1960. *The Divided Self: A Study of Sanity, Madness and the Family.* London: Tavistock.

Lam, D.H. 1991. Psychosocial family intervention in schizophrenia: A review of empirical studies. *Psychological Medicine,* **21**, 423–41.

Landeen, J., Whelton, C., Dermer, S., Cardamone, S., Cardamone, J., Munroe-Blum, H. and Thornton, J. 1992. Needs of well siblings of persons with schizophrenia. *Hospital and Community Psychiatry,* **43**, 266–9.

Langan, M., and Ostner, I. 1991. Gender and welfare. In G. Room (Ed.) *Towards a European Welfare State?* Bristol: School for Advanced Urban Studies.

Lazarus, R.S. and Folkman, S. 1984. *Stress, Appraisal and Coping.* New York: Springer-Verlag.

Lee, P.W.H., Lieh-Mak, F., Yu, K.K. and Spinks, J.A. 1993. Coping strategies of schizophrenic patients and their relationship to outcome. *British Journal of Psychiatry,* **163**, 177–82.

Leff, J.P. 1987. A model of schizophrenic vulnerability to environmental factors. In H. Häfner, W.F. Giattaz, and W. Janzarik (Eds) *Search for the Causes of Schizophrenia.* Berlin: Springer-Verlag.

Leff, J. and Vaughn, C. 1980. The interaction of life events and relative's expressed emotion in schizophrenia and depressive neurosis. *British Journal of Psychiatry,* **136**, 146–53.

Leff, J. and Vaughn, C. 1981. The role of maintenance therapy and relatives' expressed emotion in relapse of schizophrenia: A two-year follow-up. *British Journal of Psychiatry,* **139**, 102–4.

Leff, J.P. and Vaughn, C. 1985. *Expressed Emotion in Families. Its Significance for Mental Illness.* New York: Guilford Press.

Leff, J.P. and Vaughn, C. 1987. Expressed emotion. *Hospital and Community Psychiatry,* **151**, 166–73.

Leff, J.P., Kuipers, L., Berkowitz, R., Eberlein-Vries, R. and Sturgeon, D. 1982. A controlled trial of social intervention in the families of schizophrenic patients. *British Journal of Psychiatry,* **141**, 121–34.

Leff, J.P., Kuipers, L., Berkowitz, R., Vaughn, C. and Sturgeon, D. 1983. Life events, relatives' expressed emotion and maintenance neuroleptics in schizophrenic relapse. *Psychological Medicine,* **13**, 799–806.

Leff, J.P., Kuipers, L., Berkowitz, R. and Sturgeon, D. 1985. A controlled trial of social intervention in the families of schizophrenic patients: Two-year follow-up. *British Journal of Psychiatry,* **146**, 594–600.

Leff, J., Berkowitz, R., Shavit, N., Strachan, A., Glass, I. and Vaughn, C. 1989. A trial of family therapy v. a relative's group for schizophrenia. *British Journal of Psychiatry,* **154**, 58–66.

Leff, J., Wig, N.N., Bedi, H., Menon, D.K., Kuipers, L., Korten, A., Ernburg, G., Day, R., Sartorius, N. and Jablensky, A. 1990. Relative's expressed emotion and the course of schizophrenia in Chandigarh: A two-year follow-up of a first-contact sample. *British Journal of Psychiatry,* **156**, 351–6.

Lefley, H.P. 1987. Aging parents as caregivers of mentally ill adult children: An emerging social problem. *Hospital and Community Psychiatry*, **38**, 1063–70.

Lefley, H.P. 1990. Culture and chronic mental illness. *Hospital and Community Psychiatry*, **41**, 277–86.

Lessing, D. 1971. *Briefing for a Descent into Hell*. London: Jonathan Cape.

Lessing, D. 1973. *The Summer Before Dark*. London: Grafton.

Lessing, D. 1974. *The Memoirs of a Survivor*. London: Octagon.

Levin, E., Sinclair, I. and Gorbach, P. 1983. *The Supporters of Confused Elderly Persons at Home*. London: NISW.

Levine, N.B., Dastoor, M.A. and Gendron, C.E. 1983. Coping with dementia—a pilot study. *Journal of the American Geriatrics Society*, **31**, 12–18.

Levy, L.H. 1978. Self-help groups viewed by mental health professionals: A survey and comments. *American Journal of Community Psychology*, **3**, 305–13.

Levy, L. 1981. The National Schizophrenia Fellowship: A British self-help group. *Social Psychiatry*, **16**, 129–35.

Liberman, R.P., DeRisi, W.J. and King, L.W. 1973. Behavioural interventions with families. In J. Masserman (Ed.) *Current Psychiatric Therapies*. New York: Grune and Stratton.

Liberman, R.P., Falloon, I.R.H. and Aitchison, R.A. 1984. Multiple family therapy for schizophrenics: A behavioural approach. *Psychosocial Rehabilitation Journal*, **4**, 60–77.

Liberman, R.P., Massel, H.K., Mosk, M. and Wing, S.E. 1985. Social skills training for chronic mental patients. *Hospital and Community Psychiatry*, **36**, 396–403.

Lidz, T., Cornelison, A., Terry, D. and Fleck, S. 1957. The intrafamilial environment of the schizophrenic patient. II. Marital schism and marital skew. *American Journal of Psychiatry*, **114**, 241–8.

Lin, K. and Kleinmann, A.M. 1988. Psychopathology and clinical course of schizophrenia: A cross-cultural perspective. *Schizophrenia Bulletin*, **14**, 555–68.

Lukes, M. undated. *The ARAFMI Story. A Decade of Support (1975–1985)*. ARAFMI Newsletter. Australia.

MacCarthy, B. 1988. The role of relatives. In A. Lavender and F. Holloway (Eds) *Community Care in Practice*. Chichester: Wiley.

MacCarthy, B., Lesage, A., Brewin, C.R., Brugha, T.S., Mangen, S. and Wing, J.K. 1989a. Needs for care among the relatives of long-term users of day care. A report from the Camberwell High Contact Survey. *Psychological Medicine*, **19**, 725–36.

MacCarthy, B., Kuipers, L., Hurry, J., Harper, R. and Le Sage, A. 1989b. Counselling the relatives of the long-term adult mentally ill. 1. Evaluation of the impact on relatives and patients. *British Journal Psychiatry*, **154**, 768–74.

McCreadie, R.G. 1993. Relatives' expressed emotion: Does it matter and does it change? Paper presented at *A Scientific Symposium to Celebrate the 150th Anniversary of Gartnaval Royal Hospital*, Glasgow, 3 June.

McCreadie, R.G. and Phillips, K. 1988. The Nithsdale schizophrenia survey. VII. Does relatives' high expressed emotion predict relapse? *British Journal of Psychiatry*, **152**, 477–81.

McCreadie, R.G. and Robinson, A.D.T. 1987. The Nithsdale schizophrenia survey. VI. Relatives' expressed emotion: prevalence patterns and clinical assessment. *British Journal of Psychiatry*, **150**, 640–4.

McGreadie, R.G., Phillips, K., Harvey, J.A., Waldron, G., Stewart, M. and Bourd, D. 1991. The Nithsdale Schizophrenia Surveys. VIII. Do relatives want family intervention—and does it help? *British Journal of Psychiatry*, **158**, 110–13.

McCreadie, R.G., Williamson, D.J., Athawes, R.W.B., Connolly, M.A. and Tilak-Singh, D. 1994, a. The Nithsdale schizophrenia surveys. XIII. Parental rearing patterns, current symptomatology and relatives' expressed emotion. *British Journal of Psychiatry*, **165**, 347–52.

McCreadie, R.G., Connolly, M.A., Williamson, D.J., Athawes, R.W.B. and Tilak-Singh, D. 1994, b. The Nithsdale Schizophrenia Surveys. XII. 'Neurodevelopmental' schizophrenia: A search for clinical correlates and putative aetiological factors. *British Journal of Psychiatry*, **165**, 340–6.

McFarlane, W.R. 1990. Multiple family groups and the treatment of schizophrenia. In M.I. Herz, S.J. Keith and J.P. Docherty (Eds) *Handbook of Schizophrenia. Vol. 4. Psychosocial Treatment of Schizophrenia*. Amsterdam: Elsevier.

McGill, C.W., Falloon, I.R.H., Boyd, J.L. and Wood-Siverio, C. 1983. Family educational intervention in the treatment of schizophrenia. *Hospital and Community Psychiatry*, **34**, 934–8.

Maclean, U. 1969. Community attitudes to mental illness in Edinburgh. *British Journal of Preventive and Social Medicine*, **23**, 45–53.

MacMillan, A.B., Goldstein, M.J., Karno, M. *et al.* 1986. A brief method for assessing expressed emotion in relatives of psychiatric patients. *Psychiatric Research*, **17**, 203–12.

MacMillan, J.F., Gold, A., Crown, T.J., Johnson, A.L. and Johnstone, E.C. 1986. The Northwick Park Study of first episodes of schizophrenia. IV. Expressed emotion and relapse. *British Journal of Psychiatry*, **148**, 133–43.

Magãna, A.B., Goldstein, M.J., Karno, M., Miklowitz, D.J., Jenkins, J. and Falloon, I.R. 1986. A brief method for assessing expressed emotion in relatives of psychotic patients. *Psychiatric Research*, **17**, 203–17.

Mandelbrote, B.M. and Folkard, S. 1961. Some factors related to outcome and social adjustment in schizophrenia. *Acta Psychiatrica Scandinavica*, **37**, 223–35.

Marder, S.R., Van Putten, T., Mintz, J., Lebell, M., McKenzie, J. and May, P.R. 1987. Costs and benefits of two doses of Fluphenazine Decanoate. Two-year outcome. *Archives of General Psychiatry*, **44**, 518–21.

Martins, C., de Lemos, A.I. and Bebbington, P.E. 1992. A Portuguese/Brazilian study of expressed emotion. *Social Psychiatry and Epidemiology*, **27**, 22–7.

Mavreas, V.G., Tomaras, V., Karyd, V., Economou, M. and Stefanis, C. 1992. Expressed emotion in families of chronic schizophrenics and its association with clinical measures. *Social Psychiatry and Psychiatric Epidemiology*, **27**, 4–9.

Medvene, L. 1992. Self-help groups, peer helping and social comparison. In S. Spacapan and S. Oskamp (Eds) *Helping and Being Helped. Naturalistic Studies*. Newbury Park, CA: Sage.

Meichenbaum, D. and Turk, D. 1987. *Facilitating Treatment Adherence*. New York: Plenum.

Meissner, W.W. 1970. Sibling relations in the schizophrenic family. *Family Process*, **9**, 1–25.

Mendus, S. 1991. Human nature and the culture of enterprise. In J. Hutton, S. Hutton, T. Pinch and A. Shiell (Eds) *Dependency to Enterprise*. London: Routledge.

Miklowitz, D.J., Goldstein, M.J. and Falloon, I.R.H. 1983. Premorbid and symptomatic characteristics of schizophrenia from families with high and low levels of expressed emotion. *Journal of Abnormal Psychology*, **92**, 354–67.

Miklowitz, D.J., Goldstein, M.J., Nuechterlein, K.H., Snyder, K.S. and Doane, J.A. 1986. Expressed emotion, affective style, lithium compliance and relapse in recent-onset mania. *Psychotherapy Bulletin*, **22**, 628–32.

Miklowitz, D.J., Goldstein, H.J., Nuechterlein, K.H., Snyder, K.S. and Doane, J.A. 1988. Family factors and the course of bipolar affective disorder. *Archives of General Psychiatry*, **45**, 225–31.

Miklowitz, D.J., Goldstein, M.J., Doane, J.A., Neuchterlein, K.H., Strachan, A.M., Snyder, K.S. and Magãna-Amato, A. 1989. Is expressed emotion an index of transaction process? I. Parents affective style. *Family Process*, **28**, 153–67.

Mill, J.S. 1859. On Liberty. In M. Warnock (Ed.) (1969) *Utilitarianism*. London: Fontana.

Miller, P.McC., Surtees, P.G., Kreitman, N.B., Inghan, J.G. and Sashidaran, S.P. 1985. Maladaptive coping reactions to stress. A study of illness inception. *Journal of Nervous and Mental Disease*, **173**, 707–16.

Miller, T.W. 1989. Group sociotherapy: A psychoeducative model for schizophrenic patients and their families. *Perspectives in Psychiatric Care*, **25**, 5–9.

Mills, E. 1962. *Living with Mental Illness: A Study in East London*. London: Routledge and Kegan Paul.

Mintz, J., Mintz, L. and Goldstein, M. 1987. Expressed emotion and relapse in first episodes of schizophrenia: A rejoinder to MacMillan *et al.* 1986. *British Journal of Psychiatry*, **151**, 314–20.

Mintz, L.I., Liberman, P., Miklowitz, D.J. and Mintz, J. 1987. Expressed emotion: A call for partnership among relatives, patients, professionals. *Schizophrenia Bulletin*, **13**, 227–35.

Moline, R.A., Singh, S., Morris, A. and Meltzer, H.Y. 1985. Family expressed emotion and relapse in schizophrenia in 24 urban American patients. *American Journal of Psychiatry*, **142**, 1078–81.

Moore, E., Ball, R.A. and Kuipers, L. 1992a. Expressed emotion in staff working with the long-term adult mentally ill. *British Journal of Psychiatry*, **161**, 802–8.

Mozny, P. and Votypkova, P. 1992. Expressed emotion, relapse rates and utilisation of psychiatric inpatient care in schizophrenia: A study from Czechoslovakia. *Social Psychiatry and Psychiatric Epidemiology*, **27**, 174–9.

Mullen, R., Bebbington, P. and Kuipers, L. 1992. A workshop for relatives of people with chronic mental illness. *Psychiatric Bulletin, Royal College of Psychiatrists*, **16**, 206–8.

National Schizophrenia Fellowship 1974. *Social Provision for Sufferers from Chronic Schizophrenia*. Surbiton: NSF.

Niskanen, P. and Pihkanen, T.A. 1972. Attitudes of relatives of schizophrenic patients: A comparison study between home-based treatment and hospital care. *Acta Psychiatrica Scandinavica*, **48**, 174–8.

Norman, R.M.G. and Malla, A.K. 1993. Stressful life events and schizophrenia. I. A review of the research. *British Journal of Psychiatry*, **162**, 161–6.

Nuechterlein, K.H. and Dawson, M.E. 1984. A heuristic vulnerability–stress model of schizophrenic episodes. *Schizophrenia Bulletin*, **10**, 300–12.

Nuechterlein, K.H., Snyder, K.S., Dawson, M.E., Rappe, S., Gitlin, M. and Fogelson, D. 1986. Expressed emotion, fixed dose fluphenazine decanoate maintenance and relapse in recent onset schizophrenia. *Psychopharmacology Bulletin*, **22**, 633–9.

Nuechterlein, K.H., Snyder, K.S. and Mintz, J. 1992. Paths to relapse: Possible transactional processes connecting patient illness onset, expressed emotion and psychotic relapse. *British Journal of Psychiatry*, **161**, 88–96.

Nunnally, J.C., Jr. 1961. *Popular Conceptions of Mental Health: Their Development and Change*. New York: Holt, Rinehart and Winston.

O'Brien, F. and Azrin, N.H. 1973. Interaction-priming: A method of reinstating patient–family relationships. *Behaviour Research and Therapy*, **11**, 133–6.

Oldridge, M.L. and Hughes, I.C.T. 1992. Psychological well-being in families with a member suffering from schizophrenia. An investigation into long-standing problems. *British Journal of Psychiatry*, **161**, 249–51.

Pakenham, K.I. and Dadds, M.R. 1987. Family care and schizophrenia: The effects of a supportive educational program on relatives' personal and social adjustments. *Australian and New Zealand Journal of Psychiatry*, **21**, 580–90.

Palazzoli, M.S., Bascolo, L., Cecchin, G. and Prata, G. 1978. *Paradox and Counterparadox*. New York: Jason Aronson.

Parker, G. 1990. *With due care and attention: A review of research on informal care*. London: Family Policy Studies Centre.

Parker, G. and Hadzi-Pavlovic, D. 1990. Expressed emotion as a predictor of schizophrenic relapse: An analysis of aggregated data. *Psychological Medicine*, **20**, 961–5.

Parker, G., Johnston, P. and Hayward, L. 1988. Parental expressed emotion as a predictor of schizophrenic relapse. *Archives of General Psychiatry*, **45**, 806–13.

Pastor, D.L. 1981. The quality of mother–infant attachments and its relation to toddlers' initial sociability with peers. *Developmental Psychology*, **17**, 326–35.

Pearlin, L.I. and Schooler, C. 1978. The structure of coping. *Journal of Health and Social Behaviour*, **19**, 2–21.

Perring, C. 1991. How do discharged psychiatric patients fare in the community? In J. Hutton, S. Hutton, T. Pinch and A. Shiell (Eds) *Dependency to Enterprise*. London: Routledge.

Perring, C., Twigg, J. and Atkin, K. 1990. *Families Caring for People Diagnosed as Mentally Ill: The Literature Re-examined*. London: HMSO.

Perris, C., Jacobsson, H., Lindstom, H., von Knorring, L. and Perris, H. 1980. Development of a new inventory for assessing memories of parental rearing behaviour. *Acta Psychiatrica Scandinavica*, **61**, 265–74.

Perris, C., Arrindell, W.A., Perris, H., Van der Ende, J., May, M., Benjaminson, S., Ross, M., Eismann, M. and der Vecchio, M. 1985. Cross-national study of perceived parental rearing behaviours in healthy subjects from Australia, Denmark, Italy, The Netherlands and Sweden: Pattern and legal comparisons. *Acta Psychiatrica Scandinavica*, **72**, 278–82.

Peter, H. and Hand, I. 1988. Patterns of patient–spouse interaction in agoraphobics: Assessment by Camberwell Family Interview (CFI) and impact on outcome of self-exposure treatment. In I. Hand and H.V. Wittchen (Eds) *Panic and Phobias. Vol. 2*. New York: Springer.

Peters, T. 1988. *Thriving on Chaos*. London: Macmillan.

Platt, S. 1985. Measuring the burden of psychiatric illness on the family: An evaluation of some rating scales. *Psychological Medicine*, **15**, 383–93.

Pratt, C.C., Schmall, V.L., Wright, S. and Cleland, M. 1985. Burden and coping strategies of caregivers to Alzheimer's patients. *Family Relations*, **34**, 27–33.

Reilly, J.W., Rohraugh, M. and Lackner, J.M. 1988. A controlled evaluation of psychoeducation workshops for relatives of State Hospital patients. *Journal of Marital and Family Therapy*, **14**, 429–32.

Reismann, F. 1965. The 'helper' therapy principle. *Social Work*, **10**, 27–32.

Reiss, D.J. 1988. Psychoeducational family treatment of schizophrenia: Dealing with the slowness of change. *International Journal of Mental Health*, **17**, 65–74.

Richardson, A., Unell, J. and Aston, B. 1989. *A New Deal for Carers*. London: Kings Fund.

Rodger, L. and Hollingshead, A. 1965. *Trapped: Families and Schizophrenia*. New York: Wiley.

Rodnick, E.H. and Goldstein, M.J. 1974. Premorbid adjustment of the recovery of mothering function in acute schizophrenic women. *Journal of Abnormal Psychology*, **83**, 623–8.

Roth, L.H. and Meisel, A. 1977. Dangerousness, confidentiality, and the duty to warn. *American Journal of Psychiatry*, **134**, 508–11.

Rutter, M. and Quinton, D. 1984. Parental psychiatric disorder: Effects on children. *Psychological Medicine*, **14**, 853–80.

Sakamoto, Y. 1969. A study of the attitude of Japanese families of schizophrenics towards their ill members. *Psychotherapy and Psychosomatics*, **17**, 365–74.

Salokangas, R.K. 1983. Prognostic implications of the sex of schizophrenic patients. *British Journal of Psychiatry*, **142**, 145–51.

Sarbin, T.R. and Mancuso, J.C. 1970. Failure of a moral enterprise: Attitudes of the public toward mental illness. *Journal of Consulting and Clinical Psychology*, **35**, 159–72.

Scharfstein, B. and Libbey, M. 1982. Family orientation: Initiating patients and their families to psychiatric hospitalisation. *Hospital and Community Psychiatry*, **33**, 560–3.

Schwartz, C. and Myers, J.K. 1977. Life events and schizophrenia. I. Comparison of schizophrenia with a community sample. *Archives of General Psychiatry*, **34**, 1238–41.

Scott, R.D. 1991. Family relationships and outcome in schizophrenia focusing on the often unperceived role of the patient. In N.R. Punukollu (Ed.) *Recent Advances in Crisis Intervention, Vol. 1*. Huddersfield: Intervention and Community Psychiatry Press.

Scott, R. D. and Montanez, A. 1971. The nature of tenable and untenable patient–parent relationships and their connection with hospital outcome. In Y. Alanen (Ed.) *Proceedings of the 4th International Symposium on Psychotherapy of Schizophrenia*. Amsterdam: Excerpta Medica.

Secretaries of State for Health, Social Security, Wales and Scotland, 1989. *Caring for People. Community Care in the Next Decade and Beyond*. London: HMSO.

Seywert, F. 1984. Some critical thoughts on expressed emotion. *Psychopathology*, **17**, 233–43.

Sidley, G.L., Smith, J. and Howells, K. 1991. Is it ever too late to learn? Information provision to relatives of long-term schizophrenia sufferers. *Behavioural Psychotherapy*, **19**, 305–20.

Skynner, R. 1989. *Institutions and How to Survive Them: Mental Health Training and Consultation*. London: Methuen.

Smith, J. and Birchwood, M.J. 1985. *Understanding Schizophrenia 1, 2, 3, 4*. Health Promotion Unit, West Birmingham Health Authority.

Smith, J.V. and Birchwood, M.J. 1987. Specific and non-specific effects of educational interventions with families of schizophrenic patients. *British Journal of Psychiatry*, **150**, 645–52.

Smith, J. and Birchwood, M. 1990. Relatives and patients as partners in the management of schizophrenia: The development of a service model. *British Journal of Psychiatry*, **156**, 654–60.

Snyder, K.S. 1984. Education for families of schizophrenic patients: Rationale, annotated review and users' guide. In M.J. Goldstein, L. Cazalino and K. Snyder (Eds) *Education for Families with Schizophrenic Members*. Rockville MD: Office of Prevention, NIMH.

Social Work Services Group 1984. *Supporting the Informal Carers: Fifty Styles of Caring; Models of Practice for Planners and Practitioners*. London: DHSS.

Spaniol, L., Zipple, A. and FitzGerald, S. 1984. How professionals can share power with families: Practical approaches to working with families of the mentally ill. *Psychosocial Rehabilitation Journal*, **8**, 77–84.

Steinglass, P. 1987. Psychoeducational family therapy for schizophrenia: A review essay. *Psychiatry*, **50**, 14–23.

Stern, D. and Agacinski, K. 1986. Family night: One facet of family intervention in a day-hospital programme. *International Journal of Partial Hospitalisation*, **3**, 285–9.

Stirling, J., Tantum, D., Thomas, P., Newby, D., Montague, L., Ring, N. and Rowe, S. 1991. Expressed emotion and early-onset schizophrenia: A one-year follow-up. *Psychological Medicine*, **21**, 675–85.

Strachan, A.M. 1986. Family intervention for the rehabilitation of schizophrenia: Toward protection and coping. *Schizophrenia Bulletin*, **12**, 678–98.

Strachan, A.M., Leff, J.P., Goldstein, M.J., Doane, J.A. and Burtt, C. 1986. Emotional attitudes and direct communication in the families of schizophrenics: A cross-national replication. *British Journal of Psychiatry*, **149**, 279–87.

Strachan, A.M., Feingold, D., Goldstein, M.J., Miklowitz, D.J. and Nuechterlein, K.H. 1989. Is expressed emotion an index of transactional process? II. Patient's coping style. *Family Process*, **28**, 169–81.

Sullivan, H.S. 1927. The onset of schizophrenia. *American Journal of Psychiatry*, **7**, 105–34.

Tarrier, N. 1989. Electrodermal activity, expressed emotion and outcome in schizophrenia. *British Journal of Psychiatry*, **155**, Suppl. 5, 51–6.

Tarrier, N. 1991. Some aspects of family intervention in schizophrenia. I. Adherence to intervention programmes. *British Journal of Psychiatry*, **159**, 475–80.

Tarrier, N. and Barrowclough, C. 1984. Psychophysiological assessment of expressed emotion in schizophrenia: A case study. *British Journal of Psychiatry*, **145**, 197–203.

Tarrier, N. and Barrowclough, C. 1986. Providing information to relatives about schizophrenia: Some comments. *British Journal of Psychiatry*, **149**, 458–63.

Tarrier, N., Vaughn, C.E., Lader, M.H. and Leff, J.P. 1979. Bodily reactions to people and events in schizophrenia. *Archives of General Psychiatry*, **36**, 311–15.

Tarrier, N., Barrowclough, C., Vaughn, C., Bamrah, J.S., Porceddu, K., Watts, S. and Freeman, H. 1988a. The community management of schizophrenia: A controlled trial of a behavioural intervention with families to reduce relapse. *British Journal of Psychiatry*, **153**, 532–42.

Tarrier, N., Barrowclough, C., Porceddu, K. and Watts, S. 1988b. The assessment of psychophysiological reactivity to expressed emotion of the relatives of schizophrenic patients. *British Journal of Psychiatry*, **152**, 618–24.

Tarrier, N., Barrowclough, C., Vaughn, C., Bamrah, J.S., Porceddu, K., Watts, S. and Freeman, H. 1989. The community management of schizophrenia: A two-year follow-up of a behavioural intervention with families. *British Journal of Psychiatry*, **154**, 625–8.

Thompson, S.C. and Pitts, J.S. 1992. In sickness and in health: Chronic illness, marriage and spousal caregiving. In S. Spacapans and S. Oskamp (Eds) *Helping and Being Helped. Naturalistic Studies*. Newbury Park, CA: Sage.

Toner, H.L. 1987. Effectiveness of a written guide for carers of dementia sufferers. *British Journal of Clinical and Social Psychiatry*, **5**, 24–6.

Tunnell, G., Alpert, M., Jacobs, J. and Osiason, J. 1988. Designing a family psychoeducation programme to meet community needs: The NYU/Bellevue project. *International Journal of Mental Health*, **17**, 75–98.

Turner, T.H. 1986. Responding to stigma. *Bulletin of the Royal College of Psychiatrists*, **10**, 359.

Twigg, J. 1989. Models of carers: How do social care agencies conceptualise their relationship with informal carers? *Journal of Social Policy*, **18**, 53–66.

Twigg, J. and Atkin, K. 1991. *Evaluating Support to Informal Carers*. York: Social Policy Research Unit.

Twigg, J., Atkin, K. and Perring, C. 1990. *Carers and Services: A Review of Research*. London: HMSO.

Ungerson, C. 1987. *Policy is Personal*. London: Tavistock.

Vaughn, C. 1986. Comments on Dulz and Hand. In M. Goldstein, L. Hand and K. Hahlweg (Eds) *Treatment of Schizophrenia: Family Assessment and Intervention*. Berlin: Springer-Verlag.

Vaughn, C.E. 1989. Expressed emotion in family relationships. *Journal of Child Psychology and Psychiatry*, **30**, 13–22.

Vaughn, C. and Leff, J. 1976a. The influence of family and social factors on the course of psychiatric illness: A comparison of schizophrenic and depressed neurotic patients. *British Journal of Psychiatry*, **129**, 125–37.

Vaughn, C.E. and Leff, J. 1976b. The measurement of expressed emotion in the families of psychiatric patients. *British Journal of Social and Clinical Psychology*, **15**, 157–65.

Vaughn, C. and Leff, J. 1981. Patterns of emotional response in relatives of schizophrenic patients. *Schizophrenia Bulletin*, **7**, 43–4.

Vaughn, C. E., Snyder, K.S., Jones, S., Freeman, W. and Falloon, I.R.H. 1984. Family factors in schizophrenic relapse. *Archives of General Psychiatry*, **41**, 1169–77.

Vaughan, K., Doyle, M., McConaghy, F., Blaszczynski, A., Fox, A. and Tarrier, N. 1992. The relationship between relatives' EE and schizophrenia relapse: An Australian replication. *Social Psychiatry and Psychiatric Epidemiology*, **27**, 10–15.

Ventura, J., Nuechterlein, K.H., Pederson, J., Hardesty, J.P. and Gitlin, M. 1992. Life events and schizophrenic relapse after withdrawal of medication. *British Journal of Psychiatry*, **161**, 615–20.

Walker, A. 1982. The meaning and social division of community care. In A. Walker (Ed.) *Community Care: The Family, the State and Social Policy*. Oxford: Basil Blackwell.

Wallace, C.J. and Liberman, R.P. 1985. Social skills training for patients with schizophrenia: A controlled clinical trial. *Psychiatry Research*, **13**, 239–47.

Wallace, C.J., Nelson, C.J., Liberman, R.P., Aitchison, R.A., Lukoff, D., Elder, J. and Ferris, C. 1980. A review and critique of social skills training with schizophrenic patients. *Schizophrenia Bulletin*, **6**, 42–63.

Walrond-Skinner, S. 1987. Feminist therapy and family therapy: The limits to the association. In S. Walrond-Skinner and D. Watson (Eds) *Ethical Issues in Family Therapy*. London: Routledge and Kegan Paul.

Weakland, J.H., Fisch, R., Watzlawick, P. and Brodin, A.M. 1974. Brief therapy: Focussed problem resolution. *Family Process*, **13**, 141–68.

Weal, E. 1980. California parents join together. *Innovations*, **7**, 20–1.

Weiner, B. 1986. *An Attributional Theory of Motivation and Emotion*. New York: Springer-Verlag.

West, K., Cozolino, L., Malin, B., McVey, G.G., Lansky, M.R. and Bley, C.K. 1985. Involving families in treating schizophrenia: The role of family education. In M.R. Lansky (Ed.) *Family Approach to Major Psychiatric Disorder*. Washington, DC: American Psychiatric Association.

Whittick, J.E. 1993. Carers of the Dementing Elderly. Coping Techniques and Expressed Emotion. Ph.D. Thesis, University of Glasgow.

Wig, N., Ghosh, A., Bedi, H., Menon, D.K., Korton, A., Ernberg, G., Day, R., Sartorius, N. and Jablensky, A. 1987. Influence of relatives' expressed emotion on the course of schizophrenia in Chandigarh. *British Journal of Psychiatry*, **151**, 166–73.

Williams, P., Williams, W.A., Sommer, R. and Sommer, B. 1986. A survey of the California Alliance for the Mentally Ill. *Hospital and Community Psychiatry*, **37**, 253–6.

Wing, J.K. 1978. *Reasoning about Madness*. Oxford: Oxford University Press.

Wing, J.K. and Brown, G.W. 1970. *Institutionalisation and Schizophrenia. A Comparative Study of Three Mental Hospitals 1960–68.* Cambridge: Cambridge University Press.

Wing, J.K., Cooper, J.E. and Sartorius, M. 1974. *The Description and Classification of Psychiatric Symptoms: An Instruction Manual for the PSE and CATEGO System.* London: Cambridge University Press.

Wing, J.K., Bebbington, P. and Robins, L.N. 1981. *What is a Case?* London: Grant McIntyre.

Wynne, L.C. and Singer, M.T. 1965. Thought disorder and family relations of schizophrenics. I. Research strategy. *Archives of General Psychiatry,* 9, 191–8.

Yarrow, M., Clausen, J. and Robbins, P. 1955a. The social meaning of mental illness. *Journal of Social Issues,* 11, 33–45.

Yarrow, M., Schwartz, C.G., Murphy, H.S. and Deasy, L.C. 1955b. The psychological meaning of mental illness in the family. *Journal of Social Issues,* 11, 12–24.

Zelitch, S.R. 1980. Helping the family cope: Workshops for families of schizophrenics. *Health and Social Work,* 5, 47–52.

Zubin, J. and Spring, B. 1977. Vulnerability: A new view of schizophrenia. *Journal of Abnormal Psychology,* 86, 103–26.

Zubin, J., Steinhauer, S.R. and Condray, R. 1992. Vulnerability to relapse in schizophrenia. *British Journal of Psychiatry,* 161, Suppl. 18, 13–18.

Appendix 1

NOTES FOR RELATIVES

MEETING PLACE   _____

GROUP LEADER   _____

Contact at   _____

SESSION	TITLE	DATE
1	What does schizophrenia mean to you?	
2	What is schizophrenia?	
3	Why?	
4	Treatment of schizophrenia	
5	Relatives' problems	
6	The family and schizophrenia	
7	Creating a low-stress environment	
8	Managing disturbed behaviour	
9	Using services and dealing with crises	
10	Where do we go from here?	

Further Reading:

Schizophrenia. A Guide for Sufferers and their Families. Jacqueline M.
   Atkinson, Turnstone Press.

This book is available in libraries in Glasgow—if your library does not
   have it you can ask to order it.
It is also available or can be ordered from bookshops.

SESSION 1:

WHAT DOES SCHIZOPHRENIA MEAN TO YOU?

Schizophrenia is one of the most severe, and most dramatic, of the mental illnesses. It is also one of the most common, affecting approximately one person in every hundred. Schizophrenia affects the way a person thinks, and, because of this, affects every other part of their lives—how they behave, how they feel, what they believe, how they relate to other people.

It is almost impossible to imagine what schizophrenia is like—it is not the same as someone who is very depressed and anxious, when we can imagine, from our own feelings, what they are going through. It is this inability easily to understand how the person with schizophrenia feels, or what they experience, that leads to so many of the problems in families.

Here are some examples of how patients and relatives have described their experience of schizophrenia.

> Family friction was a severe problem, but for three years now he has been on regular medication, and a part time job that keeps him occupied and so we don't have to listen all the time to him and his worries. I have just spent three weeks with him trying to take him out every day for his holiday. I was worn out at the end.   Mother

> I have always tended to be somewhat lazy but my motivation problem appears to be worse now. At times it is a real effort to get involved in anything.   Male patient

> I have lost all my old friends and husband through the illness. Fortunately I have a few new friends who, knowing me only since the beginning of my acute illness, are more tolerant. Some of them I have met directly through being in hospital or at a day centre. Female patient

> He was admitted to _____ three times in as many months, having been discharged too quickly on each occasion. Finally he returned with us to (home) and has lived with us ever since. _____ Hospital has little in-house facilities and no help for discharged patients.   Father

The sufferer will not accept that she is ill.   Sister

My son was 40 last week, he has become a great worry to us as he grows older. I can't say how worried I am about what will happen to him when I am no longer here.   Mother

Discussion Questions

1. Why have you come? What do you expect from the group?

2. What are your current major problems? Are these the same as, or different from, the past?

3. What do you think schizophrenia is?

4. Is schizophrenia an illness? What other explanations do you, or others in your family, have for your relative's behaviour?

SESSION 2:

WHAT IS SCHIZOPHRENIA?

Schizophrenia is a severe mental illness, a psychosis. In this session we will look at, and discuss, what the symptoms of schizophrenia are, how these cause the patient to act, and how a psychiatrist looks for symptoms and uses them to make a diagnosis.

Acute symptoms

During the acute phase of the illness the patient shows what are called positive symptoms. This means that something is *added*, that the person has new, unusual behaviours. Many people have heard words like 'delusions' or 'hallucinations' but don't really understand what they mean. In this session we will explain what the acute symptoms are. These include:

1. Appearance and general behaviour;

2. Speech;

3. Disorders of thinking—the way a person thinks,

                    —what a person thinks, e.g. delusions;

4. Disturbances of perception—e.g. hallucinations;

5. Attention, concentration and memory;

6. Insight, or how the person views their illness;

7. Disorder of emotions.

To have schizophrenia the patient does not have to have *all* these symptoms. The minimum necessary to diagnose schizophrenia will be outlined.

Chronic symptoms

The patient does not stay in an acute phase for ever, or sometimes even for long. With treatment (see Session 4), many of these symptoms will be suppressed, or they may just disappear with time. The behaviours which are much more typical of someone with chronic schizophrenia are usually called negative symptoms. This means that something has been 'taken away' from the person's behaviour, for example, their motivation to do anything, so we are left with a person who is apathetic and lethargic.

Diagnosis

What is a diagnosis and how is it made? Does getting a diagnosis matter?

Psychiatrists talk to patients to establish what symptoms the patient has. They may also talk to relatives to find out what has been happening. Sometimes this can feel like a cross-examination, but it is important to make sure both sides mean the same thing. A clinical history will also be taken, which means: what has happened in the past, how someone was treated, how they responded, for example to particular drugs, and so on.

Getting a diagnosis is not always straightforward—it may take time for a psychiatrist to be sure whether someone really has schizophrenia or not.

Subgroups of schizophrenia

Some of you may have heard of different types of schizophrenia, although most psychiatrists do not use these categories now. The one most people have heard of, and is still used, is paranoid schizophrenia, but other types are catatonic schizophrenia, hebephrenic schizophrenia, and simple schizophrenia. These will be described.

Discussion Questions

1. Do you recognise any of the acute or chronic symptoms in your ill relative?

2. Do you think you understand the symptoms?

3. Do you think patients and relatives should be told the diagnosis? If so, when? Is it better to know as soon as possible? Or later? Why?

4. How do you feel about the way you were told?

5. Do you think your relative has been properly diagnosed?

6. Do you think they really have schizophrenia?

SESSION 3:

WHY?

What causes schizophrenia? Why has this happened to us?

These are the two questions we will be discussing in today's session. No-one knows one hundred per cent what causes schizophrenia, but there are a number of explanations which hold some of the truth.

It is likely that a number of factors contribute to the cause (the jargon word is aetiology) of schizophrenia. Or it may be that what we know as schizophrenia is a number of illnesses with different causes.

We will discuss a number of different explanations.

Genetic factors

It is suggested that schizophrenia sometimes runs in families, that it may be inherited in some way. If it is, no-one yet knows how. Evidence for this theory comes from studies with twins, and adoption studies. We will discuss the very slight risk to families (brothers and sisters, or children) of people with schizophrenia that they might develop the illness themselves or pass it on.

Biochemical factors

It might be that something is wrong with the way the brain works—that there is something wrong with the brain's biochemistry. One explanation is that a substance in the brain called dopamine is not handled correctly. Dopamine is a transmitter substance—that is, it is involved in passing on messages between nerve cells in the brain. It is as though there is a network of nerve cells, and transmitter substances help to switch cells on and off.

Drugs that suppress the action of dopamine usually improve the acute symptoms of schizophrenia. You may have heard of dopamine in connection with another illness—Parkinson's disease.

Neurological abnormalities

Some people believe that there are differences between the brains of people with schizophrenia and those who do not have it.

Environmental factors

Most people agree that environment plays some part in the development of schizophrenia, but it cannot produce schizophrenia by itself. Stress is very important—people with schizophrenia seem unable to withstand as much stress as those who do not have the illness. For some patients change seems to be the crucial factor that contributes to their illness, for others too much pressure will be a problem.

Family factors

Although in the past some people have suggested that the type of family you grow up in can cause schizophrenia, there is no real evidence to support this. We will discuss the impact of the family on schizophrenia in Session 6.

Psychological factors

There are some psychological factors which have to do with arousal, attention and perception, and thought and speech disorders which influence the way schizophrenia develops.

Why?

None of these fully answer questions like 'why now?' 'why me?' Families and patients often search through their history to try to find a cause. It is unlikely that one single thing caused schizophrenia to develop in a person, and searching to put the blame on something, or, even worse, someone, is not necessarily helpful.

Discussion Questions

1. What do you think causes schizophrenia?

2. Do you have any explanation for what happened in your family? How does it stand up in the light of what you have just heard?

3. Do you keep looking backward to try to find out why or how it started? Do you find this helpful? Why?

SESSION 4:

TREATMENT OF SCHIZOPHRENIA

At different times in their illness people with schizophrenia will either be in hospital receiving treatment, or getting treatment on an out-patient basis or possibly from their GP. Sometimes they will improve enough to go for periods with no treatment at all. Not all patients will be offered, nor would benefit from, all the treatments discussed. What treatment might a patient receive?

Drug therapy

Drugs or medication are often the first treatment method tried when someone is acutely ill. Drugs can damp down many of the positive symptoms (see Session 1) but do not do anything for the chronic, negative symptoms. Drugs are usually given either as pills or as an injection.

The drugs used may have side effects in the patient and they may have to take other drugs to control these side effects. We will discuss the form these side effects take during this session, and what can be done about them.

There are some patients whose symptoms do not appear to be influenced by drugs at all.

Psychotherapy

This involves talking to a therapist. It cannot cure, or manage, the acute symptoms of schizophrenia, but 'supportive psychotherapy' may help someone to come to terms with their situation and manage their life better.

Social therapy

This often comes under the heading rehabilitation, and involves someone learning or re-learning everyday activities ranging from caring for themselves to getting on with other people.

Behaviour therapy

This is a set of techniques to help a person learn new behaviour. Such techniques may well be used as part of social therapy or rehabilitation. It is usually used to manage chronic symptoms such as withdrawal and apathy, rather than acute symptoms.

Social skills training comes under this category and can be useful for withdrawn or socially anxious people.

Industrial therapy

Whether within the hospital or at a special unit, the aim of industrial therapy is to develop the patient's work habits and their confidence in the work situation. For some people this may be a brief period before returning to work; for others it may be as much as they can cope with.

Day care

Day wards in hospitals provide care for those not requiring inpatient hospital treatment but who still need continued supervision, and often provide a stage between in-patient care and attending a day centre. Day centres are for those who will benefit from the various social therapies, groups and activities on offer. The social contact is important for people living on their own or who are very withdrawn.

Rehabilitation

Rehabilitation includes many of the activities found under social therapy and aims to make the person as independent and capable of looking after themselves as possible. What this means, and what has to be learnt, differs from person to person, and good assessment is necessary.

Prognosis

Prognosis means how is someone going to do over time. Many factors are involved, including how the illness started, how the person responds to drugs and other treatments, and the type of environment they live in.

Discussion Questions

1. What treatments have you experience of? Were they helpful?

2. Do you have any reservations about any of the treatments? Why?

3. Are there other treatments you have heard of? Has your relative tried any? What do you think of them?

4. What do you think the aim of rehabilitation should be?

SESSION 5:

RELATIVES' PROBLEMS

So far we have been concentrating on what schizophrenia is, how it is treated, and what sort of course it follows. We have been considering schizophrenia very much from the point of view of the patient. This week we will return to some of the issues that were raised in the first session and consider how living with someone who has schizophrenia affects the rest of the family, and how some of these problems might be managed.

The problems of the family have often been described as 'burden' by professionals—objective burden being things like financial problems and disruption of daily living, and subjective burden being how you feel about the illness, about having to care for someone with the illness, and its effects on the family.

Rather than have separate discussion questions at the end, as in the other sessions, there are a number of issues and questions for you to think about. For example, do you find the concept of burden appropriate?

Anxiety

Anxiety and worry about the present, about how to manage the patient on a day-to-day basis. Worry about the future—what will happen when you can no longer look after the patient? How do you cope with anxiety? How does it make you feel?

Family friction

Do different family members expect different things of the patient? Do some think he/she is lazy rather than ill? Does this lead to family problems or arguments? Is there particular family friction between the patient and another family member? How does this affect you? How do you cope?

Blame and guilt

Do you blame yourself for the patient's condition? Why? Does this make sense? Do you blame anyone else? Does anyone else blame you?

Why? How does this affect your relationship with them? With the patient? How do you cope?

Embarrassment

Do you ever feel embarrassed by how the patient behaves? Why? When? Does this make you feel guilty? How do you cope? Are other family members embarrassed by the patient—for example brothers or sisters, children?

Burden

How great is the burden of caring for the patient? How much do you do for the patient? Do you subsidise him/her financially? Does having the patient at home stop you doing things—going out, working, inviting people round?

Health

Do you feel your health has been affected through caring for the patient? Has anyone else's health been affected? How?

Privacy

Do you find it difficult to have time to yourself because of caring for the patient? Does this bother you? If the patient is your child, do you ever get to spend time alone with your spouse?

SESSION 6:

THE FAMILY AND SCHIZOPHRENIA

Many people with schizophrenia live with their family, either because they choose to, because they could not manage on their own, or sometimes because there is nowhere else for them to go. We need to consider the effect that living with the family has on the person who has schizophrenia.

There have been several theories which considered certain types of family to be involved in causing schizophrenia. In the main they concentrated on problems in communication within the family, or disordered relationships between the parents of the person with schizophrenia. None of these family theories have any evidence to support them. What is important is to look at how the family may affect someone with schizophrenia once they get the illness.

Does the way someone is treated have any affect on how well they do? There are several important areas to be considered in relation to that question.

Stress

There is some agreement that people with schizophrenia handle stress poorly. It seems that they have a low tolerance for stress—things which would not be stressful for someone who does not have schizophrenia can prove too much for those who have it. Clearly this makes knowing how far to push or encourage someone to do something a difficult decision. On the one hand too much pushing may lead to problems and even relapse, whereas no encouragement to do things may see someone sink into apathy and withdrawal.

Criticism

Some family members may be overly critical of the patient, and this will often be experienced as stressful by that patient. This can, in turn, lead to an increase in problems, or possibly relapse. Criticism, hostility and a generally highly charged negative atmosphere can all cause problems for the patient, as well as being unpleasant for everyone to live with.

Maintaining a more low-key atmosphere and being encouraging without putting on the pressure seems to be the sort of environment in which many people with schizophrenia do well.

Over-protectiveness

This is often the most difficult to see in ourselves. It may be that someone with schizophrenia may need 'watching over' sometimes, but this can become stifling, and again lead to an increase in problems and possible relapse.

Over-protectiveness shows itself when relatives or friends do practically everything for the patient and never let them try to manage on their own. It is usually done for the best of reasons: 'he's not well, you can't expect him to cope', or 'I'm her mother. Of course I'll look after her', or 'I'm only trying to prevent him from failing/making a mess of things/looking silly/losing money/', and so on.

Sometimes the over-protectiveness is based on past experiences—things *have* gone wrong in the past, so now they are not given the opportunity to learn or try again. Or someone has behaved irresponsibly when they were acutely ill, and are then not trusted when they are better again.

Over-involvement

Like over-protectiveness, it's often hard to see if we are overinvolved and the effects are much the same. We might say it's 'only natural' to want to know what our child or spouse is doing or thinking, or what happened to them at the hospital today, or what the psychiatrist said, or whether their medication was changed and so forth. When this gets to the point of not allowing the patient any privacy, and not allowing them to make any decisions of their own, this can be experienced as extremely stressful.

Over-protectiveness and over-involvement often come together and are best summed up as saying that the person is being treated more like a child than an adult. Someone with schizophrenia may have particular problems in dealing with life but, whatever their problems, they are adults and not children. This is the role they have to learn to take, and the family have to allow them to take it.

In the next two sessions we will concentrate on how to manage some of these particular problems.

Discussion Questions

1. Do you recognise any of this behaviour in yourself or other members of your family? What do you feel about it?

2. How does it affect the patient? Are there other ways of behaving?

3. Why do you think some of these behaviours, such as over-protectiveness or hostility, may develop?

4. Does any of this sort of behaviour create friction between other members of the family?

5. Do you feel you have been blamed in the past (or even now) by professionals for causing the illness? How did this make you feel?

SESSION 7:

CREATING A LOW-STRESS ENVIRONMENT

This session follows directly on from the last and looks at how we can use the knowledge we have gained about schizophrenia to create an atmosphere at home which enables both the person with schizophrenia and the family to do as well as possible.

We have said that undue stress is bad for someone with schizophrenia. What sort of things can we do to prevent this stress?

Communication

One way to try to relieve stress and pressure is to talk about what is going on, both with the patient and with other family members. This does not mean going over something endlessly, ganging-up against someone, or pushing a person to talk at the wrong time. It does mean putting your point of view across clearly, and listening to theirs; letting someone know your feelings and finding out theirs. It *is* possible to explain to someone why something they do causes you to feel angry or worried without putting the blame for that anger or worry on the other person.

Talking about problems is usually best done away from the heat of the situation—no discussion works well when everyone is upset and feeling fraught. Sometimes this will mean leaving the discussion of a certain topic until the patient is no longer acutely ill and can handle it. Discuss bad times only when the person is well, not in order to blame them, but with a view to knowing what to do in the future. Remember that there should be no recriminations; no going back over how bad things have been; no pressure of the type: 'if you had any feelings for us at all you wouldn't behave like this.'

Involving the Patient

Encourage your relative to participate in family events, and sometimes do things together that you all enjoy.

When does encouragement become pushing/nagging? This question is hard to answer, since it will be slightly different in every case. It is important to try to establish what the patient *can* do, what they *want* to do, and what they *might want* to do. Remember that just because someone has schizophrenia it does not mean they cannot have valid opinions and interests. Concentrate, at least at first, on things the person is interested in, and wants to do.

Is it Really a Problem?

Ask yourself why certain things upset you? Does it *really* affect you? Or others? Is it disruptive or is it simply that something is not being done as you think it should? Does everyone in the family agree that there is a problem? If not, why? Whose standards/values are you imposing? Why? How does this contribute to hostility, over-involvement and over-protectiveness?

Privacy

Stress can be reduced in many cases by allowing the patient a certain privacy and independence. This may need to be negotiated so that it does not degenerate into withdrawal, but everyone needs a certain amount of privacy in their lives.

Creating Warmth

Most of these suggestions are aimed at lowering the negative aspects of interaction between members of the family and the patient, and creating a warmer atmosphere.

Discussion Questions

1. Do you think these strategies would work? If not, why? If yes, how are you going to use them?

2. How can you set about improving communication to reduce stress?

3. Do you think it is possible to put over emotional messages in a neutral way?

4. How far do you want the patient involved in the daily life of the family?

5. Who defines what is a problem?

SESSION 8:

MANAGING DISTURBED BEHAVIOUR

What families consider disturbed or disturbing will vary. Some people can ignore odd ideas or somone answering 'the voices', others cannot. The patient's inability to live by 'normal hours' is stressful for some, others worry more about lack of friends and isolation than they do about overtly 'ill' behaviour.

Different problems require different kinds of solutions—the ideas and strategies we discussed last time will come back into our discussion today. As relatives living with the problems you know as much as anyone how to handle certain situations, and by sharing your ideas and ways of coping you may learn new strategies as well as passing on your own.

When looking for ways of managing a problem, do not always expect the change to come from the patient. If they do not see a problem, or the need to change, there is little likelihood of success. Some families, however, go to the opposite extreme and try to adapt to accommodate everything the patient does. This is not necessarily the best thing for the patient, or the family either.

Setting Limits

There are some behaviours which everyone would agree are undesirable but, nevertheless, are tolerated differently by families. These include verbal abuse and swearing, being aggressive and being violent. It often helps to set limits about potential problem behaviour when someone is well. Agree with the patient and other family members what is acceptable and what the consequences of overstepping the limit are, and then *stick to it*. Physical violence to people should not be tolerated.

Delusions and Hallucinations

Remaining calm and avoiding argument is probably the best way of dealing with these behaviours. You may need to acknowledge that the patient believes what they do, but never go along with this to 'humour them', nor try to talk them out of it. You will not be able to dissuade them and may only cause more friction or distress.

Other problems you may want to discuss how to manage include:

- lack of friends, isolation and loneliness;
- depression;
- suicide attempts or talk of suicide;
- withdrawal;
- apathy;
- aggression—verbal and physical.

Discussion Questions

1. What problems affect you the most? How do you manage them?
2. Do you think you should set limits or should families adapt to the patient's behaviour 'because they are ill'? Who should change the most, patients or families? Why?

SESSION 9:

USING SERVICES AND DEALING WITH CRISES

What services are available and how do you contact them? Since it helps to go to the right person for the right thing, we will discuss what you can expect from:

- the hospital;
- the day centre;
- a psychiatrist;
- a GP;
- a community psychiatric nurse (CPN);
- a social worker;
- other people you may have come across.

There are also other people who can be helpful sometimes, or who you may need to involve:

- ministers or priests;
- solicitors;
- police;
- voluntary organisations.

Getting the Most out of your Doctor (or other Professional)

1. Be clear in your own mind what you want to discuss/ask. To do this:

    - write down a list of all the things on your mind;
    - then group the ideas under headings;
    - then decide what your priorities are.

2. Make an appointment to see the GP, psychiatrist or whoever and tell them why you want to see them.

3. Take your list with you, so you do not forget what you wanted to raise.

4. Take paper and a pen with you so you can write down what is said and you do not have to rely on your memory.

5. Be persistent—but not rude (as this only puts people's backs up). As carers you should expect some consideration and advice from professionals.

6. Do not demand the impossible! (It might be helpful to discuss in the group what is impossible and what are reasonable demands.)

7. Keep a list of who you see, when, why, what they say and what happens, as well as major happenings to the patient (e.g. hospital admissions, changes in treatment and so on). It gives you more confidence to be sure you have your facts/order of events right when dealing with people who might not have the whole picture.

Coping with a Crisis

- What is a crisis?

- Who do you contact?

- What if you are ignored?

Keep a list of useful telephone numbers together so you always have it handy. For example:

NAME	TELEPHONE NUMBER
Hospital	
Psychiatrist	
GP	
Social worker	
Day centre	
Other	

Discussion Questions

1. How many people are involved with your relative? Do you know what they do? How helpful were they?

2. Who do you think might be helpful? Why?

3. What has happened to you in the past at time of crisis? What do you think should happen?

SESSION 10:

WHERE DO WE GO FROM HERE?

This session gives you the opportunity to go over things you have covered in previous weeks, discuss anything that you want to and which has not come up yet, and look at what changes, if any, the group has made to how you think and feel about schizophrenia and how you behave towards your relative.

You will have an opportunity to discuss where you want to go from here and what sort of services or support you would (ideally) like.

Discussion Questions

1. Has the group made any difference to how I think and feel about schizophrenia? How?

2. Has it altered my behaviour in anyway?

3. Where do we go from here?

Appendix 2

NOTES FOR GROUP LEADERS RUNNING GROUPS

SESSION 1:

INTRODUCTION

WHAT DOES SCHIZOPHRENIA MEAN TO YOU?

1. Group leader introduces self.

2. Describe group. It is:

   - here to provide information and education,

   - a place to discuss problems,

   - informal,

   - confidential.

Emphasise confidentiality:

'I would ask you not to discuss details of other people's lives which you hear here with people outside the group. I will not pass on comments you make to other staff unless you ask me to, neither will any comments be passed on to your ill relative.

No-one will force you to say anything, and even if you feel a bit shy or uneasy at first remember that everyone is in the same position. You all know that living with someone who has schizophrenia can be more than difficult at times, and we know that other people often do not understand what it means or what you are going through. This group is set up to deal with some of these problems.'

3. Group members introduce themselves, giving a brief account of their problems—if they want to.

4. Describe leader's role in group:

'My role is to give you some information and help you think about problems and discuss them amongst yourselves. It is not just to answer questions, nor is it to discuss how your relative is being treated by the hospital, nor to discuss particular doctors.

You have a booklet which describes what we are going to talk about over the coming weeks. For example, next week we are going to look at what the symptoms of schizophrenia are, and how it is diagnosed. The week after, why it happens, and then what can be done about it, how it can be treated, and so on. This is so that we can make sure that we cover all the topics which are important, and let you discuss all aspects of schizophrenia and not just some. This means that we will need to try to stick to the topic to be covered. Of course there will be some overlap, but we do not want to get stuck in a rut, talking about the same problems every time.

Today, however, we are going to be fairly general in our discussion and talk about what schizophrenia means to you as relatives.'

In all handouts to relatives there are questions for discussion. You can use these to get the ball rolling if necessary, but do not feel yourself limited to them.

SESSION 2:

WHAT IS SCHIZOPHRENIA?

1. Introduce the concept of schizophrenia as psychosis. Explain the difference between psychosis and neurosis.

2. Acute symptoms.

   • Explain what is meant by 'acute', 'positive symptoms' and 'florid symptoms'.

   • Go through the list and outline each symptom, giving a clear example of each. Be careful to avoid using too many jargon words, and be sure to explain *everything* you think is not, or may not be, understood. Words like 'insight', 'affect', 'thought disorder', 'perception', 'paranoia', 'hallucinations', 'delusions' will have to be explained.

3. Chronic symptoms.

   • As above.

4. Discuss how symptoms may be understood.

5. Diagnosis.

   • Explain that it is a psychiatrist who makes the diagnosis and how this is done.

   • Explain what is meant by 'present state' description, a clinical history, and an interview.

   • Explain that there are no physical tests to diagnose schizophrenia *positively*, but some might be used to eliminate other disorders.

SESSION 3:

WHY?

In this session it is more important to let people deal with the wider issues of 'why has it happened to us?' than it is to get across details of dopamine theory! Some people will not be able to deal with much more information than 'it seems that to get schizophrenia you need to be born with a predisposition to develop it, and encounter sufficient environmental stress to trigger it.' Although a few people may want, and understand, quite detailed explanations, this should not take up all the group's time—it is easy to alienate or bore people over this topic.

It is also easy to use too many difficult or jargon words in this session. Be sure to explain (and not use too often) 'aetiology', 'predisposition', 'trigger', as well as more obvious terms like 'transmitter substances'. It might be particularly important in this session to ask for, and encourage, questions as you go along, so that people do not get too confused or bored.

Explain

1. Genetic factors:

    • risk, incidence,

    • twin and adoption studies.

2. Biochemical theories.

3. Neurological abnormalities.

4. Environment:

    • stress.

5. Family:

    • explain that this will be discussed in detail in Session 6.

6. Psychological mediating mechanisms.

Allow people to express their feelings of 'it's not fair' and 'what have we done to deserve this?', and discuss the arbitrariness of the illness. Discuss with them their 'search after meaning'.

Some esoteric theories of causation may come up, most notably allergies. Be prepared to deal with this!

SESSION 4:

TREATMENT OF SCHIZOPHRENIA

It is likely that in this session more time will be spent on dealing with drugs and side effects than on other aspects of treatment. Although people may have a lot to say on this aspect, try also to focus on rehabilitation and optimistic, but realistic, outcomes.

We have left out ECT as it is now rarely used for schizophrenia, but since some patients may have had it in the past, be prepared to explain and discuss it. Reassure people over its current usage.

Some unusual treatments may come up for discussion—notably treatment of allergies, megavitamin therapy, and hypnosis. Hypnosis (which is the easiest to get at!) should be strongly discouraged, and it should be pointed out that it could easily make someone worse. People may also want advice about getting second opinions, private treatment, and so on.

Main points to be covered.

1. Treatments

   - Drug therapy and side effects.

   - Psychotherapy.

   - Social therapy.

   - Behaviour therapy.

   - Industrial therapy.

   - Day care.

2. Rehabilitation

3. Prognosis

SESSION 5:

RELATIVES' PROBLEMS

This session will probably work best as a general discussion almost from the first. A brief description of some of the burden research may be useful—particularly that which suggests that families with the greatest objective burden do not necessarily experience the greatest subjective burden.

Rather than conveying a lot of information, it will be more important to make sure that everybody has an opportunity to speak and air their views. Bring the discussion around to talking about how they cope, and what their strategies are, rather than just expressing all negative comments or moaning.

Main points to be covered.

1. Anxiety, particularly about the future.

2. Family friction.

3. Blame and guilt.

4. Embarrassment.

5. Burden.

6. Health.

7. Privacy.

SESSION 6:

THE FAMILY AND SCHIZOPHRENIA

During this session it is important to *avoid* sounding as though you are putting any blame for schizophrenia on the relatives themselves. Not unnaturally many will be particularly sensitive to this issue, especially those who have felt themselves blamed by professionals in the past.

Putting over information about expressed emotion requires sensitivity and care, but as long as people are given a chance to discuss the information and express their feelings about it, it can be done. Other relatives can often point out what is, for example, reasonable behaviour and what is over-protectiveness in a more acceptable way than the group leader.

It will be worth stressing that the focus of this session is whether any of these behaviours happen, how they happen, and why they happen. What to do about them comes in the next session. If you move too quickly into what to do about these behaviours it gives people less chance to appraise their own situation honestly—and it is *this* which is the main aim of this session.

Main points to be covered.

1. Stress.

2. Expressed emotion.

   - Criticism.

   - Over-protectiveness.

   - Over-involvement.

SESSION 7:

CREATING A LOW-STRESS ENVIRONMENT

Concentrate in this session on the relatives' responses to patients' behaviour. This includes making them take responsibility for their feelings, i.e.

'when you do "X" I feel . . . '

NOT

'you make me feel . . . '

The discussion should be about putting over (negative) messages in a more neutral way. This can be translated into positive discussion about ways of talking to patients about problems, and suggestions about lowering the negative tone of communications and creating more warmth.

As in the last session, make good use of relatives who already have this mode of communicating (if there are any!) to describe what they do and encourage others. Again avoid any sense of blaming relatives for the way they react. Point out that changes are being expected of the patient as well as of them.

Main points to be covered.

1. Communication.

2. Involving the patient.

3. Is it *really* a problem? *Whose* problem is it?

4. Privacy.

SESSION 8:

MANAGING DISTURBED BEHAVIOUR

This should be another relative-led session. Discover what are common problems and spend most time discussing these. Fears about what *might* happen, e.g. someone becoming suicidal (although they have shown no evidence of this as yet), can be dealt with in less detail. (It might be worth trying to find out why someone is worried about this behaviour—are they picking up real, subtle signs of this, or is it something they have 'read somewhere'.)

Successful instances of coping from other relatives may prove to be of more use to others than discussing coping in the abstract.

It may be necessary to go back to the issue of 'whose problem is it?', and discuss the difference between disturbed and disturbing behaviour.

Setting limits is an important topic to cover, and relatives should be encouraged not to accept violence, particularly towards people, just because someone is ill. You may have to discuss police involvement, although this could come up next week.

Be prepared to discuss management of both acute and chronic problems:

1. Delusions and hallucinations.

2. Aggression and violence.

3. Suicide.

4. Withdrawal, apathy and isolation.

5. Depression.

SESSION 9:

USING SERVICES AND DEALING WITH CRISES

Outline briefly the roles and responsibilities of the main professionals involved:

- psychiatrist
- GP
- CPN
- social worker

It is important to make it clear who has responsibility for drugs and overall management. It may be necessary to clear up unrealistic expectations or views of roles.

Add others as they are mentioned or when relevant. Too many descriptions of roles at one time are confusing.

Describe techniques for making the most of any interview with a professional. Stress that the aim is for them to get what they want, even if some of it looks like making life easier for professionals.

Probably much of this session will be devoted to describing how to get help at time of crisis. *Do not* assume a GP or psychiatrist will answer a distress call from relatives. Discuss why they may not, and what to do. Try to avoid getting into a 'them' and 'us' situation by always taking the part of professionals, but explain why they may not always appear (to relatives) to be totally cooperative. Discuss issues of confidentiality, lack of resources and lack of answers. Do relatives think that a psychiatrist/whoever is deliberately withholding a cure/day centre place/whatever it is they want.

Do not get involved in defending or commenting on a particular

Discuss the use of other people, e.g. ministers or priests, as a source of support, and occasionally the involvement of police or getting legal advice. Introduce the use of voluntary organisations—to be taken up next time.

SESSION 10:

WHERE DO WE GO FROM HERE?

This is essentially a summing-up session, with revision of any points which are unclear and discussion of anything which has not yet been covered. (Please keep a note of any topics which come up which have not been mentioned before.)

Discuss how useful the group members have felt the group to be. Would they have liked it earlier (in the patient's career)?

Where do we go from here?

Is there any interest in setting up a self-help group? If yes, take names, find out thoughts about time, place, etc., and tell them about the NSF(S) and what will have to happen if a group is going to be set up.

INDEX

Advocacy, 74, 118, 123, 124, 127, 129, 133, 204

Affective style, 12, 14, 19

Alliance for the Mentally Ill of Dane County, USA, 125–6

Association of Relatives and Friends of the Mentally Ill (Inc.): Australia, 121–3

Attitudes to the family, people with schizophrenia, 30 professionals, 42–4 *see also*: Blame

Attitudes to mental illness/schizophrenia, 23–9, 40, 42–3, 76, 77, 142, 145, 156

Autonomy, 97, 111, 150, 205–9, 217, 221

Behavioural interventions/programmes, 54–6, 56–60

Biological vulnerability, 21–2, 146

Blame, of family, 5, 6, 14, 17, 18, 22, 41, 62, 66, 67, 69, 83, 99, 129, 133, 150, 184, 189, 199 of patients, 29, 41, 51

Burden, 32–3, 40, 58, 66, 81, 87, 91, 93, 94, 96, 98, 101, 103–4, 110, 113, 116, 130, 134, 149, 211, 217

Camberwell Family Interview, 7

Cape Support for Mental Health: South Africa, 126–7

Care models of, 93–5, 101–3

Carers, 33–4, 36, 73, 89, 91–113, 114, 205, 207, 208–9, 212, 215–17 as clients, 65, 93, 94, 96, 97–8, 101, 105, 206 as co-workers, 83, 93, 96, 97, 98, 99, 101, 105 as resources, 93 as superseded carers, 93, 94, 104

Carers National Association, 91

Caring, 30, 36, 91–8, 101–3, 106, 205–9, 212–13, 214, 215–17

Caring for People (White Paper), 93, 158, 204, 215

Change, 45–7, 50, 58, 79

Child rearing, 15–16, 40, 213

Children of people with schizophrenia, 39–40

Communication, 54, 55, 74, 185–7

Communication in families, 4–6, 15, 39, 64

Community care, 43, 86, 89, 91–5, 158, 159, 216, 217, 219

Community Care: Agenda for Action, 92

Confidentiality, 42, 48, 171, 192, 205, 209–12

Contacting relatives, 171–2, 174–5

Coping, 60, 80, 106–13, 152–3

Coping skills/strategies/styles, 15, 21, 31, 33, 41, 49, 74, 106–9, 111–13, 152, 199
Costs of care, 86, 91, 158, 163, 168, 219
Crisis intervention/management, 49, 55, 59, 153–4, 201
Critical comments, 7, 13, 14

Dependant, the, 93, 97, 105, 203, 215
Dependency, 29, 33, 105, 215–21
Diagnosis, 144–5, 169, 170, 193
Double bind, 4

Education, 46, 49, 50, 53, 54, 55, 56, 62, 69–90, 93, 114, 117, 127, 139, 155–6, 181–3, 221
Education groups
  setting up, 138–56, 157–78, 210, 212
    accommodation for, 163, 166–7
    budget, 162–4
    contacting patients, 170
    group membership, 173–4
    interactions within, 185–9
    justification for, 88–9, 159–60
    resources required, 162–4
  notes for, 140–1
  staff involvement, 160–2, 164–6, 167–8, 179
Education programmes, 69–90
  content of, 70–80, 82, 141–55, 191–202
  impact of, 79–80, 80–3
  style of, 78–80, 139–40, 182
  with patient or relatives, 71, 79
  see also: Education groups
ENOSH: The Israel Mental Health Association, 120–1, 127
Expressed emotion, 6, 7–18, 33, 40, 56–7, 58, 70, 84, 85, 87, 100, 103, 104, 106, 128, 133, 150–2, 180, 187, 198–9, 208, 213

assessment of, 7–8, 14, 56
concept of, 7, 10, 18
and coping, 109, 110–11
definition, 7
and contact, 8, 10–11, 110
future of, 17–18
history of, 6, 8–11
as interactionist concept, 14–17
and life events, 19–21
reducing, 49–54
and relapse, 8–9, 11, 13, 14, 20, 21, 22
stability of, 14, 18
and staff, 17–18
transcultural implications, 12–14

Family
  adjustment to illness, 40–2
  causal themes, 2–6, 77, 129
  contact with professionals, 40–1, 42–4
  effect of schizophrenia on, 33–42, 150–1, 198–9
  and guilt, 29, 32, 37, 38, 41
  health of, 34–5
  maintaining in group/treatment, 64–7, 176, 191, 213
  relationships in team, 36–40, 151, 202, 209–10
  relationship with professionals/ therapists, 62–3, 97, 103, 128–9, 183–5, 189–91
  see also: Expressed emotion
Family intervention programmes, 49–51
Family-orientated treatment programmes, 46
Fathers, 3, 37, 207
Financial problems, 36, 99–100

Gender, 10, 37, 92, 98, 212, 216, 219–20
Genetics, 38, 146, 195, 212, 216

Griffiths, Sir Roy/Griffiths Report, 91–2, 93, 95

Health education/promotion, 82, 86, 89, 128
Helping the Community to Care, 94
Homework, 75, 78

Information, 63, 76, 80, 83–5, 108, 117, 125, 139, 140, 180, 183, 195, 204, 211
Information wanted, 38, 43

Knowledge About Schizophrenia Interview (KASI), 76
Knowledge Interview, 70

Life events/stressors, 19–21, 98

Media, 155–6
Medication (drugs), 8, 9, 20, 52, 53–4, 60–2, 72, 77, 83, 84, 113, 147–8, 195–6
Mental health law, 203–4, 206
Methodological problems, 9–10, 56–60, 80
MIND, 120, 135, 204
Models of schizophrenia/illness, 2–6, 11, 16–17, 21–3, 85, 86, 114, 139, 142, 144, 146
Mothers, 2–3, 15, 16, 29, 37, 214

National Alliance for the Mentally Ill, 100, 116, 125, 127, 133
National Schizophrenia Fellowship, 95, 114, 117–20, 127, 158
National Schizophrenia Fellowship (Scotland), 118, 154–5, 169
A new deal for carers, 95–6

Over-involvement/protection, 7, 11, 13, 16, 17, 41, 63, 66, 105, 151, 208, 214

Parents of people with schizophrenia, 37
see also: Expressed emotion, Carers, Mothers, Fathers
Paternalism, 136, 205, 206–9
Patient Register, 171–2
Patient rejection scale, 7
Patients' rights, 105, 167, 201, 203–5, 207
Problem solving, 52, 54, 55, 64, 74, 108, 139, 149
Prodromal signs, 61, 68, 72, 79
Psycho-education, 62, 69, 79, 81, 85–7, 122
see also: Education
Psychotherapy, 47–9

Relapse, 6–20, 46, 51, 52, 53, 58, 61, 82, 83, 84, 88, 93, 174, 201
Relatives' groups, 49, 52, 79, 88, 89–90
see also: Education groups
Relatives' involvement, emergence of, 114, 128–31
see also: Self-help groups
Relatives' rights, 204–5
'Right to know', 47

SANE, 134–5
Schizophrenia Society of Canada, 123–4
Search after meaning, 63, 194–5
Self-help groups/movement, 83, 89, 114–37, 154, 158, 159, 175, 211, 221
and campaigning, 118, 126, 132–3, 135
and education, 114, 115, 130, 135
and funding, 117, 130, 131, 133, 134, 136
and the future, 131–5
role of professionals, 136–7

Self-help groups/movement (*cont.*)
  and service provision, 114,
      118–19, 120, 121, 122, 123–4,
      125, 126, 127
  see also: Voluntary groups
Services, 31, 68, 77–8, 95–9, 153–4,
    158–60, 161
  carers' views of, 99–101, 143
Siblings of people with
    schizophrenia, 38–8
Social skills training, 52, 53, 54
Spouses of people with
    schizophrenia, 36–7
Stigma, 24, 29, 35, 37, 41
Stress, 6, 11–12, 21, 32, 150
Stress management, 12, 79, 83, 89,
    151–2, 199–200
Support groups, 117, 121, 122, 125,
    130, 154, 221
Supporting the Informal Carers, 95
Survival skills, 51, 53, 84–5

Therapy
  and families, 45–68, 213–14

see also: Education groups,
    Expressed emotion, Family,
    Relatives' groups
Training, 59, 165, 172, 179–202

Untrained staff, 87, 101
User-movement/groups, 114,
    115–16, 133, 168

Value judgments, 86, 189, 203
Value systems, 159–60, 189, 203
Voluntary organisations/agencies,
    83, 115, 119, 127, 128, 135, 154,
    162, 168, 175, 201, 204, 208

World Schizophrenia Fellowship,
    127

ZENKAREN: National Federation
    of Families with the Mentally Ill
    in Japan, 124–5, 127

Wiley Titles of Related Interest

COGNITIVE BEHAVIOUR THERAPY for PSYCHOSIS
Theory and Practice
David Fowler, Philippa Garety *and* Liz Kuipers

A practical guide that highlights some of the difficulties encountered in working with psychotic patients and ways of overcoming them.

0-471-93990-3 200pp 1995 Hardback
0-471-95618-X 200pp 1995 Paperback

PERSONALITY DISORDERS: CLINICAL and SOCIAL PERSPECTIVES
Assessment and Treatment based on DSM-IV and ICD-10
Jan J. L. Derksen

Explores the process of the diagnosis and treatment of DSM-IV and ICD-10 personality disorders, using case studies to illustrate methods used.

0-471-94389-4 374pp 1995 Hardback
0-471-95549-3 374pp 1995 Paperback

Psychological Management of Schizophrenia
Edited by Max Birchwood *and* Nicholas Tarrier

Offers a practical guide for mental health professionals who want to develop and enhance their skills in new treatment approaches.

0-471-95056-4 176pp 1994 Paperback

Symptoms of Schizophrenia
Edited by Charles G. Costello

Approaches the psychopathology of schizophrenia from the perspective of symptoms rather than the more common view of disordered systems. Chapters cover symptoms such as thinking disorders, hallucinations, delusions, and social withdrawal.

0-471-54875-8 320pp 1993 Hardback